FEMINIST THEORY AND THE PHILOSOPHIES OF MAN

FEMINIST THEORY AND THE PHILOSOPHIES OF MAN

Andrea Nye

ROUTLEDGE

NEW YORK • LONDON

Published in 1988 by Croom Helm

Paperback published in 1989 by

Routledge, an imprint of
Routledge, Chapman and Hall Inc.
29 West 35 Street
New York, NY 10001

Published in Great Britain by

Routledge
11 New Fetter Lane
London EC4P 4EE

Library of Congress Cataloging in Publication Data

Nye, Andrea,
  Feminist theory and the philosophies of man.

  Includes bibliographical references.
  1. Feminism—Philosophy. 2. Patriarchy.
3. Women's rights. I. Title.
HQ1154.N93   1989   305.42′01   89-10651
ISBN 0-7099-1852-6; ISBN 0-415-90204-5 (pb)

British Library Cataloging in Publication Data

Nye, Andrea
  Feminist theory and the philosophies of man.
  1. Feminism
  I. Title
  305.4′2′01   HQ1154
  ISBN 0-7099-1852-6
  ISBN 0-415-90204-5(pb)

*For Deirdre, Stephen, and Anna
who almost always waited
at the bottom of the stairs
until I finished my work*

Contents

Contents

Prologue

Ovid in his Metamorphoses *(Book VI) tells the story of Athena's revenge on the Lydian weaver Arachne.*

Athena, patron goddess of Hellenic Athens, was jealous of Arachne's legendary skill. Even the Muses came to watch Arachne rolling the wool, softening the fleeces, moving the spindle, and embroidering colourful designs with her nimble fingers. One day, Athena, disguised as an old woman, went to spy on Arachne. In the voice of the old woman, she warned Arachne to concede to Athena's superiority. Arachne, impatient and scornful of this interference, retorted that Athena could come herself if she liked, and they would see who was the better weaver. At these presumptuous words, Athena cast off her disguise and accepted Arachne's challenge. The looms were set side by side and both began to weave — but they wove two different designs.

Athena embroidered the monumental symbols of Athenian sovereignty: the rock of Mars, the citadel of Cecrops, the twelve Olympian gods with Zeus at their head. In each corner she added an object lesson for Arachne: Rhodope and Haemus turned to mountains, the Pigmy queen turned to a crane, Antigone to a stork, and Cinyras weeping immobile on the stone steps that once were his daughters. All had been punished for challenging the authority of the Olympian gods.

Arachne chose another theme. Her tapestry was alive with action, with violence, and with grief. She vividly painted, in picture after picture, the crimes of the Olympian gods against women. She showed Zeus as a bull carrying off Europa, as an eagle raping Asterie, as a swan raping Leda. Not only did Arachne show the crimes of Zeus, she also showed the weeping victims of lustful Apollo and Poseidon. Her tapestry mercilessly depicted the brutality and deception of men, and the pitiful pleas of women, carried off, away from children, family, homeland.

Athena stared at Arachne's weaving in rage. Even she could not deny its superiority. Furious, she took up the offending tapestry, ripped it, tore it to shreds, and, taking her wooden shuttle, beat Arachne repeatedly over the head. Arachne, harassed, terrified, threatened with her life, put a noose around her own neck in despair. However, just as Arachne fell, the noose tightening around her throat, Athena relented and turned her into a spider scurrying up a slender thread to safety.

'Live,' Athena said to Arachne, 'live wicked girl, but stay hanging. So that you will expect nothing better from the future, let this same punishment fall on all your race and descendants.'

Reborn as the spider, Arachne resumed her weaving.

Acknowledgements

The original research for this book was made possible by a Fellowship from the United States National Endowment for the Humanities in 1982–83.

Some of the material of this book has been previously published as follows:

Parts of Chapter III as 'Preparing the Way for a Feminist Praxis' in *Hypatia* Vol. I, No. 1 (Sp. 1986) 101–16

Parts of Chapter V as 'French Feminism and Philosophy of Language' in *Nous* Vol. 20, No. 1 (1986) 45–51

Also parts of Chapter 5 will be forthcoming as 'The Inequalities of Semantic Structure' in *Metaphilosophy*. All are reprinted here with the kind permission of the publishers.

1

Introduction:
The Designs of Feminist Theory

Contemporary feminist theory is a tangled and forbidding web. Familiar slogans of equality and freedom have been replaced by the intricate embroidery of Marxist economics, the hermetic mysteries of psychoanalysis, and inaccessible theories of the signifier. Practising feminists — struggling with abusive marriages, pay scales that devalue the work of women, repressive laws against homosexuality, lack of funding for social services — approach the proliferation of feminist theory with an acute sense of frustration. Constantly confronted with the defeat or neutralisation of feminist projects, wearily seeking fresh insights into mechanisms that perpetuate women's oppression, searching for the new vision needed to begin again, women urgently require the answers that feminist theory promises. Faced, however, with multiple volumes of Marx's *Capital*, Lacan's *Écrits*, or Irigaray's *Speculum of the other woman*, a woman may easily decide that theory is a luxury which she cannot afford. It will take years, she might say, years, to understand all this; and in the meantime, there is a meeting of women employees, a class to teach, a court date, a child to pick up at school, or an urgent call on the woman's hot line. And Marx goes back to the library unread. Maybe there will be time next week.

Is it such a loss? Does a practising feminist need theory? Perhaps she does not, she consoles herself: her convictions, her energies, her relations with other women are enough. Philosophy is a luxury for ivory tower intellectuals. At other times, however — when her efforts, and other women's efforts, fail, when she feels herself drawn back into destructive relationships, when the court refuses to mandate comparable worth, when her lover is fired from her teaching job for coming out as a lesbian, when the funding for the rape centre is withdrawn — she goes to the library and checks out the books again. She must understand, she tells herself, how to confront a government bureaucracy that takes no account of human needs, an education system that denies knowledge, a constitution that allows discrimination, a sexual ethics that sets different standards for men and women. There are also choices she must make. Who is she to listen to? — the Marxist feminist who tells her she has abandoned poor women in her drive for equal democratic rights?; the radical feminist who tells her she has compromised her primary commitment to women in her involvement with leftist politics?; the lesbian feminist who tells her she is a collaborator because she lives with a man?; the French feminist who tells her that in being rational she denies her femininity?

In thinking about these conflicting prescriptions — for equal rights, socialist revolution, sexual revolution, women's writing — we cannot avoid either our sexist past or the various ways women have tried to escape from the past. Any theory we might use to understand our situation already has a history, a history in which its meaning was shaped in feminist and non-feminist practice. There can be no fresh start that analyzes sexism authoritatively into discrete units with scientific precision in order to infer the correct feminist intervention. There is no infallible logic that avoids the constant and painful adjustments between what one is doing and what one thinks one is doing that characterise any progressive action. Women, becoming aware of their exclusion from a male culture in which they have little power, in which women's values are not expressed, in which they may not be considered persons or even God's creatures, find no pure feminist theory.

Nor will they find it in feminist history. Matrifocal culture lies deep in prehistory, accessible only when mediated through male archaeologists who had their own reasons for searching for the White Goddess. To women struggling with property law, prostitution, wife beating, homophobia, and racism, the story of a feminist Golden Age remains a myth not substantial enough to be translated into any insights that can guide current practice. Instead, feeling the injustice everywhere around them, looking for some way to make sense of their experience and to project an effective programme for future action, women have adopted theories, systems, and categories invented by men to rationalise and justify men's activities. Perhaps in these theories which men devise to regulate their relations, they reasoned, there might be something that women could adapt to feminist purposes. Women could take their opponent's own argument, turn it against him, and generate a human society inclusive of women.

The first systematic justifications of women's rights in the nineteenth century were borrowed from liberal and democratic theory. The democratic panacea of the vote was the focus of feminist struggle. Locke, Rousseau, and the utilitarians had fashioned a world in which men could be free and equal, a civil society in which men would determine their own fates. These ideas, which were never meant to be applied to women, were taken up by reformers such as Mary Wollstonecraft and Harriet Taylor. At the same time, socialists attacked liberalism. Capitalism, they charged, did nothing to change the economic and social degradation of women, and the bourgeois family provided only domestic servitude. Marxist analysis of class relations and economics became the focus of a more radical feminism. However, feminists also found Marxist theory inadequate. The failure of Marxist revolutions to change substantively the position of women, or to bring about, even for men, the Utopia promised by Marx, led feminists like Simone de Beauvoir to a deeper study of the existential relations between self and other described by philosophers such as Hegel and Sartre. Feminist psychoanalysts, in turn, went beyond existential relations to a study of the feminine psyche generated in family structures that survived even a Marxist revolution. Finally, structuralist theories of language located sexism at the very origins of culture. If the language that women speak, in which they must speak, is tainted with sexism, a sexism deeper than a revisable lexicon, if the grammar of language is itself reflective of male thought, then nothing women can say or write in existing language can ever be truly feminist.

Each time in the continuing struggle for coherent practice and revolutionary theory, there is a spinning out, a drawing of conclusions, an expansion of hope and of conviction, and then a disappointment, a painful drawing up at the limits of a theoretical orientation, which in turn forces a new beginning. Will these borrowed ideas ever work? Can feminists take the thread offered by the collaborating Athena and the male gods to whom she has pledged allegiance and make it into an escape?; or will such a thread always lead back to unreflective collaboration? Is it possible to discern among the complex patterns of feminist thought a reoccurring design of male supremacy which makes feminist theory ultimately self-defeating?

This is the dilemma that feminists confront. A sporadic,

reactive, unthinking response to injustice has little practical force. There must be a centre from which to begin weaving feminist theory, a foothold from which action can be initiated and take on meaning and strength. At the same time, that ideological foothold may have to be borrowed from the only ideas available. If culture is sexist culture, feminist theory may have to be generated out of whatever lifelines that culture concedes. This borrowing, this adaptation, this continual outgrowing of a theoretical stance that restricts feminist practice, that leaves too much of what remains alien to feminine experience intact and untouched by women's thought and action, is the history of feminist theory. It is also a history re-enacted each time women begin again to repair the damaged web of understanding that must support any meaningful feminist action.

What follows is not objective. I write from a particular position in space and time that I share with other women. Nor is it disinterested. I do not pretend to assess fairly all previous feminist theories from a position of removed authority. My project is a personal one, to think through a concrete, immediate problem. What should we/I do now? What is the adequate understanding of women's situation that will inform that practice? The point is not to make a catalogue of mistakes but to learn to own the past, to remember how we thought a certain way for the first time, and went on thinking that way, and the difficulty we had in acting on that thought. This, it seems to me, is the only way to learn to be the past and at the same time not to be it, as each new attempt at understanding what was thought and done creates a new past and a new future.

2

Liberté, Egalité et Fraternité: Nineteenth-century Liberalism and Women's Rights

The philosophical inheritance

When a woman in the United States or Western Europe first identifies herself as a feminist, it is often as a liberal feminist, asserting her claim to the equal rights and freedoms guaranteed to each individual in democratic society. In doing so she follows those nineteenth-century feminists who found in the democratic ideals of equality and liberty, that marked the change from feudal Europe to an industrial economy, a coherent systematic body of doctrine from which to argue for women's rights. These ideals, reflected in and inspired by bourgeois revolutions in the United States and France, took shape in the political writings of philosophers such as Locke, Rousseau, and Bentham. All men were to have the same rights; all men were to be equal before the law which would only be imposed with the consent of those who were to obey it. Although contract theorists such as Rousseau might differ from utilitarians such as Bentham over the terms of political participation, the vote pragmatically represented for all aspiring groups the minimal sign that their members were fully functioning and self-determining in the new civil society. Accordingly, in the first great wave of feminist activity in the nineteenth century, the primary issue was suffrage. Other issues such as property rights, marriage reform and sexual freedom were discussed, but democratic theory encouraged feminists to see the vote as the correct and most practical way of achieving their goals. When suffrage was granted, women would be able to vote for the legislation that would correct injustice to women. Unfortunately, there was much in the theorising of the founding fathers of democratic theory that stood in contradiction to this feminist logic. Philosophers such as John

5

Locke, who argued against the absolute power of the king and for free contractual relations between men, did not include women as participants in civil society. Although Locke argued against Adam's absolute monarchy and also against the eternal inevitable submission of Eve, it was still the case that when there was a dispute in the family, a 'different understanding' between husband and wife, 'the last determination, i.e., the Rule . . . naturally falls to the man's share as the abler and stronger'.[1] Although for the contractualist Locke there are limits to the rule of the husband, the elements constituting civil society are households with male heads. The woman's place is in the home where she is subordinate to the better judgement of the man. Although the possibility is left open that there might be exceptional women (God did not give man universal authority), still in his punishment of Eve ('and thy desire shall be to thy husband and he shall rule over you' — 3 Gen. 16), God foretold woman's lot. It has, Locke pronounced with some satisfaction, worked out *in fact* that women are subject and also that there is a foundation in nature for their subjection.[2]

David Hume, the defender of the virtues of sympathy and rapport with other's suffering, also took a traditional view of women's place. Men are the natural rulers in the home.[3] Women do not participate in the moral relations established between men in which natural sympathies are replaced by rules of justice. Men are the proper spokespersons for the family. As Aristotle before him, Hume argued that there are different virtues for women. Modesty and chastity are virtues for women but not for men. Women are the 'fair sex' with 'female virtues'. Because men must know when they are fathers if they are to take on the responsibilities of supporting a child, these restraints on women are necessary. It is therefore shameful for a woman to invite adultery or even to allow herself to be approached.[4]

Rousseau, the great democrat, elaborated on the feminine nature that subjects women to male authority. Women he argued, are naturally weaker, suited for reproduction but not for public life. In *Emile*, in which Rousseau described the ideal natural spontaneous education for a man away from the corruptions of society, the education of his female counterpart, the unfortunate Sophie, is very different. Women are to be educated to please men and to be mothers. They are to be trained in the sexual restraint and chastity that ensures paternity. They must learn to stimulate male desire and at the same time to restrain men's lusts. Seductiveness suits their nature; they are desiring to please, modest, tolerant of

6

injustice, manipulative, vain, and artistic in a minor way. In the family, men must rule these frivolous creatures.

This view of women's place was ratified, though in a different tone, by the celebrated Madame de Stael. Writing in 1796, still stunned and horrified by the 'unleashed passions' of the French Revolution, she analysed *(De) L'influence des passions sur le bonheur des individus et des nations*,[5] hoping to make clear the ways in which uncontrolled emotions destroy happiness both for individuals and societies. However, with respect to emotions, women are in a different position from men. Ambition and pride in a man *may* bring his downfall; in a woman such sentiments are *never* conducive to happiness. When a woman meddles in politics, if she is young she is considered immodest; if old, disgusting.[6] If she desires power she is always judged harshly by both men and women, by men because she can no longer be a love object, and by women out of either jealousy or principle. The only acceptable passion for women is love, but even there, true happiness is impossible. She is adored when young and beautiful, only to be inevitably ignored when she loses her beauty.[7] Love for men is just an episode in their lives, while for women it is everything; and so for women, after a few years of romance, life is finished.[8]

Men in love are bound by no principles of honour or constancy. For them love does not involve obligation: even the best of them only love for the moment. Consequently it is better for a woman when her passionate life is over, when she is no longer tempted to this, in de Stael's words: . . . 'devastating feeling that like the burning wind of Africa dries in the flower, knocks down in violence, bends finally to the ground the stem which dreamed of growing and dominating'.[9] Though love is the province of women it is better not to be loved, because if you give in to the need to be loved, you give yourself over to men, 'overturning your existence for several instants of theirs'.[10] However, a woman should not hope to escape the misery of love by emulating male ambition. She must, with all of its dangers, be content with being loved. She is irrevocably dependent, and nothing can extricate her from the control of men. Even if she achieves celebrity, like Madame de Stael herself, and produces great works, this can never bring her happiness. She has too much imagination, is too agitated, has too many illusions and fears, is too 'sensible', too 'mobile', and so any achievement is always at the expense of her happiness.[11] As Stael observed, rather surprisingly for a woman whose literary gifts were so obvious, the worst situation is when

7

women reject 'the distinctive character of their sex' for literature.[12] The only possible consolation is motherhood where at least a woman's affections may have some reward.

Madame de Stael, like Rousseau, saw these deficiencies as a result of nature. Women's nature determines their destiny and they should not go against it. They owe their powerlessness to 'the route nature has traced for them'. They must accept 'the insurmountable faculty of their nature'.[13] However, in Stael's description of the woman's proper role, there was a new tone. Women accept a 'situation in the social order',[14] and furthermore, the role that women are to play is impossible. In it there is no happiness: from it there is no escape. Not only are women what they are by nature, they are also what men wish them to be; they are judged harshly when ambitious because 'men do not see any kind of general utility in encouraging the success of women in this career'.[15] In Stael, Rousseau's mute Sophie begins to speak and in her voice emotions unbefitting a properly feminine woman are already beginning to sound: bitterness, contempt for male values, resentment of her position. The revolution, whose excesses Stael so much regretted, did nothing directly to change the situation of women, but it had initiated in women like Stael a reflection on woman's lot that would eventually flower in feminists like Mary Wollstonecraft and Harriet Taylor. These women would argue beyond Stael that the logic of the revolution, if properly employed, demanded a radical change in the attitudes of those men who saw no 'utility' in female success.

The democratic reforms of the French Revolution were originally theorised as benefiting women only indirectly: women are dependent upon men, therefore, women will be better off because men will be better off. Unsuited to civil responsibility with its necessary rationality and autonomy, they cannot enter into the social contract which Rousseau urged as the basis of any legitimate authority. In the perfect equality that Rousseau envisioned for his ideal republic, in which no one was to be a servant of anyone else or lesser than anyone else, women would not be counted. In turbulent years of struggle in England and France, the majority of reformers did not question women's unacceptability for public life. The positivist Auguste Comte, for example, argued that women's brains are smaller then men's and that women should therefore be subordinate. The philosopher and utilitarian James Mill, father of John Stuart Mill, politicking for the right of all men to decide their own interests in a democratic vote, thought that women's interests would be better protected by men. Even socialists, such as Saint Simonians, who claimed complete equality for women, tended to surround women with an aura of sentimentality that validated them as spiritual leaders but threatened to raise them above petty civil disputes.[16] It was therefore not surprising that the French Revoluton brought about little change in women's situation. Women might march to Versailles because their shrill voices better expressed hunger,[17] hold coats, cook dinners, be inspiring as Empire odalesques swooning on couches in filmy draperies, be celebrated as Greek goddesses at the Pantheon, but they were not envisioned in responsible political roles.

It was not that women's rights were not brought to the attention of the new law makers. In France, Olympe de Gouges presented to the reforming and courageous Assemblée nationale her *Déclaration des Droits de la Femme et de la Citoyenne*.[18] In her 17 resolutions were admirably and succinctly expressed the conditions for women's equality:

(1) Any distribution of social goods must depend on 'utilité commune' (Resolution 1) where 'common' must be taken to include women. Here Gouges referred to the utilitarian theories that would be so important in the British reform movement.

(2) Political association must conserve natural rights (Res. 2), authority is vested in the people (Res. 3), and a law, to be valid, must be an expression of general will (Res. 6). Certainly women are also people, have desires, and therefore natural rights. Here Gouges drew on Rousseauian social contract theory which claimed that a government is only legitimate if it preserves the natural liberty of men by allowing each to participate in public decision making.

(3) Government authority is only valid when harmful action is in question (Res. 5) and freedom of speech and thought should be guaranteed (Res. 11). Gouges expressed the libertarian principles worked out later more fully by John Stuart Mill.

Women should have all the rights that men have, including property rights and freedom of speech, and in addition they are to have all the reciprocal responsibilities. If they commit a crime they are to be punished with the full severity of the law. Certainly,

Gouges argued, if a woman can mount the scaffold, she may mount la Tribune. Women must pay taxes, and perform all public duties.[19] She appealed to women to take heart and make their claim to the new democratic freedoms. 'What are the advantages that you have amassed in the revolution? A distrust more marked, a disdain more attenuated?' Gouges, in an optimism which was the reverse of Stael's pessimism, reasoned that if women use 'the force of reason', 'the standards of philosophy', they will succeed; if they do not, the revolution is a sham.

Judging by the results of the French Revolution, Stael's pessimism would seem to have been more in order. None of the leaders of the revolution except Condorcet called for women's suffrage. What emerged in the great rhetoric of social upheaval was a theory of the rights and dignity of *man*. It was in men's nature to be free, to be equal, and it was men who required the protection of democratic institutions. Rules of justice would regulate the dealings of men; women were not to be included, any more than the insane, or criminals, or children. The revolution would improve women's lot, but only because men would learn to treat them better in the new moral atmosphere.

Certainly capitalism and industrialism had not improved women's economic situation. Although the woman was subordinate in feudal society, her work was an economic necessity. The family's dependence on her contribution gave her a certain position and power. With wage earning work being increasingly located outside the home and being done by men, women's at-home work decreased in apparent value.[20] Furthermore, workers' associations and unions kept women who did work out of skilled jobs, forcing them to the very lowest levels of the labour market. Women were increasingly excluded from the public world of business and affairs where power was located and barred from voting or participating in the new Parliaments and General Assemblies where commercial interests were represented.[21] Without the property rights that replaced feudal tenure, without the ability to enter into the contractual relations that took the place of feudal responsibilities and duties, without the access to education that allowed men to compete, without the access to employment that guaranteed that the skillful and hardworking would get jobs, women's situation in capitalist society was hardly better than it had been under feudalism. Participation in democratic institutions, property rights, contractual rights, public education, competitive markets, and all the mechanisms of democratic functioning were now closed to women, and the more secure the establishment of the new institutions, the more complete was women's exclusion.

Nevertheless, there was a logic in democratic theory that feminists found encouraging. Firstly, there was the fact that a truly great social revolution had taken place. Feudal privileges and aristocratic rules, seemingly so natural and permanent a part of social life, had given way to a new kind of society in which relations between men were to be regulated by law and not by birth. No longer did pessimism seem necessary simply on account of the longevity of male domination. If feudal lords could lay down their privileges, so too could men. In the United States the success of the abolitionists and the struggle to give black men the vote was also initially heartening. If the suffrage was to be extended to black men, certainly the question of women's inclusion would then be raised and discussed.[22]

Secondly, even though equality and liberty seemed to mean only fraternity, once equality was seriously put forth as a value, how could democrats consistently resist the implications? Whether or not it was contemplated at the outset that women be included, how after reflection could they be denied, and on what logic? Were women not human beings? If so they also must be equal. Did women have interests? Then they also were the best judge of how those interests would be served. Was this democratic freedom only the freedon of the male *entrepreneur* to make money? Was this equality only the equality of the self-made male capitalist to sit in Parliament with earls? Or were equality and liberty really *principles* of justice? If so, they must not just protect established commercial interests, but the interests of everyone, including women.

Mary Wollstonecraft in her *Vindication of the rights of women* reopened the question of the extension of the ideals of the French Revolution to women. The female character described by Rousseau and Stael, Wollstonecraft argued, is not natural but is formed in the kind of education Rousseau prescribed for Sophie. Once women are educated, like men, to be citizens, the logic of the revolution must apply to them also. *The Delaration of the Rights of Man and Citizen*, passed by the reforming French Assembly[23] in 1789, and the American *Bill of Rights* both proclaimed that all human beings had rights. Is a woman a human being? Is a woman moral in the same way as men? If women are not animals but human, if the have immortal souls and are morally perfectable, then they should have the same rights as men.

11

Wollstonecraft acknowledged the actual political incompetence of women. As degraded sex objects, they cannot even perform their duties as wife or homemaker properly. Wollstonecraft's recommendation was simple; women should be educated like men. They should read philosophy, logic, and mathematics. They should be encouraged to exercise; whatever physical weakness they possess should be overcome, not magnified. When they are afraid, they should not be cuddled but should be called cowards. In this way, women will become economically independent and fully capable of political participation. If women in their present state are degraded creatures, the reason is not in women's nature, but in the closely woven complex of attitudes and practices that, especially for the young girl, form feelings, thought, and character into the narrow lines prescribed by a stunted male lust. When women are treated differently, they will, on the other hand, make efficient, faithful, and chaste wives and citizens.

The electorate in a democratic society must be rational, but Wollstonecraft exposed as circular the argument that women are not capable of such rationality. Women are too degraded to vote, but they are degraded because they have not been educated to vote. Once the self-serving male presupposition of difference is removed, once it is seen that women are like animals because they are treated and trained like animals, there can be no more resistance to their inclusion as fully functioning members of society.

More than half a century later, Harriet Taylor and John Stuart Mill were still arguing the same points.

An application of principle: the liberal feminism of Harriet Taylor and John Stuart Mill

From 1790 to 1850 the excitement, confusion, and enthusiasm of revolution, channelled into new social and political structures, gave way to a more sober and specific consciousness of women's exclusion. It is fitting that the first systematic, detailed defence of women's rights came from John Stuart Mill and Harriet Taylor. Both were placed ideologically and pragmatically in the midst of currents of democratic reform in nineteenth-century England. Furthermore, their collaboration[24] brought together two divergent strains in the reform movement and in democratic theory. Mill was a utilitarian in the Benthamite tradition, an active member of the Philosophical Radical group which took

Bentham's ideas as the basis for Parliamentary reform. After a painful period of self-questioning, and after meeting Harriet Taylor, Mill was also increasingly drawn into her circle, the Unitarian Radicals,[25] more literary, more radical and more libertarian than the utilitarians, especially in matters of the family and sexuality.

In the work of Taylor and Mill, these two sometimes conflicting strands in democratic theory came together: firstly, utilitarian demands for a society in which there is the greatest happiness of the greatest number, and secondly a libertarian, Rousseauian, claim that freedom is the natural right of every human being. Both doctrines had weaknesses — utilitarianism because, if applied strictly, it seemed to allow actions that were clearly and intuitively wrong;[26] and the doctrine of natural rights because it could too easily, as argued by critics such as Edmund Burke, degenerate into the dangerous metaphysical fictions which led to the excesses and destructiveness of the French revolution.[27] In Mill's political theory, a synthesis of utilitarianism and libertarianism structured the final balance of the functioning democratic state. In arguments for a society in which the interests of every man would be considered and, at the same time, in which the individual rights of each man would be protected, Mill and Taylor found the justification for a corresponding feminist revolution. These arguments would provide the agenda for the next 200 years of liberal feminism. Women should be granted all political privileges including the vote and the right to run to public office. They should also have available to them the choice to enter a profession rather than to marry and the education necessary for the fulfilment of that ambition. According to the principles of democratic theory, such reforms would eventually lead to equality.

The argument was simply and rationally stated by Mill's utilitarian mentor, Jeremy Bentham.[28] Human affairs are regulated by two sovereign masters, pleasure and pain. It is for these masters to tell men both what they will do and what they should do. Because society is only a collection of pleasure-seeking, pain-avoiding individuals, a just society is one in which the maximum amount of pleasure is produced together with the minimum amount of pain. Accordingly, in order to decide whether any individual action or piece of legislation is to be chosen, one can do a calculus of pains and pleasures. One should take each individual affected by the action or law, estimate the pain and pleasure which will result for that individual as exactly as possible, and then make a sum total. Whatever action or law causes the most happiness and the least pain is right.[29]

From this theory of the nature of men, and of the morality appropriate to that nature, came two important pragmatic principles of political reform. First, since no pleasure is to be considered superior to any other except on the basis of quantity, each person in society is considered to be the best judge of their own pleasure. Consequently, the only way to guarantee the greatest happiness of the greatest number is to allow each to register his own preference and vote for the representative who will legislate for the voter's greatest pleasure. When everyone votes, everyone's interests will be served and the greatest happiness will result. Therefore, the primary political goal of the utilitarian Philosphical Radicals was the extension of suffrage. The vote would set into motion the mechanisms of self-interest that would ensure a just society.

The older social contract theory of Locke and Rousseau added further arguments for the importance of the vote. Locke was more specific than Bentham as to the nature of the transition from an aggregate of self-interested pleasure-seeking individuals to civil society. Men, realising the impossibility of achieving reliable pleasure in the anarchy of a 'state of nature' agree to co-operate for their mutual advantage. However, an individual only enters into a social contract with its attendant duties and responsibilities on the condition that through representative institutions he will have a say in the making of law. Only if everyone makes the law will it be legitimate and binding: if the responsible members of the community are not consulted then there is no obligation to obey it.

There was yet another way in which individual interests must be registered and served, developed by the utilitarian contemporary of Bentham, Adam Smith. Utilitarian pleasures are real, countable, physical, and do not include any mystical satisfaction in poverty and self-denial for their own sake. Pleasure means productivity, industrialisation, more consumer goods: the more productive a society, the more pleasure and, according to utilitarian principles, the more justice. Only with a free and open market for the exchange of goods can the most efficient production be guaranteed. Each will buy according to his pleasure. Each will compete on the open market for jobs. The market will produce what people want and in the press of competition produce it in the most efficient manner. In Smith's economic theory, a mechanism is provided to bridge the gap between Bentham's self-interested individuals and the greatest happiness of society; not only a social contract but also economic law turns selfishness into social good. Only *if* everyone is self-interested and tries to get as much for himself as possible will the interests of society be served. When each person is free to pursue his own interest and each person's integrity as a consuming unit is preserved, separately striving egotisms will fuel the requisite expansion of an ever more pleasure-producing economy.

These utilitarian principles were used to argue the case for women's liberation in Taylor's 'The enfranchisement of women' and Mill's *The subjection of women*. Women's suffrage was the mechanism by which other reforms could be achieved and women's interests best served. At the Worchester, Massachusetts convention whose notice is the topical introduction of Taylor's article, that right was unambiguously stated.[30] The right to a voice in government is the basis, Taylor argued, for democratic institutions both in the United States and in England.

Everywhere it is claimed that there must be a vote for all, and all cannot mean the male half.[31] On what basis can women be excluded? The Declaration of Independence states than 'All men are created equal'. Certainly Bentham's arguments apply. Women have interests, suffer pain, enjoy pleasure. And on what basis would they not be the best judge of how those interests are to be served? The only possible argument against women's inclusion is the simplest: because they are not men. However, this is, Taylor argued, a 'dishonest or ignorant subterfuge'. What other possible reasons could be given for women's exclusion? — that women are physically weaker? . . . but modern institutions do not depend upon physical strength; certainly it takes no strength to vote. Custom? — not a very convincing argument when such sweeping social changes have already taken place.

Mill's defence of women's right to vote in *The subjection*, more extended if not more powerful than Taylor's clear, unequivocal statement, also depended on utilitarian principles. It is the vote alone that guarantees full and just consideration of interests. Why should women be treated differently? The answer, Mill considered, was that they think in a different way. Mill accepted this judgement, although he left open the question as to whether it is due to nature or nurture.[32] Women are less logical than men, more practical, less interested in general principles than in concrete facts. Men tend to get lost in empty abstractions, ignore counter examples, and forget the original reasons for theorising.

15

However, women's thought processes, different as they are, could bring a healthy pragmatism to political questions, could temper masculine dogma, could bring theorising back to reality. Whether or not one suspects here the well-known, celebrated Mill, kept on the track by his faithful disciple Harriet, it is clear that Mill meant no offence. If women lack speculative skills they can get them by education; in any case, their pragmatism would be welcome in political disputes.

For Taylor the vote was not enough: participation in the free market of capitalist society is also necessary. Women must contribute economically to the family for the simple reason that a woman who contributes cannot be 'treated in the same contemptuously tyrannical manner' as when the 'male is the sole dispenser of what is earned'.[33] Women's participation will also, in good utilitarian fashion, contribute to the happiness of all. The market functions best when everyone, in open competition, decides what he or she will do best. The most qualified person gets the job, and so the more they compete, the better filled jobs will be. The underlying reasons, Taylor argued, for women's exclusion from the market, or inclusion only at the lowest levels, have to do not with the supposed unfemininity of competition but with the determination that women's labour be reserved for their function as mothers, and the fear that women might take jobs from men. These are not, however, valid arguments: 'There is no inherent reason or necessity that all women should voluntarily choose to devote their lives to one animal function and its consequences.'[34] As far as men's jobs are concerned, Taylor invited a utilitarian look at the balance sheet of pleasures and pains. The worst that could happen is that men would make half as much and contribute only half of family income, a result not so bad at all. Perhaps even this will not happen as the pressure of women on the job market is eased with the elimination of abuses such as child labour. In any case, it is elementary economics that competition only works if everyone is allowed to compete.

Aside from the utility of the vote and professional opportunities for women, Taylor and Mill considered some utilitarian calculations that should appeal to men as well as women. How much pleasure does the subjection of women really provide for men? In place of the emotion and prejudice that surrounded the issue, Taylor and Mill invoked 'an enlightened estimate of tendencies and consequences'.[35] Men, Taylor argued, think they like having someone to support, someone who depends on them for everything. Here they may be mistaken.[36] Associations between unequals are deleterious even to men, weakening, ignobling, boring. Is there really any pleasure in the society of one of Wollstonecrafts's degrading female spaniels? Mill was even more eloquent than Taylor on the consequences of women's subjection for men: 'All the selfish propensities, the self-worship, the unjust self preference, which exist among mankind have their source in, and derive their principle from the present constitution of the relations between men and women'.[37] However, Benthamite utilitarianism, as noted by both Taylor and Mill, had a dangerous weakness. What if women do not *want* to vote, to hold jobs, to be educated? Certainly in the mid-nineteenth century the majority of women did not support women's suffrage, nor were they eager to enter the job market unless absolutely necessary. If the vote was given to women, they might easily vote to remain the way they were, claiming that this is where their true happiness lay. Custom and conditioning could prevent women from taking advantage of opportunities legally granted; as Mill pointed out, 'Custom hardens human beings to any kind of degradation, by deadening part of their nature which would resist it.'[38] If women's assessment of their own pleasure cannot be trusted, then utilitarianism by itself is an inadequate basis for a defence of women's rights. There is no reason to think that women will vote for liberalising laws or for feminist candidates, no reason to think that they will rush to register at universities, or to apply for jobs. In most cases, the consequences can hardly be assessed as pleasurable when women attempt to trespass into male areas.[39] If it is only pleasure and pain that rules, women will stay home, rightfully choosing to avoid the frustration, alienation, insults, of any other course of action. Added to their satisfaction is the seeming happiness of the traditional male, undisturbed in the domestic comforts of his household.

The danger of such a stasis built into utilitarianism was one of the reasons given by Mill for his revision of Bentham's utilitarianism. People cannot be left to judge their own pleasure. They must be educated away from the lower, animal pleasure of physical gratification for intellectual and moral fulfilment. Higher spirits, such as he and Taylor, would lead the way. The masses cannot be relied upon to see the future; this is the privilege of the intellectual elite, and actually to have the feeling of the future was for an even 'rarer elite'.[40] Mill hoped to provide such superior guidance in the inspiring portrait of his and Taylor's marriage at the end of *The subjection of women*, where he presented their achievement not as a state which everyone can reach but as an ideal toward which everyone might strive.[41]

In addition, in *On liberty*, Mill — and Taylor as his acknowledged collaborator — tried to make consistent with utilitarian theory a doctrine of personal and individual rights applicable even when pain might result from the exercise of those rights. On this reasoning, not only can women's pain be ignored in their struggle for justice, but the fact, if it exists, of male pleasure in their subjection can also be discounted. Human rights, Mill argued, guaranteed to each person, are essential to the long-term health and happiness of society, and so are more important than any individual's short-term pleasure or pain.[42] Each person must have the right to speak and live as she or he wishes. Mill's justification of civil liberties was ultimately utilitarian. He did not use the alternative explanation from social contract theory of a natural right reserved from the social contract, preferring to rest on long-term effects on human happines rather than on quasi-metaphysical rights. Harriet, consistent with her libertarian, Rousseauian convictions, suggested in her 'Enfranchisement' that there is also inherent in mankind a natural right; no social contract can require that they give up freedom and equality. Women in sexist society are like Rousseau's slaves, whose acquiescence in their own enslavement Rousseau claimed to be invalid. If women are human, they must also, on Rousseau's logic, be free. They must have a right to choose their lifestyle, whether in relatively superficial matters such as restrictive and concealing dress, or in more controversial areas such as marriage and sexuality. Instead, women are restricted to the home, condemned to repetitive activities of child rearing, visiting, and charity. Their sexual freedom is limited; they cannot divorce or retain custody of their children.

However, a woman's legal right to choose a 'non-traditional' lifestyle does nothing to mitigate the social stigma and practical difficulties that must result from the choice. The cruel force of public opinion might destroy the happiness of rebellious women such as Taylor or Wollstonecraft; it might even completely crush other less hardy spirits, but it was not clear that there existed in democratic theory any principle that could justify interference in private life. More often, democratic principles were used to reinforce traditional morality.

Typical are the views of the popular American reformer Thomas Wentworth Higginson, who considered himself a feminist, and whose marriage of Lucy Stone and Henry Blackwell, under feminist protest against existing marriage laws grossly unfair to women,[43] is often cited as a milestone in the fight for women's rights. In his *Common sense about women*, appearing some 20 years after *The subjection of women*, Higginson echoed Mill's defence of the institution of marriage in a book that ostensibly defended women's rights. Women, Higginson said, should have the vote, not on the grounds that they are the same as men but on the grounds that they are different. Being different, wearing the 'halo of motherhood',[44] they cannot be represented by men. Women are weaker, more sensitive than men and should accept their deficiencies as men accept theirs. Suffrage, Higginson argued, certainly will *not* mean that women will give up their role as mother, homemaker and wife: 'For every thoughtful person sees that the cares of motherhood, though not the whole duty of women, are an essential part of the duty, wherever they occur.'[45] Certainly married women should not work, but should stay home while their husbands work. It is *because* of this difference that they must vote. Each person, Higginson agreed with the utilitarians, should vote according to his or her interest, and women, playing such a different role, must especially have the right. The tone of *Common sense* was reassuring: suffrage will not disturb the social fabric; women will still be to men what they always have been; their vote will only strengthen the traditional society in which they play such an important role.

In France also, a defence of women's rights was not inconsistent with traditional roles for women. In *La femme au XIX siècle*, an emotional *exposé* similar to Higginson's of the sad lot of women and of the need for laws that offer protection, Madame Romieu also described the differences between men and women. The vocation of women was to give hope and encouragement, to be the centre of family life; the vocation of a man was reflection, energy, analysis. 'La femme' was a secret and mysterious power.[46] Although she should be better educated and legally protected from husbands and prostitution, and although the choice of a public or artistic life should be open, the majority of women will find their 'real sanctuary' in the home.

Romieu was as eager as Higginson to dissociate the 'women question' from any tampering with family life. The concerns of Mill and Taylor, firstly, that public opinion could make the right to a free choice of a profession unexercisable for women and secondly (in the case of Taylor), that the role of a dependent wife and mother was inconsistent with marital equity and personal development, were not shared by Romieu and Higginson. Democratic reforms, they insisted, would leave the position of the woman in the family unchanged. Women might have the right to vote and to participate politically, but they would be unlikely to exercise those rights in any way inconsistent with their primary duties. Given that a woman's sexuality is only respectable in marriage, given that in marriage her professional life is discouraged or limited in commitment, given that she is expected to stay at home, only exceptional women will choose to be educated. Rousseau's humanity may essentially involve freedom, but regardless of metaphysical principle, women are still in chains, imprisoned in the private sphere which the social contract between men was never meant to invade.

In his view of marriage, Mill proved to be not that different from Higginson. A woman's proper place is as an educated companion to her husband. When Mill said it is not a 'desirable custom' that married women work, the tone of deadening public opinion that Mill in other contexts so deplored is clearly audible. Also apparent is the limited viewpoint of someone whose class allows him to support a wife comfortably. Mill's and Taylor's 'ideal' marriage, inevitably associated with a well-off and educated middle class, could hardly have relevance for the poor, downtrodden, beaten wives for whom Mill professed sympathy in *The subjection of women*. To women who had to make a living in the degrading working conditions of nineteenth-century England, and whose moral superiority was unprotected by independent wealth, the Mill's marriage was a sham supported only by privilege. Marriage partners were to be equal, Mill claimed, but if women were not to work, then that equality could obtain only if both were idle rich. If there is to be a real association of equals and no hierarchy in marriage, than there must be economic equality. How is it that Taylor was always supported by men? What right had she to talk about the right to work when she never had to exercise it?

Mill's educated higher faculties and individual rights did not cure the weakness in utilitarianism. The example of Mill's enlightened marriage which was to encourage women to rebel, depended on class privilege and was irrelevant for working-class women. The right to education, even if legally granted, would be exercised by those who could afford it and would remain subject to ideas of what constitutes a feminine role. The right to work was no more than a right to work at those poorly paid jobs which were considered suitable for women. The competitive market economy which was finally established in nineteenth-century Europe was an arena for the activities of men, those men whose nature was the starting point for democratic theory. Men, said Rousseau, had a natural right to get all they wanted; men, said Bentham, were motivated only to increase their pleasures and possessions. Women were not to be expected to compete with men as entrepreneurs or participate in the violent confrontations between male industrial workers and capitalists which were beginning to force from these entrepreneurs some of their profit.

In fact Taylor and Mill doubted whether women could be easily integrated into competitive capitalism even when they left marital obligations aside. Taylor, for example, hesitated at the hardening effects of capitalism, ultimately admitting that competition may not be the best method of economic regulation.[47] Still capitalism exists, and given the existence of that economic system, women should be able to compete. Reassuringly, she added that in any case public life today is not so very vicious; at least physical aggression is no longer necessary and disputes are settled with words at court. Mill also expressed doubts about capitalism. Freedom of choice means a healthy society, but wealth when it is passed on confers special privileges. The difficulties in amassing wealth may be insuperable for the majority,[48] certainly even more insuperable for women who are without property and are not left family fortunes. These economic barriers to success in capitalism, Mill admitted, may have to be accepted. In democratic society, at least women would not be denied the acquisition of property by law.

Mill's critique of utilitarian economics, elaborated in detail in *Political economy*, undermined the arguments of *The subjection of women*. Would the achievement of a legal right to property make any real difference in women's position? Would it actually give them property or power? At best it might allow a few exceptional women to overcome their handicaps, and, if they were willing to give up an intimate relationship with the opposite sex, to exercise the choice to compete freely. The selectivity of this liberation is not accidental but endemic, built into the very logic of democratic theory, in which success of the few provides the incentives that fuel economic activity.

21

All men are created equal

There is nothing in either utilitarianism or social contract theory that supports economic equality for women. Social contract theory promises equality before the law, but leaves a private sphere subject to natural law in which each has a right to whatever he can get and retain. The utilitarian's greatest happiness of all is a sum, an aggregate of happiness, used not to forbid inequality but to justify inequality as an incentive that will result in the utility of increased production. The liberated woman, even if she escapes from the private authority of her husband, will not compete as an equal. Her equality is only — as for any worker — to bargain with an employer who controls the means of her subsistence. As Mill admitted, the odds against her success are overwhelming. If women enter into the labour market they enter it at the lowest level and with liabilities not suffered by the poorest man.[49]

These doubts of Taylor and Mill become reality as the freedom and equality of democratic society are extended to women. Women, often out of economic need rather than choice, work outside the home. Because of continuing marital responsibilities, because of discrimination in the private economic sphere, because of dissatisfaction with the terms of economic success, they remain in low-paid, low-status, jobs. Even when they escape from marital responsibilities, they find themselves in a work place which is a replica of the patriarchal family with man at the top and women servicers at the bottom. Women run for political office, but when they overcome the prejudice of voters, male and female, and win, they remain clustered at the lower echelons of power. Once in office the woman legislator must be careful to court conservative interests who can finance her next campaign.

For the most part, women in Western countries are now 'free': free to vote, free to run for public office, free from protective labour laws to work where and how they choose. What this means, however, is that there are no legal barriers to doing any of these things. Discrimination by employer, hostility of co-workers, socialisation in the family, cultural stereotypes that convince women that they are sex objects, family responsibilities — these are barriers beyond the law. Women are free from child care, from unwanted pregnancy, from the prejudice of employers exercising their propety rights, from mass media depicting women in subordinate roles. Although a few exceptional women may occupy positions of power, the great majority remain clustered in low-paid, low-status professions. Given her economic situation, a woman is free to bargain but is in no position to do so profitably; free to travel or to go out alone, she is still too poor to pay her own bill. Forced to pay a kind of feudal dues of labour in the family, at a disadvantage in the job market, the liberated enfranchised woman might complain that democratic society has only returned her to a more profound subordination.

Furthermore, feminist proposals to correct these persistent inequities often come into conflict with the logic of democratic theory. Equal pay acts to guarantee that women with the same jobs as men are paid equally or civil rights acts that forbid sexual discrimination in employment should not, in theory, be necessary. In its purest form, especially as revived by contemporary neo-classical economics and the New Right, utilitarian economics guarantees that a free market will be free from discrimination.[50] Male employers faced with a choice between a qualified woman and less qualified man will, for economic reasons, choose the woman. They will also have to pay her the market rate for her services to convince her to accept and remain on the job. Theoretically, therefore, there is no need to extend the power of the state and restrict the economic freedom of individuals with legislation that forbids discrimination in employment or that insists that women have equal pay for the same job. If women remain in low-paid jobs, it must be because they either choose to do so or are not qualified for any other. On this reasoning, repeal of protective labour laws and discriminatory legislation, along with increased competition, should be sufficient to bring about equality.[51]

Even when implemented, civil rights acts and equal pay acts have not substantially changed women's position in the work force.[52] The more radical principle of comparable worth cuts deeply into democratic economic theory. This principle — that work not necessarily the same but of camparable value must receive equal pay — applies directly to women in low-paid female professions, such as nursing, teaching, and clerical work, and would require employers to adjust women's wages to match those of workers in male professions of equal value. Because enforcement would involve extensive determinations of the relative value of jobs, comparable worth would consitute a substantial state interference in the free market activities of employers.[53] The feminist, once she confronts such theoretical barriers, must begin to share Mill's and Taylor's doubts as to the adequacy of democratic economic theory.

23

Democratic insistence on the freedom and priority of the individual might seem to compensate for these inadequacies, and in some cases, a recognition of individual rights has advanced the cause of women. However, even when a right, such as the right to legal counsel, is established, a woman may be in no position to exercise that right. Her empowerment may again require state interference with the free market in the form of legal-aid funds, state-run child care centres, or free medical care.

In addition, women's rights often conflict with other interests in democratic society. A woman's right to an abortion, recognised in the United States in 1977,[54] rests partly on a right to privacy. Claims to the right freely to express one's private sexuality have been advanced to protect lesbian women from harassment and discrimination. These rights, however — to abortion, contraception and homosexual expression — are nowhere firmly established. In the United States, the constitutional right to abortion is eroded by legislation that denies funds for abortion to poor women, flaunted in harassment and terrorism against private abortion clinics, and in danger of being overruled by an increasingly conservative supreme Court. The right of homosexuals not to be discriminated against in employment has not yet been clearly asserted, with the result that many lesbian women must still live their familial and sexual lives in destructive secrecy. The failure of democratic society to allow women to exercise these rights suggests that the doctrine of rights may bring with it designs antithetical to feminist purposes.

In the case of rights to abortion, contraception, and homosexual expression, women's rights conflict with the concern expressed by Higginson and Mill that woman's role in the family be preserved. Recent feminist social theorists have argued that this concern is inevitable. Democratic theory required that the family persist as an institution. Theoretically, the democratic construction of society as made up of competing individuals can only be maintained if non-competing individuals remain in the privacy of the family to be represented by the male head of the family.[55] Furthermore, the family must survive to perform the practical functions of socialisation of children, and the care of the ill, aged and handicapped not included in the appropriate sphere of state action.[56] If the family is necessary for the functioning of democratic society, a woman's right to avoid unwanted pregnancy and her right to homosexual expression cannot be recognised because the exercise of such rights would deflect her from marriage and motherhood.

In some cases, the logic of rights is inadequate for deeper reasons. The right to privacy of the pregnant woman wishing an abortion immediately conflicts with the right of the foetus to life. In many discussions of abortion framed in the language of rights, a sterile debate follows on the definition of person; but the concept of person, whether used by pro-choice or anti-abortion activists, already carries an atomistic logic which obscures the real dynamics of the abortion issue. Instead of a negotiated clash between two individuals, one of whom's person status is debatable, abortion from the beginning is an interpersonal problem. To claim that the right to an abortion is based on a woman's claim to do as she likes is to apply a logic inconsistent with the place that a choice for or against abortion has in a woman's life. Carol Gilligan's influential argument for a distinctive feminine moral sensibility, *In a different voice*, analysed the actual reasoning involved in abortion decisions. The women she studied saw abortion not in terms of abstract determinations of individual rights, but in terms of conflicting responsibilities to lovers, families, and potential children that could only be resolved in an ethic of care for self and others.[57]

In other areas, individuals' rights to freedom of sexual expression directly impede feminist projects. Pornography, for example, after the defeat of the Equal Rights Amendment, was perhaps the best publicised feminist issue in the United States. However, proposed extensions to civil rights legislation which acknowledge pornography as discrimination, are easily defeated on the grounds that such legislation restricts freedom of speech and freedom of sexual expression.[58] There is nothing in the logic of rights that can distinguish between the right of a pornographer to depict or enjoy women as degraded sex objects in humiliating and painful positions and the right of a woman to express love for another woman. Both can shock, and, in the logic of Mill's *On liberty*, shock must not be allowed to legislate against private behaviours and attitudes. The case against pornography must be established outside democratic theory which recognises neither economic exploitation of poor women by pornographers nor the power politics played out in women's private lives.

The resistance to a woman's right to choose abortion and the insistence on the rights of pornographers suggest that the adjudication of rights may not be appropriate in areas of special concern to women such as abortion and sexuality. These aspects of women's lives cannot be analysed in terms of the world of economically competing individuals that democratic theory projects. For this reason the rights of pornographers, who are busily making money, are more defensible than a woman's right to an abortion unrelated to commerce. Nor can sexuality and child-birth be thought of as private recreations engaged upon in one's own time. Sexuality and birth necessarily involve others: sexual partners, family, and society as a whole. They cannot, therefore, be analysed in terms of rights that mark out spheres of competing economic or private interest.

It is not out of simple, correctible exclusion that the founding fathers of liberalism spoke of the rights of man. Utilitarianism and social contract theory begin with a theory of man. Men are self-interested, pleasure-seeking, acquisitive, competitive.[59] The arrangements that democratic theory proposes are to mediate the selfishness of these men and prevent them from killing each other. It is therefore not surprising that women are only included with difficulty. Women, it is acknowledged by democrats such as Rousseau, are different and need not participate in democratic institutions. Liberal feminism demands that women be guaranteed the rights of man, but it is not necessary to propose an essentialist feminine altruism or passivity to see the limitations of such an achievement. The 'man' of democratic theory is no natural human being, or even 'natural man'; he is instead man in nineteenth-century industrialised Europe, separated from feudal ties to place and extended family, independent economic units bargaining for decisive economic advantage in the midst of the uncontrolled and often destructive expansion of capitalist production. All that liberal theory recommends to feminists in the way of strategy, all the legislating and constitutional reform that still predominate as feminist practice in many Western countries, can never accomplish more than that women take *his* place.

Notes

1. Peter Laslett (ed.), *Two treatises on government* (Cambridge University Press, Cambridge, 1970), II, Sec. 82 on husband's authority.

2. Ibid., I. Chapter V, Sec. 44–7, pp. 89–92.

3. David Hume, *Treatise on human nature*, ed. Selby-Bigge (Clarendon Press, Oxford, 1965), Book III, Part II, Sec. VIII. The natural state of society here is claimed to be a 'conjunction' of patriarchal families.

4. Ibid., Book III, Part II, Sec. XII, 'Of Chastity and Modesty'.

5. Louis Harimen, Bruxelles, 1830 (written in 1796).

6. Ibid., p. 17.

7. Ibid., p. 96.

8. This view of women as first and foremost susceptible to love is echoed in the romantic fiction of the nineteenth century. One can see it even in Nathaniel Hawthorne's unflattering portrayal of a feminist in *The Blithedale romance*. Zenobia considers herself a feminist and a reformer but only orates on women's rights when she is thwarted in love. Hawthorne's narrator's comments: 'What amused and puzzled me, was the fact, that women however intellectually superior, so seldom disquiet themselves about the rights or wrongs of their sex, unless their own individual affections chance to lie in idleness, or to be ill at ease' (Ohio State University Press, Cent. Ed., vol. III, 1964), p. 20. Once her love affair with Hollingsworth fails, Zenobia ends her life with a romantically staged suicide. Verena Taggart in Henry James's *The Bostonians* is similarly deflected from her feminist activites by the seductive courtship of a chivalrous sexist.

9. Stael *De l'influence des passions sur le bonheur des individus et des nations*, p. 101.

10. Ibid., p. 100.

11. Stael's examples here are the overworked Sappho and Queen Elizabeth. Sappho jumps to her death out of unrequited love; Elizabeth makes a fool of herself over Essex (ibid., p. 76).

12. Ibid., p. 76.

13. Ibid., pp. 72–3.

14. Ibid., p. 74.

15. Ibid., p. 73.

16. Harriet Taylor also objected to this tone in the otherwise admired resolutions of the first 'Women's Rights Convention' in her 'Enfranchisement of women', first pub. 1851 in the *Westminster Review*; reprinted in Alice Rossi (ed.), *Essays on sex equality* (University of Chicago Press, Chicago, 1970). Taylor deplored the irrational demand for 'social and spiritual union', for a 'medium of expressing the highest moral and spiritual views of justice', rightly suspicious of the delegation of women to any kind of 'spiritual priesthood'.

17. Here the Paris left, agreeing with Plato that women's voices are more complaining, shriller, better at lamentation, finally manages to put them to some good use.

18. Printed in Hubertine Auclert, *Le vote des femmes* (V. Giard and E. Brière, Paris, 1908), p. 78.

19. Gouge's declaration might be held to be radical even today when issues such as women's inclusion in the draft are controversial. In the United States, for example, the defeat of the Equal Rights Amendment was at least partly due to the fear that such an Amendment would make unconstitutional the limiting of conscription to males.

20. See for example Alice Clark, *Working life of women in the seventeenth century* (Augustus Kelly, New York, 1968), 1st edn 1919, who argued that capitalism is responsible for a decrease in women's status as women's work becomes nonproductive domestic labour.

21. That women were not specifically excluded from the suffrage until 1832 in England shows the depth of a discrimination that did not have to

be written into law. The fact that women did not vote was used as proof that not everyone has that right. See Ellen Carol Du Bois, *Feminism and suffrage* (Cornell University Press, Ithaca, NY, 1978), p. 44.

22. Nothing was as bitter to American feminists as the inclusion of 'male' in the 14th Amendment which guaranteed to the black man his rights. Women, many of them front runners in the abolitionist movement, when the gains were to be registered, were again excluded, and explicitly, by the male leadership. At the time, there was certainly no doubt that 'male' meant just what it said. See William O'Neill, *The women's movement: feminism in the United States and England* (George Allen and Unwin, London, 1969) for a full discussion.

23. Not that the British Wollstonecraft had any illusion about the French. She commented on their cult of 'la femme': 'The very essence of sensibility has been extracted to regale the voluptuary, and a kind of sentimental lust has prevailed which, together with the system of duplicity, that the whole tenor of their political and civil government taught, have given a sinister sort of sagacity to the French character, properly termed finesse, that injures the substance by hunting sincerity out of society.' *Vindication of the rights of women* (Walter Scott, London, 1792), pp. xxv–xxvi.

24. As always with a collaboration it is not always possible to say who wrote what. Mill, himself, claimed that from the *Principles of political economy* onward, his work, including *On liberty*, was a joint project with Taylor. Certainly there is substantial evidence in correspondence and notes that they thoroughly discussed all aspects of his works, with Harriet a critic to whom Mill often demurred. Why Mill did not acknowledge her authorship more publicly is probably explained by the unconventional nature of their situation (most of their friendship was carried on while Harriet was still married to John Taylor). Also, Mill's name was better known and would add respectability to the cause. See Alice Rossi's *Introduction to essays on sexual equality* (University of Chicago Press, Chicago, 1970), for a full discussion of the question of authorship, esp. p. 41. Harriet, it would seem, was primarily responsible for the 'Enfranchisement of women' published in the *Westminster Review* in 1851. Mill's *The subjection of women* was written after Harriet's death but, Mill says in the introduction, to make clear *her* ideas.

25. Wollstonecraft was also a Unitarian. The Unitarians had for many years published articles championing the cause of women in their journal *Monthly Respository* and the *Westminster Review*.

26. The classic example, originally given by E. F. Carrett: an innocent man is hung for the utilitarian purpose of deterring future crime.

27. Edmund Burke, *Reflections on the Revolution in France* (Penguin, Harmondsworth, 1969).

28. There has been enough said about Mill as child prodigy and his awesome feats in Greek and mathematics. Perhaps the most interesting is his own account of the deficiencies of such an education in his *Autobiography*. His mind was developed, he said, but not his emotions. He became like Hume's rational man who would not raise a finger even if by the gesture he could save the world. The result is a nervous breakdown, when at 20 he realises that even if the whole utilitarian

programme were successful, it would not matter to him at all.

29. Jeremy Bentham, *An introduction to the principles of morals and legislation* (Clarendon Press, Oxford, 1876).

30. Rossi (ed.) *Essays*, p. 94.

31. Ibid., p. 97.

32. Mill's discussion of the 'natural' is elsewhere admirable: see ibid., pp. 190 and 203, where he pointed out the difficulties in the Comtean biologism that attempted to establish the difference of male and female.

33. Ibid., p. 105. This is a point on which Taylor and Mill were not in accord. Mill agreed that education and jobs should be open to exceptional women. At the same time, he believed that once married, a woman's place was in the home.

34. Ibid., p. 104.

35. Ibid., p. 147.

36. Ibid., p. 107.

37. Ibid., p. 218.

38. Ibid., pp. 117–18.

39. Taylor and Mill certainly suffered their own large share of frustration and animosity because of their views and because of the irregularity of their relationship (intimate friends of 20 years, notwithstanding Taylor's marriage to John Taylor) and so furnished an example that not every couple would be brave enough to follow.

40. 'The subjection of women' in Rossi (ed.), *Essays*, p.173.

41. How ideal their relationship really was is another question. Friends often complained of Taylor's dictatorial hold on Mill who suffered a series of physical and/or mental breakdowns. A seemingly severe sexual repression clouded unreserved intimacy. It is hard to see Mill's idealisation of Taylor as any basis for real mutual understanding. Perhaps it was just exactly that notion of themselves as an elite that so marred their sought-after perfection.

42. Mill's *rapprochement* between rights and utilitarianism was subtle. Rights did not depend on any abstract essence with its necessary and dangerous absolutism, therefore in extreme cases in which a right to speak or assemble clearly meant a public danger, one could judge that the greatest happiness demanded their infringement. Stealing when starving, for example, could also be justified, whereas in a strict adherence to moral law, no exceptions are justified.

43. See O'Neill, *The woman's movement*, pp. 112–13 for the text of the protest.

44. Thomas Wentworth Higginson, *Common sense about women* (Lee and Shepard, Boston, 1882), esp. p. 41. It is also important to remember Higginson as the correspondent and mentor of Emily Dickinson. His well-meant misunderstanding of the great poet's innovations did nothing to improve either her style or the increasing unhappiness of her restricted life.

45. Ibid., p. 135.

46. *La femme au XIX siècle* (Amyat, Paris, 1859), pp. 293–6.

47. 'Enfranchisement' in Rossi (ed.), *Essays*, p. 104. Taylor seems to be on record as a socialist. In the 'Enfranchisement', she may be deliberately downplaying this conviction for rhetorical purposes. Taking

the capitalist world as it is, she argues for women's inclusion. See also Zillah R. Eisenstein, *The radical future of liberal feminism* (Longman, New York, 1981), who argued that capitalism's hierarchical inequalities will always be uncomfortable for women who will naturally move from liberalism to radicalism.

48. 'Subjection' in Rossi (ed.), *Essays*, p. 146.

49. See Juliet Mitchell, *Women and equality* (University of Cape Town Press, Cape Town, 1975), for an extension of these arguments.

50. The ideological defence of the New Right can be found in Milton Friedman or Frederick Hayek who urge a retreat from the welfare state and a return to the free market of the nineteenth century.

51. This is the argument, for example, of Judy Barnes, *The case for women's rights* (Society for Libertarian Life, undated).

52. Although an Equal Pay Act was passed in the United States in the 1960s, 20 years later women's wages remained at about 60% of men's.

53. Although the principle of comparable worth is recognised in the United Kingdom, it has had little success in the United States courts and has been implemented by only a few liberal state governments.

54. Roe vs. Wade (1977) established a woman's right to choose abortion on the basis of a right to privacy and the lack of a compelling state interest in regulating abortion.

55. Michele Barrett and Mary MacIntosh, *The anti-social family* (Verso, London, 1981). Cf. Locke's argument on p. 6 above.

56. Wagner, 'Women and neo-liberalism' in J. Etons *et al.* (ed.), *Feminism and political theory* (Sage, London, 1986).

57. Carol Gillingan, *In a different voice: psychological theory and women's development* (Harvard University Press, Cambridge, Mass., 1982), esp. Chapter 3, 'Concepts of Self and Morality'.

58. The proto-type legislation drafted by Andrea Dworkin, Catherine Mackinnon and others was first introduced in Minneapolis, Minnesota.

59. Again the range of opinion accounts for variety in democratic theory. Hobbes's natural man is a brute and so must submit to authority; Locke's, softened by an innate sense of natural law, is allowed more freedom; Rousseau's is capable of sympathy but is still self-interested enough to amass fortunes that must be protected by force. See also Nancy Hartsock's description of a historically specific and 'truncated' 'rational economic man' who is part of a particular kind of alienated community based on 'exchange'. *Money, sex and power* (Longman, New York, 1983), Chapter 2, pp. 38–54.

3

A Community of Men:
Marxism and Women

A working woman's feminism

Rousseau's Sophie, the bird in a cage so accurately described by
Wollstonecraft, the woman to be liberated by way of natural rights
to freedom and equality, was not a woman with whom a working
woman of the nineteenth century could easily have identified.
Feminists like Harriet Taylor or Margaret Fuller lived in well-
insulated environments of ease and refinement which, even when
tempered by a weekly visit to the settlement house or soup kitchen,
were not conducive to any feeling of commonality with the poor.
Although the plight of poor women was almost always described
and deplored, as feminists returned to their comfortable living
rooms, the less fortunate must have wondered how deep their
sympathies really ran. In the end, class interest and class privilege
would prevail no matter how fashionable feminism might
become.[1]

Certainly working women who, even in the 1900s already
constituted 38 per cent of the labour force, would have trouble
recognising themselves in the stereotype described by Romieu,
Higginson and de Stael. That 'woman' was rich, pampered,
married, and anything that could be said about her liberation
seemed to have little to do with a poor factory worker struggling
at home with an out-of-work husband who drank to soothe his
wounded ego and beat her on Saturday night. Whatever Harriet
Taylor might have suffered from her husband John, it was, one
must think, radically different.

Working women had no time for lectures or philosophical
speculation, or even perhaps for the instruction that such lectures
were to provide. The Rousseauian woman, passive, frail, a

31

supporter by nature, was defined by her role in a social order, an order that liberal feminists showed no signs of completely rejecting. Working women, occupying a very different place in society, could not be expected to sympathise. They were more likely to view liberal feminists with suspicion, or even contempt for their softness, for their pretension, for their hypocrisy. These feelings were often reciprocal, as the reformers looked with some condescension at the 'squalor' and 'moral decay' of working-class life. As the popular defender of women's frail nature, Michelet observed: 'ouvrière' is a word impious and sordid.

Socialism claimed to speak for these working women and men whose interests the bourgeoisie had so conveniently conflated with their own: socialists argued that the supposedly universal equality and freedom of a democratic society were part of the deception of bourgeois ideology. As reformers, as the proper antithesis to the feudal aristocracy, the bourgeoisie presented itself as a defender of universal values, but it was soon clear that concrete reforms would be to the benefit of their own class, not to workers. The philosophical radicals, with whom Mill was allied, were themselves unpleasantly surprised by this failure to attract worker support. In their rational utilitarian reforms, no distinction had been made between the propertied and the labourer. Nor did Mill make such a distinction in *The subjection of women*, although the presumption of inherited wealth alone could allow the equality he proposed between a non-working wife and her husband.

Socialism, on the other hand, promised to provide a theory of change that would engage the differences in wealth and power that made liberal feminist liberation superficial. As with democratic theory, however, socialism did not immediately or wholeheartedly embrace the cause of women. Saint-Simonians, for example, advocated complete emancipation. At the same time, they were careful to defend themselves from the charge that they advocated anything that could be labelled the 'community of women'.[2] In an address to the President of the Chambre des députés,[3] the Saint-Simonians denied that they had any intention of abolishing the 'sacred law of marriage': they wanted only to strengthen it. In fact, they argued, in their system, the couple, surrounded by religious mysticism, would be the basic social unit, not the individual. In a Saint-Simonian marriage there would be strict equality. Divorce would be available, but, given the happiness of the reformed marriage, would in all probability seldom be necessary.[4] The bourgeois marriage survived, this time made happy by the disappearance of private property that would in turn eliminate differences in power between husband and wife.

In England, Robert Owen argued against the ties of marriage for free love, but female Owenites demurred. What was needed was child care and relief from housework, not a sexual freedom that might leave women more exploited and more vulnerable than when they were married. Even these reforms were unacceptable, however, to male workers recruited by the Owenites, who were not pleased with the prospect of an influx of female labour into the market. Male authority in the home would have to be maintained. In this clash between the idealism of Owen and the concrete situation of male workers, the workers prevailed, and Owenites reverted to a more moderate support of women's rights and marriage reform that did not go far beyond the programme of liberal feminism.[5]

Fourier, unembarrassed by his failure to attract a mass of followers, goes further. In his *Théorie des quatre mouvements*[6] he advocated the complete breakup of the family, and the bringing up of children by the state. Each sex was to receive an equivalent education and there was to be no restriction in healthy sexual activity. Women would work, but — and here again the gentle Sophie must come to mind — there would be differences. 'Respected' and 'appropriate' places would be found for women in industry. It was understood that they would not do the rough work of men. This caution, ominous though it may be for the future of women under socialism, was at the same time far preferable to the outright misogyny of many socialists.

Proudhon, whose ideas were so prominent in the French syndicalist movement, was the most unequivocal in his views: women were physically, mentally, and morally inferior; they were a passive receptacle for sperm; they were given to men to serve them as auxiliaries. Proudhon adds the usual accompaniment of compensating reverence.[7] These degraded and inferior creatures were also the 'étoile de sa vie' (the star of his life), 'la fleur de sa vie' (the flower of his life). Socialism would, of course, make their lives better, but it would do so because marriage would be made stronger for women's protection. Most importantly, each husband would be guaranteed the means to support his wife. Proudhon deplored any movement in socialism to weaken the family.[8]

Leaving such excesses aside, many moderate socialists also took a view of women's rights that owed much to Rousseau. Cabet, for example, good democrat and defender of the Paris Commune, described the liberated position of women when collectivism is finally realised. In his *The woman, her unhappy lot in contemporary society, her happiness in the commune*,[9] he begins with homage. Women are extolled as wives and mothers, as what makes the life of man worthwhile: 'I would see her under an image that no man could see without emotion, under the image of a mother, a sister, a wife, or a daughter.'[10] Not, however, as workers or citizens. Cabet deplored the sad lot of these mothers and sisters in sweat shops, prey to prostitution, wife-beating, drunkenness. 'A drunken woman,' exclaimed Cabet, 'what spectacle more humiliating for Humanity than a drunken woman.'[11] The cause, he claimed, is privilege and money. The answer is the 'Communauté', organised on the principles of 'égalité, fraternité and unité, a society of citizens, all *brothers*, and all with equal rights'.[12]

Cabet was more precise as to what this fraternity would mean for women. The first articles of the Constitution of the Communauté are that men should recognise women, should give them their respect, devotion, affection, protection, care, and regard:

> In all their sessions, the representatives of the People must occupy themselves first with laws and measures that interest women . . .[13] Each must conduct himself toward his fellow citizens and *brothers* as he desires them to conduct themselves to him; each owes to other women, old and young, the same regard that he desires to see in other *men* for *his* mother and *his* sister.[14] (my emphases)

A man should always be working to embellish, to perfect, to make the woman happy. A woman's education should cultivate her intelligence and her heart to make her 'a companion worthy of man and capable of making him happy'.[15] Women, he assured his readers, also prefer institutions that will give them a husband, a friend, a protector.[16] These are the benefits that will make of revolutionary France 'le paradis des femmes'. In his novel, *Voyage en Icarie*,[17] Cabet further elaborated the sort of society he had in mind. Women will have equal legal rights and an equal education. Each 'jeune fille' will then choose 'a profession that is not tiring' leaving the demanding jobs to men. Each girl will marry. Furthermore, in marriage, since it is necessary that someone have the final say, it will be necessary to give the man the greater weight of authority.

A difference in women's role in work and in the family also prevailed in actual utopian experiments. Even when, influenced by communal ideals, women like Melusina Fay Pierce or Charlotte Perkins Gilman deplored women's exploitation in the home and proposed co-operative housekeeping, it was still women who continued to be responsible for housework. The difference was that they would organise it more efficiently than in private households and, perhaps, receive a remuneration for their service. Such modest Sophies still had behind them no force that could overcome the inevitable husband's opposition, and were soon absorbed into 'home economics' and the development of labour-saving devices for the housewife who could pay.[18]

This weakness in practice was, perhaps, inevitable. In the first place, utopian socialism's strategy was deceptively moral. Reformers dreamt that if the rich and powerful could be made to see the error of their ways and the justice of communal existence, they would then give up wealth and power. Much emphasis was given to persuasion and argument, and the positive force of examples and models. Utopians like the Saint-Simonians or the Owenites set up model communities in which their ideas could be lived out, hoping that the peace, harmony, and happiness that would prevail in these communities would be the best argument for the superiority of their views. In this strategy, utopian socialists had much in common with feminists like Taylor or Wollstonecraft who also argued and attempted to persuade that the rule of superior strength should give way to a rule of morality. Would men but 'snap our chains', said Wollstonecraft,[19] appealing to men's reason and moral sense. Taylor and Mill, in their ideal society *à deux*, hoped to show what a feminist utopia could be — but there was no reason to think that male property owners securing male heirs for their fortunes and free household labour would give up their privileges; no reason to think that isolated exceptional experiments, whether communal or marital, could bring societal change. Utopian experiments could even function as useful safety valves, creating comforting conduits for the moral uneasiness of a middle class sufficiently well off to dabble in a socialism that in no way threatened real power relationships.

There was, however, in the mid-nineteenth century, another kind of feminist — not a well-off, frustrated wife, but a woman who worked. Increasingly women were employed in industry, usually in the lower paid, most menial capacities. New categories were being invented for female labour, such as secretary or dactylo, for someone who would do the work of a male assistant for half the wage. The socialist feminist Flora Tristan, for example, was able to speak at first hand of poverty, poor working conditions, and the despair of prostitution. One might also compare Emma Goldman, born in Russia in 1869 into a poor family where relationships had all the brutality of poverty.[20] By age 16, Goldman was on her own in New York, supporting herself in a factory. These women had none of the advantages of class standing or wealth of liberal feminists. They did not see themselves as oppressed women, but rather as part of the oppressed poor. Their allies were not lecturing reforming suffragettes, but the women and men who were their fellow workers and fellow sufferers. Their strategy for change was correspondingly different. The antidote for women's oppression was not legislation but an organisation of workers. Feminists should not try to find within existing socio-economic structures the legal means to advance women's interests, but should work to destroy those structures. Women's oppression, they argued, is only superficially caused by laws, or lack of laws; instead it is located deeper in the very essence of capitalism — the exploitation of one class by another.

However, again, the initial gains for women in the new workers' movement were disappointing. Although working-class power, augmented by almost universal male suffrage and trade union activity, increased in the latter half of the nineteenth century, although there was a strong Marxist Social Democratic party in Germany and the French had managed a Commune in Paris for 70 days that Marx took as a working-class revolution, women were not prominent either in trade unions or in socialist parties. In France, for example, in 1900 34.5 per cent of the workforce was female, but only 6.3 per cent of the French syndicalists were women.[21] The workers' movement in France, developing in an atmosphere of small trade and guilds, rather than large-scale industry, was traditionally anti-feminist, taking its justification from Proudhon. In 1866 the Association Internationale des Travailleurs, meeting in Geneva, had condemned women's work as a degeneration of the race, affirming that woman's place was in the home as mother and as keeper of the hearth for men, and that only in this way could men have order and morality in their lives.

In 1877 the Trade Union Congress in England passed a

resolution that women's place was in the home and man's job was to provide. Certainly the increased use of machinery put women's finesse and delicacy in demand instead of brute strength; and as in France, English male workers were persuaded that if women were encouraged to work, unemployment would result along with a decrease in wages. Working men, just like middle-class men, demanded reassurance that homes would not break up, and that there would be continuity to family life. Claims of women to the right to contraception or divorce were also seen as threatening. At the International Anarchist Conference in Paris in 1900, Emma Goldman was prevented from reading her papers on sexuality on the pretext of a possible bad press.

In the Marxist Social Democratic party in Germany matters were little better. In 1875, at the Gotha Congress where the German Socialist party accepted a Marxist orientation, Bebel's proposal that women be given equal rights was rejected on the grounds that women were not ready. Even when in 1891 the German party, pushed by Bebel, finally accepted women's rights, they were limited and narrowly legal. Women were allowed to join the party but by late 1900 they were still not allowed to attend 'mixed' meetings and still struggled to win the right to speak. Especially when women did not have the vote, their addition seemed uselessly to swell the ranks of the party, with no political advantage.[22]

Still, no matter how discouraging the record of worker organisations and parties in practice, again there were elements in Marxist theory that seemed promising to feminists. The surge of hope that came with the French and American Revolutions had faded, the vote seemed further away than ever, and although reforms had been accomplished giving women some right to their property and to divorce and, especially in the United States, some right to higher education, women's situation had not substantially changed. Marxism offered an alternative to apparently failed democratic ideals, a new way of conceptualising the root causes of sexism, and, even more important, new strategies for change.

The attack on the bourgeois family

These new theoretical underpinnings were set out by Engels in *The origin of the family, private property and the state*.[23] Working with both Marx's notes and the observations of the anthropologist, Lewis

Morgan, Engels began with the basic premisses of Marxist theory. Communism is not utopian and idealistic, but materialist and realistic. The determining factor in history is the production of the means of existence (food, clothes, shelter). The structure of society depends on how this production is accomplished. Furthermore, as structures change and succeed each other, one can see a progression, a development, a progress.[24] Given these premisses, Engels proceeded to analyse the family, the domain of women. The origin of the family, like the origin of everything else, he argued, is economic. For the liberal, Mill, sexism is a result of the individual brutality of men, combined with the individual physical weakness of women; for Engels, society is always social, always a particular kind of economic arrangement, never reducible to the individual. Sexism, Engels argued, was not universal. There was a time when land was owned communally, when inheritance was through the mother, when women's work was valued as much as men's. Mill placed oppression from the first 'twilight' of history; Engels said once women were 'free and honored'.[25]

The family as we know it, comes into existence with private property which also brings about 'the world historical defeat of the female sex'. Given the power which this property confers on the men who own it, given the fact that men wish to pass property on to their sons, mother-right is defeated. After that 'overthrow of the female race', 'Men took command in the home also; the woman was degraded and reduced to servitude; she became the slave of his lust and a mere instrument for the production of children.'[26] Thus, according to Engels, is created the family which survives in capitalism as a kind of slavery or serfdom. 'It contains in miniature all the contradictions which later extend throughout society and its state', Engels read from Marx's notes.[27] There are several important advantages to Engel's Marxist analysis of sexism.

Firstly, sexist institutions are explained as social phenomena, as events in time, as one possible response to human problems, and not as a natural and irrevocable fact. There is no question here of nature, neither men's nor women's, and what is not 'natural', what did not exist once, may not exist in the future. Mill saw clearly enough that to take women's present 'nature' as natural was a mistake when one considered the conditioning and role modelling to which they were subjected. One would never know, he conjectured, what women's nature is until they are allowed to live freely. There is no conjecture with Engels; the character of an individual is always determined by social function, by the aggregate of relationships in which she or he is defined. Therefore, the structure of the family should never be justified as dependent on a 'nature' of any kind, female or male.

Secondly, Engels' analysis of the origin of the bourgeois family cuts through all the protective sentimentality that had insulated the family from liberal reform. The family is a functioning social unit, not a God-given necessity. It serves an economic purpose — to ensure to men heirs of undisputed paternity. That economic purpose demands a double standard, for a woman must not be unfaithful. A man, of course, is in a different position. What is in question here is not morality, not the superior virtue of women as made out by Stael, Higginson, or Romieu, but a social function. Because there is no social function for a man's fidelity, it is only to be expected that the bourgeois marriage as outlined in the nineteenth-century Napoleonic Code has different standards for male and female sexual behaviour.[28] Marriage is based not on love but property; it is a way for a man with property to make sure he has someone to whom he can leave it. A worker who has no property will have no need of marriage, nor will he be able to afford the slave labour of a wife.

In answering the old charge that communists advocated the community of women, Marx and Engels claimed that it was really the bourgeoisie who used women in common, for what else was prostitution?[29] The bourgeoisie had, in marriage, carved out of this community a kind of private property where each single man owned a woman. Now all they can imagine is that when this private property is taken away there will be only prostitution left. Bourgeois moral outrage at prostitution is only a facade covering the similar relation of bourgeois men to women in both prostitution and marriage.[30] Women are to be owned, whether in common or privately. Instead, Engels proposed that women be treated as human beings, not as objects or 'instruments of production'.

Thirdly, a programme was prescribed for radical action. Liberal feminism concentrated on legal reform: there must be equal rights in marriage and a contract freely made. Marxists pointed out that these reforms could alleviate but not essentially change the position of women as long as the economics of marriage remained. The free contract of the liberated woman will be as free as the free contract which a labourer makes with his or her employer. Given the fact that he must eat to live, given the fact that the employer owns the means of production, the labourer is hardly in an equal bargaining position. He is under duress, which makes any freedom illusory. Nor has he any adequate remedy if the contract is not kept. A woman also has no means of support. She has no property and is under an extreme disadvantage in the labour market. She must marry to live. No contract made in such a situation could be free.[31] Marxism proposed an alternative strategy; feminists can turn from narrow concerns with the vote and marriage law to socialist revolution. Once capitalism is eliminated, women's oppression will disappear.

In *Capital*,[32] Marx described the economic mechanisms of which the family is a part. In feudalism, the family was an economic unit, the institution around which production is organised. The industrial revolution replaced the family as a productive unit with the factory and with the distinctive relations of capitalist production. Labourers sell their labour power for wages and produce surplus value that is returned to the capitalist as profit. The family becomes only a unit of consumption. With a socialist revolution, inevitable as the proletariat become conscious of their common oppression and their power, the family will be economically useless. The state will take over many of its functions, such as day care for children, care of the ill and the aged, and perhaps even some personal services. For feminists, the actual, already occurring, breakup of the family meant that there was now some existing place where change could take hold, where it was already taking hold. The family was not immortal; in fact, it was obsolete, and, as obsolete, it would begin to disappear regardless of any individual action. It was by aligning themselves with these real existing material changes that feminists could bring about liberation. Unfortunately, again practice had a sobering effect on theory. In Russia, where a socialist revolution seemed to have been accomplished, the question of women did not resolve itself as easily as Marxist feminists had hoped.

Marxist feminists: Zetkin, Kollontai, Goldman

Marxism was made accessible to Alexandra Kollontai in Russia and Clara Zetkin in Germany, by Engels's follower, the German Social Democrat, August Bebel. His *Women under socialism*,[33] once it escaped Bismarkian censorship, was well circulated. Bebel's Marxism, applied to women, filled a growing vacuum in feminist theory. Less technical than Marx himself, who was still for the most part unpublished in Germany, often using arguments similar to the patient persuasions of Mill, again relying on Morgan's, and now Bachofen's studies of matrilineality, Bebel attempted to win over his fellow social democrats hostile to women workers, to the realisation that there must be full equality for women as well as men in the socialist state. He repeated Engels's genealogy of sexism: the monogamous, male-headed family develops out of private property. Women's character defects, emphasised by Bebel, are due to their debased situation, are inherited by each generation, but could be corrected in the new socialist society. After the dawn of socialism, women will have a right to work that is equal to men's, and will be educated and participate politically just like men. In the new socialist marriage, women will choose a mate freely and have the right to divorce. Once property is out of the picture, marriages will be happy, Bebel assured his readers, and divorce will only be necessary in exceptional cases.

Because these benefits will automatically follow from socialism, much of Bebel's *Women under socialism* does not need to mention women at all. After a description of women's problems in the present, the central chapters describe the mechanisms by which private property would be collectivised, with no reference to the female sex. After this groundwork, the last chapter, 'Woman in the future', can be, as Bebel said, very short. She will have equal rights with men and a happy marriage, both results of the previously described social revolution.

Similarly, in *The traffic in women*, Emma Goldman used a materialist, economic analysis of marriage and prostitution to expose the shallow moralising of American suffragettes. The supposed advantage of women's suffrage was to be the restoration of decency and morality in public life; but what decency was this to be? — the decency that would outlaw and punish prostitution, making poor women's lives worse. Prostitution was not moral but economic. There were prostitutes because women could not get work, were economically powerless, and, when they did work, were not paid a living wage. Furthermore, married women who deplored the immorality of prostitution were no different. They had also been bought, the price they paid for their security, even higher than the price the prostitute paid for her living. The married woman gave up 'her name, her privacy, her self respect, her very life',[34] Furthermore, the prospect of such a marriage, even for a single woman, made her professional life more tenuous, because she must see her work as only temporary, not a matter of real commitment.

Liberal feminists thought they could correct these evils with, firstly, the vote, and then with legislation, but as Goldman argued in 'Woman suffrage',[35] the vote had become a fetish that was to solve all problems. In fact, the vote would only make things worse. Women, whether voting or not, embrace what enslaves them: religion, home, and war. A voting woman, therefore, will only be a better Christian, homemaker, and citizen, and vote accordingly. The vote had become a new idol for women to worship just as they worship male gods. Women's voting had not been progressive; if anything, it had been reactionary.[36] Women voters became merely 'political spies' blowing the trumpets of decency and temperance.[37] They had not supported change in family law, sexual freedom, separation of church and state, or labour parties. Instead, they had supported non-threatening humanitarian causes, such as prevention of cruelty to children and animals, or aid to the handicapped. They might have better reflected on why there were so many battered, defective children to rehabilitate. Even the supposed benefits of the vote, that women would then get property rights and equal pay, were shams, firstly because property rights could be of little use to women who would never have any property, and secondly, because pay in a capitalist country was not determined by legislation.

In Germany, Clara Zetkin also saw Marxism as the theory that would be the basis of the new women's movement. In her 'What women owe to Karl Marx',[38] she argued that Marx provided a precise and sure method for studying and understanding women's struggle. Marx did not so much provide specific answers for women as give them a means to situate their struggle in history, and in the light of general social relations. Through Marx, women could come to understand their own practice and thereby develop objectives and strategies that would bring liberation. Marx's analysis of the family had shown that women's role is not eternal or immutable, not produced by either God's law or by moral law. Instead, family structures, like any other structures, change and disappear. Marx demonstrated that the 'motor' of such change is economics. This is proven in Engels's *Origin of the family*, and then more technically in Marx's *Capital* where Marx described the irresistible economic forces which are at work, breaking up the family and so clearing the way for the equality of women. Marx had opened women's eyes and given them the certainty that something new and better would result. In *Capital*, in his discussion of the supposedly 'little chores' of women workers, he had given them heart to demand specific reforms in work conditions, along with a view of the whole that would lead to change on a much grander scale.

Similarly, Alexandra Kollontai, prominent in the Russian Revolution both before and after the Bolsheviks took power, argued that only under socialism could specific women's problems such as child care, maternity, and housework be solved. The first proviso of socialism is that everyone is a worker; women will therefore work. There will immediately appear an obvious contradiction between their roles as wives and mothers and their professional responsibilities. Only a socialist society can resolve these contradictions. Socialism will handle these contradictions in women's lives in the same way that it will handle any conflict — by meeting human needs. Women will be given maternity leave with pay, access to child care and socialisation of domestic work.

In the early days of the Russian Revolution, Kollontai proceeded to attempt to implement actively these socialist ideals, both making the connections with masses of women that would allow their needs to be voiced, and then drafting proposed legislation to meet these needs. An unprecedented social revolution seemed to be taking place in Russia: civil, easily dissolved marriage, complete legal equality between men and women, maternity leave, and a growing range of support services, child care centres, communal kitchens, and so on. These improvements, Kollontai believed, were only possible within socialism, never under capitalism where the economics of marriage and child-bearing barred any such blurring of marital obligation.[39]

However, as the Russian Revolution proceeded, the question of women did not resolve itself as easily as Marxist feminists had hoped. When the Stalinist policies of the 1920s required rapid industrialisation, military development, order and discipline at all costs, Zhenodtel, the women's branch of the party, the means for the realisation of much of Kollontai's programme for women, was dissolved; programmes and reforms initiated by Zhenodtel were cancelled. The family was restored, homosexuality and abortion declared illegal, child care centres closed, and a socialist morality was encouraged not much different from Victorian propriety. It had been established that women would work, but

by 1930 women had all but disappeared from positions of power.[40]
War, hot or cold, was not the time for social experiments.

Difficulties in realising Kollontai's socialist programme for
women, however, went deeper than Stalinism. To judge the
failure of emancipation in Russia as the effect of an accident of
personality would be both non-Marxist and shortsighted. Even
Kollontai, the great sexual revolutionary, certainly willing to take
risks in the past, acquiesced in Stalin's decisions. Nor is it enough
to cite the 'special' circumstances of Russia, underdeveloped
industrially and encircled by hostile capitalist powers. In fact,
there were theoretical barriers to women's emancipation from the
very beginning. Although Lenin never equivocated in his verbal
support for women's equality in work and family, once he was
functioning head of the new Bolshevik government, he was
immediately in conflict with feminist demands.

Kollontai's Zhenodtel had always faced considerable opposition and criticism. Why should there be a separate Women's
Bureau of the Party? Why should there be any specific women's
organisations? When Stalin finally decided to dissolve Zhenodtel
it was a decision shared by the Bolshevik leadership and also by
much of the rank and file. There had always been reservations as
to the premiss on which any women's organisation was based —
that there were special women's problems, problems that women
had as women, not as workers. This premiss was not just offensive
to certain re-educatable male interests, but also theoretically
inadmissible. There should be nothing outside materialist
economics, nothing unexplained and unconnected to economics,
and it seemed that to admit specific women's problems was to
deny this basic tenet of Marxist theory. Certainly, at best, the
tenure of such organisations was expected to be brief and a
temporary 'transition-stage'[41] phenomenon.

Even Zhenodtel had to accept the limits of possible reform.
The possibility of divorce in rural areas, for example, could not
stop a husband from beating his wife. Women could be given
equality in the work place, but it did not prevent men from
taking the skilled and high-status jobs. If the patriarchal family
seemed to survive stubbornly any legislative measures and,
perhaps worse, to be repeated in hierarchical structures in the
work place,[42] this might be necessary for industrial efficiency. It
was impossible to legislate so deeply into private lives, and also
distasteful and unseemly, Lenin complained, for socialists always
to be 'looking under bed covers'. Unfortunately, that was the

place in which much of women's humiliation occurred.

This disparity between feminist hopes and communist practice was recorded in encounters between feminists and the male leaders of the Party. These discussions centred around the question of crucial and special interest to women: the new sexual and familial relations promised by socialism. The answer most consistent with Marxist theory was that no definite answer could be given; new relations would develop out of new practices that were responses to specific situations and were not foreseeable. We would never know, Engels said grandly, what a socialist sexual relationship would be like until there is:

> A generation of men who never in their lives have known what it is to buy a woman's surrender with money or any other social instrument of power; a generation of women who have never known what it is to give themselves to a man from any consideration other than real love.[43]

It is not, Kollontai claimed, a question of dreaming up, imagining new forms of sexual union: 'All one can do is to grasp the trend of evolution which is already in process of being accomplished in the social organism and accelerate the rhythm of this process of transformation.'[44]

Engels, however, was unwilling to leave totally undescribed the new socialist sexuality. Still echoing Marx's early romanticism, a sentimentality which he was in the process of rejecting in other areas of materialist analysis, Engels in his *Origin of the family* is a committed monogamist. With property out of the picture, sexual union could be based on inclination or sexual love alone which is by nature, Engels made clear, exclusive, although in capitalism it is only felt to be so by women. In socialism, the romantic union-for-love will finally be possible.[45]

Bebel, Engels's populiser, further elaborated Engels's picture of the happy socialist family. Now women will make a free choice, their own contract, and will be able to obtain divorce. Since there will be roughly the same number of women as men, no one need be celibate. There will be nothing in the way of conjugal happiness. With Bebel's more complete description of socialist marriage, left sentimentally vague by Engels, the contradictions began to develop which would later put Soviet women at odds with Party leadership. Women will be mothers and home makers without losing their independence, Bebel reassured, because there will be readily available guardians, teachers, women friends, and young girls who will help them. They will also be relieved of much heavy work by new products and technology.[46]

However — and here Bebel imagined an anti-feminist critic's response — what is to stop the liberated woman from becoming like the notorious George Sand, expressing herself sexually each night with a different man? Much as one must admire him for raising the obvious objection to his idyllic description of socialist marriage, Bebel's answer was at best elusive. Firstly, there should be no double standard between rich and poor. Secondly, no woman will want to be promiscuous because in socialism she will have a free and happy marriage. Perhaps some *men* — Bebel does not mention women here — may not want or feel capable of monogamy. What of it?, he asks cryptically; still, the acknowledged, undeniable power of the sexual instinct has an equilibrium and we do not have to worry that society will destroy itself.[47] One could only guess what it is that Bebel meant to say faced with this obvious dilemma — after all, men are uncontrollable?; eventually the worst of them will settle down? In any case there is no further mention of promiscuous women who, once property issues are removed, will settle down happily to marriage and motherhood.

Certainly it is to be expected that Marxist feminists would have found here a theoretical hiatus of worrying dimensions. Questions of sexuality could not be disposed of in a few paragraphs at the end of an economic treatise: they required a full discussion and it was precisely this proposal which proved unacceptable to the Soviet leadership. Lenin criticised Zetkin for only discussing issues of sex and marriage in meetings with her comrades in the German Social Democratic Party.[48] Surely, Lenin said, these problems had been disposed of by Engels and Bebel?; and what, Lenin went on, was all this talk of Freud?[49] He chided Zetkin: perhaps thus to enlarge the question past Engels and Bebel's economic analysis was 'cultivated', even scientific, but it was just another fashionable eccentricity. Sexual theory is only a way to justify perversion and there is no place for it in the party.

Zetkin's reasonable answer was that the situation was not so simple. The old forms and institutions were falling away, and new social forms must be created. All this requires discussion. Lenin was not impressed with this 'excuse'. Were these meetings truly scientific? If so, they should have a text to read and study,

46

instead of treating the subject in this mediocre non-Marxist fashion. In any case, sex was not what women should think about; instead, they should discuss salaries, unemployment, taxes. When these economic matters were disposed of, the rest would fall into place. Not only is discussion of sexuality unnecessary, it is dangerous. It leads to excess, especially among the young who should be encouraged to divert their energies to exercise, study and politics, not romantic distraction.

There are several aspects to be noted in what must have been a frustrating interview for Zetkin, who nevertheless loyally praised Lenin after his death for all he had done for women.[50] Firstly, the radical Lenin is a conservative in sexual matters, content with what has gone on before. Perhaps it was not, he implied, necessary that socialism should profoundly restructure bourgeois sexual habits, although it must always continue the struggle with bourgeois economics. He did not see the problem with male-female relations which so interested Zetkin and her comrades, nor was he interested in developing the new forms of relationship which she and her group were attempting to work out.

Secondly, the economic restructuring that is to guarantee justice for women appears here in a new light — not as the means to liberation, but as an *ad hoc* mechanism introduced to avoid a disquieting and inconvenient problem in the working of socialism. Theory functions no longer as a liberating promise of things to come, but as a self-justifying silencer of agitation and unrest.

Thirdly, Lenin's idea of proper socialist practice was very much at odds with Zetkin's. Zetkin took seriously the ban on visionary solutions. To propose new forms of reality in an idealistic way, Marx had argued, would always be conservative, would always be a reflection of existing reality and not revolutionary. Socialist sexuality, Zetkin argued, would have to develop with socialist practice, as the proletariat worked out new forms of relationship. It is in this light that she and other Social Democratic women saw their discussion of sexuality. Lenin opposed such 'self-organisation'. Women's spontaneous feelings and experiences, as they test the new reality, are not 'scientific': instead he said, they should have a text to study, perhaps Engels or Bebel — that is, they should consult an authority and *then* discuss the ways in which their practice can fit authoritative pronouncement. Lenin made clear the basis of his tolerance of women's organisations: women's organisations are not to generate new relationships but are a method of rousing and organising the masses of women around established Bolshevik dogma.

Marxist feminists did not immediately take account of the depth of the chasm opened between their aspirations and Marxist leadership. Marxist feminists had long claimed that socialist women must resolutely distinguish themselves from liberal feminists and that there could be no common ground. This denial of the priority of the tie between women as women in favour of the tie between workers had caused tragic bitterness between liberal and socialist women. Zetkin advised non-co-operation with such seemingly common goals as a 'petition for freedom of assembly',[51] and often ridiculed the 'myth of great sisterhood'. Now, however, in the struggle for women's organisations and women's issues, she seemed to reinstate lines of solidarity between women that cut across working-class solidarity. Kollontai had also unequivocally rejected feminism as a woman's movement; only socialism could create the environment in which women's lives would be bettered. Liberal feminists, she argued, in their reformist attitude toward bourgeois property and marriage, show themselves to be the class enemies of proletarian women.[52] At the same time in Zhenodtel she had created a specifically women's organisation. In practice, if not in theory, there were issues that united socialist women and put them in conflict with socialist men — issues like maternity care, marriage and sexuality.

Kollontai, participating actively in shaping a socialist reality for women, was the major spokesperson for these feminine interests. Lenin had shown himself willing to discuss such practical matters as child care and communal housekeeping, and had seemed sensitive to the contradiction between woman as worker and woman as homemaker/mother.[53] He was, however, as was clear in his talks with Zetkin, much less willing to discuss sexual matters. In 1908 Kollontai had already noted an ominous 'silence' in this area. New sexual practices might be tried out in reality, but still no one wanted to talk about it. At the same time there was occurring what Kollontai termed a 'sexual crisis', growing even greater as bourgeois family institutions were strained by the new status of women workers, and no new forms of familial relationships were available. Furthermore, Kollontai argued, some sexual norms were necessary. The purpose of norms, she argued was to facilitate healthy reproduction and to promote beneficial sentiments of solidarity and sympathy. Bourgeois marriage did neither, resulting in loveless relationships and unwanted children. However — and here she provisionally accepted Lenin's interdiction on the 'drink of water theory' of sexuality[54] — its supposed opposite, promiscuity or the treating of sex as the satisfaction of a simple biological need, was also unhealthy. There must be a commitment, a relationship formed. The need for a great monogamous passion had disappeared. The search for a great love had always been reserved for the few and was in part a reaction to the frustrations of bourgeois life. Now in proletarian life, there is what Kollontai calls 'the love game', a looser relationship in which each cares for the other but sees the union as dissolvable. Such love would naturally lead to a kind of serial monogamy.[55]

There will also be a new kind of woman, who sees things differently, responds differently, has new needs and feelings, an independent working woman whose new situation necessitates a change in her love life. This is Kollontai's 'single woman'.[56] Kollontai discovered such a woman in literature and described her traits.[57] She is not sentimental but purposeful, not jealous but an individual, does not worship men but expects something of them, faces rejection not with pain and humiliation, but with relief that she may now return to her work without the distraction of passion. She is not full of shame, but rather of self-affirmation. As the bourgeois marriage breaks up, this new woman emerges, the woman for whom Kollontai's 'free union' is the appropriate style of sexual relationship.

Goldman, as an American anarchist, unrestricted by Leninist authority, but subject herself to anarchist censorship, carried this notion of free sexuality even further. Liberal feminists spent much time showing their superior morality; most of them, Goldman noted drily, are very much married. These women, thinking themselves free, are really slaves to inner tyrants, the internalised authority of parents, society, religion that says that sex is evil and must be expressed only in strictly defined ways. This puritanism can never be consistent with emancipation. By focusing on the vote and ignoring the issue of sexuality, American feminists only conceal the real sources of their subjection. Women's freedom must mean the freedom to love, and this right to love is more vital to their emancipation than the right to the vote.[58] There is in fact no good reason why women should wait for marriage or even for a 'meaningful relationship' to experience sexuality:

Can there be anything more outrageous than the idea that a healthy, grown woman, full of life and passion, must subdue her most intense craving, undermine her health and break her spirit, must stunt her vision, abstain from the depth and glory of sex experience until a 'good' man comes along to take her unto himself as wife?[59]

The sex experience described by Goldman may be more intense than the casual drink of water, but at the same time it lacks any of the monogamous seriousness that Lenin thought necessary. Nor are there Kollontai's new socialist norms.[60] For Goldman, love is to be completely free, without restrictive norms, not sacrificed to any authority.

This discussion of sexuality carried on by feminists with the disapproval of socialist authorities, both Leninist and anarchist, was in one sense simply improper: sex was something private, something not to be spoken of. Prudery, however, only partly explains socialist disinclination to go any further into sexual revolution. In addition — and this is especially true for Kollontai, so often in conflict with Bolshevik authority — the discussion touched on some fundamental and sensitive theoretical issues. Kollontai agreed that socialism created the favourable terrain on which liberation could be achieved. However, she also argued that a new organisation of production was not itself adequate to bring about the liberation of women. What was also needed were new 'social relations', and specifically, it was men who must learn to behave in new ways. The socialist state had been created but there was still the male habit of jealousy, of property right in a woman, 'body and soul', a man's incapacity to defer before a manifestation of individuality on the part of another.[61] Are men, individual men, who must, after all live in a socialist society, capable of community? 'Is modern *man* capable of working with the collective in such a way as to feel the mutually interacting influences? Is the life of the collective really capable of replacing the individual's petty personal joys?'[62] One can see here the depth of Kollontai's revisionism. She implies that women and not the proletariat are in a kind of privileged position to see the truth and to be progressive.[63] Even the poorest male worker can have property in a woman and so be corrupted. Women, on the other hand, have not owned property, have not owned anything or anyone. By way of this logic, not expressed explicitly, but hinted at by Kollontai, women, having the proper character, should *lead* the way into socialism. This the male leadership of the Party was hardly ready to allow.

However. Kollontai's exploration of personal dynamics outside economics went beyond noting the differences in the male and female character. It is, she said, a fact of life, that whether capitalist or socialist, we are to some extent alone. Given the pain and anxiety of this realisation, our security is precarious. Will men be able to give up the idea of a wifely appendage that assuages this sense of aloneness? In the meantime the new 'single woman' emerges; her new work responsibilities make her unwilling to perform any longer a support role for the insecure male ego. Men, one could say, are dragging behind and have not yet been able to enter into the new relations which require new orientation in respect to a lover. They must learn to be attentive and sensitive to another's needs, considerate of her desires, take account of her personality, offer mutual support.[64] Women have learned to do all of these things, but men have not: and until they do, there can be no good socialist marriage. Here Kollontai had moved far from Bebel's socialist union. Changing the social structure is not enough; there must also be a change in personality. Otherwise, new structures operated by still-possessive males begin to look increasingly like the old ones. The dilemma was put succinctly by Goldman, and as a dilemma any human being must face. More important than the vote, or even economics, she argued, is the relationship between people. There one must find 'how to be oneself and still find unity with another, how to feel oneself in profound communication with all human beings and conserve intact one's characteristic qualities'.[65] This reconciliation, so paradoxical, seemingly so difficult between self and other, finds its paradigmatic expression in the confrontation between lovers. Here there is no avoiding the issue in etiquette or evasion. How is a woman to be reconciled with a man, or with a woman lover? How can the two learn to live together so that both remain full human beings?

This problematic, although it was neglected in Marx's later economic analyses as well as in Leninist and Stalinist practice, was at least touched upon by the early Marx. In Marx's remarks on alienation, he also questioned what it is to relate to another human being, to live as a human being among other human beings. He posed, though in different terms, Goldman's question:

> The immediate, natural necessary relationship of human being to human being is the *relationship of man to woman*. In this *natural* species-relationship, man's relationship to nature is immediately his relationship to man, as his relationship to man is immediately his relationship to nature, to his own *natural* condition. In this relationship the extent to which the human essence has become nature for man as nature, has become the human essence of man, is *sensuously manifested*.[66]

In this somewhat overinterpreted comment, Marx approached the problem of self and other from the other direction. What is in question are not the dynamics of personal relationship but social progress, and Marx inherited from the utopian Fourier the idea of the male–female relationship as indexing that progress.[67] There is, however, a significant difference even with Fourier. In Fourier's formulation it was women's emancipation that came first, whereas for Marx, it is man's progress. The crucial gauge of that progress, Marx suggested, is the extent to which nature for man has become human nature, where nature means either women[68] or man's desire for women. In his relation with women, one can see how human man is, how far he has understood himself, in Feuerbachian terms, as a 'species-being'. It shows how far he has come from an individual to a social existence. Marx here, like Kollontai, put the accent on new non-alienated socialist relations.

However, Marx's formulation places women in a false position. They are identified with the material, natural stuff that men are to make their own in a truly socialised society. Ownership of property, whether private or state,[69] must cease altogether and new co-operative productive attitudes be developed between workers. Ownership and use of women must also cease and women must be acknowledged as human beings. However, it is not at all clear, given the identification of women with nature, whether this will be possible. Woman is to be treated like a human being but her presence as human being is always as the 'other' human being. Women are not active and productive; they are the means by which *men* realise their humanity. It is how they — whether wife or prostitute or fellow worker — are treated by and thought of by men that is the gauge of human progress. Again, as with Cabet, male-female relations are of interest in socialism, but of interest from the male point of view which continues to see women as the 'other', as a problem in male experience, as dependents whose interests will be served by non-alienated social relations between men.

Goldman, on the other hand put her question outside this 'humanism'. The problem is not to realise the 'human essence of man', but, more simply, to establish a relation between one person and another. How can each person in a relationship relate and yet realise themselves individually? Put this way, the dilemma cannot be simply solved by economics: even if class differences are eliminated, what will prevent managers from dominating workers, or husbands from dominating wives? What will prevent careerism and opportunism? This problem of alienated personality, never discussed or resolved in Marxist theory, necessitated in Soviet practice a theoretical extension to the materialist mechanics that proved insufficient in themselves to bring about a change in personal relations. Character and relationships would be formed in the new socialist society, but in the mean time, such a society would in reality inherit many ways of relating from the old order. As Engels noted, for socialist relations one needed a new generation which had never lived or been corrupted by capitalism. Even a new generation might be tainted by the old, therefore the contagion must be checked. Economics must be supplemented with temporary repression; bourgeois attitudes must be treated with 're-education', psychiatric treatment, arrests, and forced collectivism.

Kollontai, among others, questioned this solution. Increasingly, the organisational work done by her, Luxemburg, and Zetkin[70] was criticised as non-Marxist. In fact, it represented an alternative to Bolshevik repression. Old attitudes were to be corrected, new social forms were to be created, not by repression but by spontaneous action; more and more, local organisations would take over co-operatively the administration of society, working out new ways for people to inter-relate. For this, the work to be done was not in an interrogation room but out among the people. Zhendotel is perhaps the most striking example of such an organisation as Kollontai and others went to the countryside to organise women and to help them devise socialist ways to deal with problems in child care, housework, sexual relations, and work.

These socialist projects of mass organisation had to be considered subversive to a party increasingly centralised, increasingly bureaucraticised, increasingly intent on industrialisation at all costs. Kollontai's *The workers' opposition*,[71] suppressed in 1918, expressed socialist frustration with the tactics of the Bolshevik leaders.[72] Changes, Kollontai argued, should come from the bottom up, from the initiatives of the people; links had to be established between masses and party, links which would facilitate communication not only downwards but also upwards. There should be within socialism no chiefs, no top-heavy bureaucracy. These were considerations, however, that would have less and less place in Soviet domestic policy, which was concerned instead with discipline, with organisation, with making sure that directives from the top were properly interpreted.

It could be argued that such an authoritarianism did not necessarily have to implicate Marxist theory. Lenin's view of Russia as an exception allowing a different route to socialism has often been cited to relieve Marxist theory of that burden. It can also be used to bracket Stalin's closure of the feminist programme. The phenomenon of Stalinism, however, just as it forced European Marxists to reconsider the foundations of their commitment, must raise the question of the adequacy of Marxist theory for feminist goals. Whether or not Marxism was successfully practised in one historical instance is one question; whether or not it is theoretically adequate for feminist liberation is quite another. This is especially true given that the bracketing, the putting aside, of the 'woman question' both pre- and post-dates Stalin and the Russian Revolution.

The perimeters of Marxist theory

Marxism neglects familial and sexual relations because these are private and have nothing to do with production. Marxist theory explains social relations with reference to economic arrangements in which labour is sold for wages and a product manufactured for profit. Not only do many women live and work in the home outside of these 'economic' arrangements, but even working women are defined, to their detriment in the workplace, by familial roles of mother or wife. Therefore women's oppression remains outside the mechanics of Marxist explanation and Marxist revolutionary practice, subject to Engels's and Bebel's sentimental restoration of the socialist family.[73] The suggestion that new sexual and familial forms might be developed by women, meeting to discuss their situation, is met with disapproval; such discussions are not consistent with the trade union model of workers' organisation; are not properly informed by Marxist economic theory; are focused on non-productive activities such as sexuality and domestic labour instead of on wages and work hours; and are conducted by women, as women, not as gender-free 'workers'.

In the years after the failure of Soviet feminism, Marxist feminists, unwilling to give up a materialistic analysis of women's situation, continued to struggle to revise or supplement Marxian theory so that it could accommodate feminist practice. There were several different possibilities:

(1) Feminists could retain Marx's economic determination and analyse women's oppression as a functional part of the economic arrangements of capitalism.
(2) They could resurrect Marx's undeveloped notion of the 'reproduction' of the means of production.
(3) They could place women's oppression in a semi-independent ideological sphere.

Typical of the first alternative is an attempt to show that women's domestic labour in the family is 'value producing' and therefore subject to Marxian analysis.[74] In the 1970s, this issue was vigorously debated by Marxist and socialist feminists. The case for treating housework as productive labour had a strong emotional appeal. The decision to the contrary, that women's work in the home produces no value and is non-productive, sounded like a crass disparagement of women's accomplishments and importance. Nevertheless, this conclusion may be necessary given the Marxian concepts of value and production. Marx not only excluded wives as productive workers; he also excluded servants, craftspeople, state employees, and workers in commerce and merchandising. Capitalist society, for Marx, is driven by capitalist production — that is, by production of commodities by labourers whose labour power has been purchased by capitalists and whose product is sold by the capitalist for surplus value or profit. Marxian value is not 'anything of importance'; it is not 'use-value'. It is the particular result of a capitalist mode of production in which concrete labour is reduced to abstract labour power and produces exchangeable goods for the profit of a capitalist employer.

Capitalist exchange is possible because abstract labour power produces goods whose value is a function of the labour time that produced them. Surplus value, realised by the capitalist as profit, is the excess time or value not returned to the labourer in wages.

Women's labour in the home is in no way subject to this analysis; and neither, furthermore, is most of women's wage labour outside the home in the fields of state employment, welfare, teaching, nursing, and clerical work. For Marx, this 'unproductive' labour might complement capitalist production and often help the capitalist realise profits, but it is subsidiary to and parasitic on the productive base of capitalist society. Clerks and sales girls may allow a merchant capitalist to appropriate some of the surplus value of commodities; they do not, however, produce any value themselves. Women's work in the home is even further removed from capitalist production. The wife, in Marxian terms, produces use-values for immediate consumption, not value; she does not sell her labour to a capitalist; she does not produce a product that will be exchanged. Her activity is not in any way regulated or allocated by the capitalist system of production.[75]

Another attempt to accommodate domestic labour to the Marxian concepts of value and productive labour focused on a wife's servicing of the labour power so essential to capitalist production. On this argument, the labour sold by the capitalist male worker is in part the product of his wife's care and the employer can pay the labourer less than would be necessary for maintenance than if the labourer had to purchase services like food preparation and laundry. Therefore, the argument continued, the work of the housewife contributes to the surplus value of the product made by her husband.[76] However, this approach also dilutes the Marxian concept of value. The characteristic reduction of the individuality of specific jobs in capitalist assembly-line production and the resulting uniform counting of work hours allow there to be value that can be exchanged by capitalist owners. In the case of housework there is no way to determine which are labouring hours and which are not, which activities should count as housework and which should count as leisure.[77] The housewife punches no time-clock and puts in no hours. Therefore, even though her activity may produce what is useful or even necessary, she produces no exchangeable value. Unlike industrial production, she continues to work to service her husband even when her product cannot be sold — that is, when her husband is out of work. When he is employed, there is no showing that the value of his work is in any relation to the amount of her care. In capitalist production, when a product is devalued or unsellable, labour is immediately diverted to other production. A woman continues to care for her husband even when she has to find a (non-productive) job to support their family. Domestic labour is an anomaly unable to be assimilated by the mechanisms of capitalist commodity production.

This is not to say that domestic labour is not indirectly functional in relation to capitalist production, as is other nonproductive work such as law, medicine, and so on. Women's role in the family provides a reserve labour force that keeps down the wages of full-time workers and allows employers to weather times of full employment without raising wages. A woman's role in the family may provide an excuse for paying her a lower wage and so generally lower wages.[78] However, these claims do not have the same practical consequences as the claim that housework is productive. They place women's work as subsidiary to the great engine of capitalist production that, on Marxist reasoning, continues to grind out commodities, whether or not wives refuse to do housework. The claim that housework is productive seems to put the housewife within reach of Marxist revolutionary action. If women are part of capitalist production, they can take over the means of production by industrial action, they can strike, demand wages, better working conditions, and managerial control. The incoherence of the theory behind this optimism is reflected in the incoherence of the proposed remedy. Women are not in the same position as industrial workers to organise or make demands.

Marxist economic theory is a theory of change. Its description of capitalism includes a description of capitalism's final defeat. That defeat is directly related to the quality of industrial work and the special position of industrial workers. Workers collected in large factories are situated so that they can develop a consciousness of their collective exploitation; they are situated so that they can implement collective action. Because they are in this position of power, by Marxian reasoning they will be able to change the very foundations of society. Women in the home are in no such position. Firstly, men can do without their services if necessary and many single male workers do so. Secondly, women are isolated in separate establishments and are in no position to organise, act collectively, or develop a common consciousness. Although the consciousness-raising groups of the 1970s constituted an attempt to overcome this lack of commonality, with no stable institutional support, they were typically ephemeral and temporary. To extend 'productive' to household work is to promote a dangerous illusion. It suggests that an ineffective Marxist praxis is appropriate to the housewife's situation; 'productive' loses its practical force and becomes only an honorific.

The point of Marxian analysis of capitalist economic arrangements is to locate the contradictions that will destabilise, transform, and eventually destroy capitalist production. There is no comparable analysis of sexual and procreative production. The result is that the Marxist or socialist feminist must fall back on the utopianism and voluntarism criticised by Marx. The socialist feminist Alison Jaggar, for example, argued for an extension of Marxist concepts of production and exploitation to women's procreative and sexual labour. For remedial action, however, she could only suggest that women must 'name' the constraints on their free sexual and procreative activities.[79] They must see how the unavailability of abortion and conception and the imposition of compulsory heterosexuality allow them to be exploited by men, and they must 'seek the possibility of eliminating them'.[80]

Jagger, however, cannot provide any of the reassurance that Marxian materialism is meant to give. There is no positive programme for carrying out a feminist socialist revolution, nor any hope that it could succeed. Why would men, if they have all the coercive power that Jaggar proves that they have, give up that power? Jagger identified no material conditions, no movement in the material base of procreation, that could suggest a direction for progressive action. On the other hand, if Marxist remedies are adopted, contradictions develop in feminist practice. Should mothers go on strike and abandon their children? Should women appropriate the products of their labour and claim ownership of a product-child? The only alternative would be to further drain Marxian analysis of its content and claim that production does not necessarily mean there is a product. The more consistent Marxist view of domestic labour, held by Zetkin, is that domestic labour is economically anachronistic and will be increasingly socialised under capitalism.

That domestic labour persists, and that working women return at night to domestic chores at home, has to be seen as an important failure in Marxist prediction that cannot be covered up by an *ad hoc* application of the categories of industrial production to domestic work. The fact that women do housework even in socialist countries is further proof that, however economically functional women's privatisation in the family may have become within capitalism, economics does not seem to be a sufficient explanation.[81] In a labour-supported welfare state, the family structure of husband and dependent wife is maintained in the demand for wages high enough to support a wife, in welfare laws that assume a woman's dependent status, and in programmes that facilitate a woman's return to the workforce *after* she has raised her children. At the same time, issues such as abortion or child care, potentially damaging to the family, are avoided in labour politics. The welfare state is a place where the interests of male capitalists and male workers coincide; the capitalist state maintains the worker in his family retreat where the frustrations and alienation of his work can be forgotten. The argument can then be made with Kollontai that in family matters, male workers are no longer the progressive class. Their revolutionary zeal has been bought off, and until their familial retreat from alienation is destroyed, no progress can be made in the elimination of capitalism.[82]

The second approach is to focus upon what Marx called the 'reproduction' of the means of production. For production there must be labourers. For Marx, reproduction of the worker was a simple economic marker, indicating the level of wages corresponding to a labourer's ability to maintain himself and also the children who will replace him. Some Marxist feminists, however, argued that 'reproduction of the means of production' could be expanded to include woman's role in the family, giving birth to and raising children. Juliet Mitchell, for example in *Women's estate*,[83] argued that there is a 'mode of reproduction' as well as a mode of production, and the former does not necessarily change with the latter. Orthodox Marxism had made invisible the mode of reproduction by treating the family as if it were natural and biological and therefore inevitable.[84] Instead, Mitchell argued, just as there can be contradictions in the mode of production, there can also be contradictions in the mode of reproduction. The family, as the form of reproduction, changes. In capitalism the family decreased in size as industry's need for large numbers of workers gave way, with increased mechanisation, to a demand for fewer skilled workers. Although more lengthy and concentrated socialisation in the family may be required to produce workers with needed skills and discipline to function in hierarchical organisations, women still found themselves less occupied with reproduction and child-care. An illusory mystique of motherhood was necessary to keep women in the home. Even more importantly, under capitalism the source of the unity of the family had disappeared. The members of the feudal family had a common economic purpose. In capitalism each individual is expected to make his or her own way in the world. Family members are separated for most of the day;

conflicts inevitably develop in interests and values, resulting in family dysfunction and mental illness. These changes in the material base of the mode of reproduction, Mitchell argued, point the way to its possible dissolution. The family, satisfying only an anachronistic desire for private property eliminated in socialised production controlled by a few capitalists, had to be held together by women. The impossibility of this task could lead to women's revolutionary action.

Mitchell, however, immediately retracted her 'materialism'. Women are in an impossible situation, but *will* they revolt? 'The difficulties', she said, 'that confront us are not just the opposition of the system we are confronting, but also its influence.' Women, because of their situation, become petty, possessive, passive, lacking in vision. Like the feudal peasantry they are backward and although oppressed, may be unable to do anything about their exploitation.[85] Changes in the techniques of reproduction can be neutralised in the same way. Contraception and safe abortion constitute potentially radical material changes.[86] Attitudes about women and women's place may keep women from using them. Marx's proletariat was in a different position. Its members, admitted Mitchell, are already involved in 'socially organized' work in an 'antagonistic form' and so are in a position to identify and overthrow their oppressors. The simple fact of oppression, on the other hand, is not enough to guarantee revolution. Nor is a materialist analysis enough to point the way to corrective action. Mitchell had to go elsewhere, to psychoanalysis, to find the structures that keep the family in place even when it is no longer economically functional.[87]

Mitchell's feminist recovery of the much criticised Freud was part of a larger effort to cure Marx's narrow economism. Women's oppression has a life of its own which survives changes in economic arrangements. Rather than conflating biological reproduction with Marx's economic concept of reproduction, many Marxist feminists focused on revisions in another Marxist concept, 'ideology'. In the *German ideology* Marx defined ideology as a false representation, reflected in consciousness, of material reality. On this view, even if women's oppression is ideological — that is, located in literary, philosophical, theological, and historical representations that define women's nature and role — these representations, distorted or not, must be a reflection of economic reality. To escape yet another eclipsing of the woman question, many Marxist feminists followed the suggestion of Louis

Althusser that ideology is to some degree autonomous of economic structure and therefore requires a separate analysis.[88] Juliet Mitchell, for example, claimed an ideological role for the family that was not limited to its function of reproducing capitalist workers. The family provided a kind of nostalgia, she said, for private property no longer in existence within capitalism.

The family was not the only ideological structure of concern to women. Rosalind Coward, in 'Sexual liberation and the family',[89] found in *Cosmopolitan* magazine and the movie *Emmanuella* an image of the new, supposedly liberated, woman. This is an image that eroticises new areas of the body, that provides an arena for competing definitions of feminine sexuality, that encourages consummation of beauty products. All of this, Coward argued, assumes that a woman's true realisation is sexual. These ideological representations of women may have 'conditions of existence' in the advent of the pill or the working woman, but they do not simply reflect existing conditions. They have a life of their own and can be examined apart from institutions of social control. Analyses followed of representations of women in films, in fashion, in popular romance, and television.[90]

Although in these analyses, ideology or discourse,[91] as it soon will be called, is still loosely related to economic structures, again the analytic categories owe little to Marxist theory. Furthermore, with the idea that ideological representations of women are semi-autonomous, the advantages of Marxist theory have been lost. Marxism no longer provides an historical explanation of women's oppression or a way to locate that oppression in specific material realities; nor does it provide a course of action. Representations of femininity and masculinity — whether in people's minds, or in popular culture, or in science, or in philosophy — are to be examined independently of whether they are bourgeois or proletarian. One can get right on, Coward implied, to say what is progressive or reactionary. However, there are no longer any stable criteria. Sado-masochism may be an expression of male hostility to the feminine or an essential aspect of female sexuality. Clothes may be a male plot to enslave and objectify women or a legitimate expression of feminine taste. You can ask what are the effects of certain ideological representations, but there is no longer any standard by which to gauge their progressiveness. In the end all judgements must be based on one's political perspective.[92] At this point, Marxism contributes only its name to feminist analysis.

Women's subordinate role in the family, their exploitation in the media, their victimisation in sexual assault and harassment, cannot be accommodated within Marxist theory. One aspect of women's lives, such as domestic labour, may submit partially to economic analysis, but the more wide-ranging dynamics of women's oppression are untouched. It is not that Marxist theory omits one particular kind of oppression in an oversight which can be remedied in a simple extension of Marxist concepts such as 'reproduction' or 'ideology': either these concepts remain narrowly economic in application and so fail to capture women's situation, or alternatively they are extended so as to become vacuous. Marxist theory cannot analyse the reproduction of human personality in the family because in Marxist theory it is not personalities which are responsible for social change. Marxist theory cannot give an account of the dynamics of familial relations because in Marxist theory relations are a result of the mode of production. Marxist theory cannot provide a textual analysis of popular film, because in Marxism, texts must reflect economic realities. Nor can psychoanalytic theory as suggested by Mitchell, or discourse theory as suggested by Coward, be grafted onto Marxist economics. If historical changes in means of production are subject to universal psychic structures, or to universal ways of conceptualising reality, then both the explanatory force and revolutionary programme of Marxist theory are lost.

Jaggar, and others such as Christine Delphy in France,[93] proposed to reinterpret Marxist theory so that it could support feminist action outside the mechanics of capitalist distribution and production. Others proposed a 'dual systems' approach that would save the Marxian analysis of class relations, but supplement it with a feminist analysis of sex-class relations.[94] Marxist analysis, however, carried a resistant logic. 'Production' and 'value' are not neutral explanatory terms; they also validate and place as central in human life a certain kind of activity. Marx himself explained what must remain constant in all historically specific forms of production: 'The subject, mankind, and the object, nature, remain the same.'[95] 'All production is appropriation of nature by the individual within and through a definite form of society.'[96] The idea of property, if not of private property, is therefore 'tautologically' connected with the idea of production. Marxist man must tame nature, must make it human, must impose his image upon it: this is the substance of Marxist materialism. This activity of appropriation leads directly to clashes between competing owners, and between owners and those who have failed to appropriate. If democratic theory attempts to construct a world in which men can compete less destructively, Marxist theory constructs a world in which a violent class struggle between competing capitalist men and propertyless working men is resolved in communal control of the means of production. Much of what has gone on or goes on in society, even of an economic nature, is not included; not nurturing, not services, not production for use, not education, not medical care. In all of these activities there is no production and no relations of production. The conflict that Marx described is a conflict among men — men involved in a particular kind of project.

This is not to say that women did not, and do not, work in factories or that they are not exploited by employers; but unlike men, their identity as appropriators is always in question. Marx himself showed considerable ambivalence when talking about women workers, usually combining them with children and often deploring the 'moral' effect of factory work on young women and the neglect of children by working mothers. If women are forced into factory work, it is often as a last resort or as a temporary necessity. When it is clear that a woman must work she often chooses a non-productive profession in a typically feminine area such as nursing, social work, or teaching. No explanation can be given in Marxist theory as to why women would choose professions removed from capitalist production. In so far as women can involve themselves in the struggle between male entrepreneurs and male workers, they can be social agents. Even then, as the experience of Zetkin, Kollontai and Goldman in the union movement illustrates, their participation may not be welcome and, when accepted, may be limited. Whether this exclusion can be blamed on the innate hostility of men towards women, on the structure of male and female personalities, or on the way we think and talk about masculinity and femininity, is beyond the scope of Marxist theory.

Marxism focused on a particular activity of man, rationalised that activity, and theorised a world in which conflicts between men will be resolved. In Engels's *On the origin of the family*, this man and this world have already come into being; primitive man is already busy, producing and humanising the natural world. Also already established is a sexual division of labour between men and women:

The division of labor is purely primitive, between the sexes
only. The man fights in the wars, goes hunting and fishing,
procures the raw materials of food and the tools necessary
to do so. The woman looks after the house and the preparation of food and clothing, cooks, weaves, sews.[97]

To procure the necessities of life had always been the
business of the man, he *produced* and *owned* the means of
doing so. (my emphasis)[98]

In his description of primitive societies before the advent of
private property and the 'downfall of the female race', Engels had
already detached the sphere of male production and endowed it
with an illusory importance, a theoretical move repeated in the
Stalinist drive for production at all costs. The human world
theorised by Marx and projected back onto human history by
Engels is a world that excludes women. At the very dawn of
Marxist history, women exist apart from the economic activities
that will eventually develop into means of production;[99] at the
very dawn of Marxist history, women are doing women's work,
a work which they will double in the sex-segregated capitalist and
socialist work places. This work is not women's work because
women are too weak to do real work.[100] In primitive societies
women's gathering, agriculture, and food preparation not only
provide the bulk of food for the community, but also require
more heavy manual labour than the hunting and domestication
of animals which is men's work. Nevertheless, it is the men's
work that becomes the subject of Marxian analysis.

Productive Marxist *man*, the man to be liberated in the
socialist state, depends from the beginning on the nurturing
home and non-productive services that provide for him the
necessary mental and material antidote to his exhausting and
destructive humanisation of the physical world and his obsessive
craving for products which reflect his image. The great projected
triumph of socialist production is no more than the final mirroring of this Marxist man in the authoritarian state. Again the
same question must be asked that Marxist women asked of
democratic theory: do women want to achieve the status of
comrades in such a society?

Notes

1. This is the portrait of liberal feminists supplied by Henry James in *The Bostonians*, from Olive Schneider's comfortable well-appointed drawing room to the great salons where the evening's entertainment might be the charming and beautiful new feminist speaker, Verbena Tarrant.

2. This damning phrase occurs and reoccurs in anti-socialist and socialist literature. In the rhetoric of the nineteenth century there seemed no other imaginable alternative to monogamous marriage but a situation in which all men had a right to all women. The immorality of this community, not of women but of men, was no doubt enhanced by the expectation of the fighting and quarrelling that would occur if property in women was not more carefully established.

3. Quoted in Bebel's follower, Charles Thiebaux's *Le féminisme et les socialists* (Arthur Rousseau, Paris, 1906), p. 15.

4. Traditional Saint-Simonians were careful to distinguish themselves from the Enfantin 'heresy' which somewhat more shockingly advocated the use of sexual initiation of neo-phytes and couple-priests. Enfantin also proposed a short-term marriage with no children and easy no-fault divorce. Thiebaux is shocked, as he is so often in his exposition of radical socialism. This 'scabreuse' sacradotal prostitution, this 'right to inconstance', must not be confused with orthodox socialism such as Bebel's.

5. See Barbara Taylor, *Eve and the new Jerusalem: socialism and feminism in the nineteenth century* (Pantheon Books, New York, 1983) for a complete account of the Owenites' history and for an analysis of their views on women.

6. Bureau de la Phalange, Paris, 1841.

7. This exaggerated view of women's virtues is a frequent accompaniment to their inferiority. Either an unconscious guilt at the oppression of women provides a compensating glorification of their mystical powers, or, what is perhaps more likely, the religious power of women so marked in primitive society, to which perhaps their degradation is a response, surfaces after the fact to justify the assertion of male authority.

8. See, for example, *La justice dans la révolution et dans l'église* (Garnier Frères, Paris, 1858).

9. Populaire, Paris, 1848.

10. Cabet, *The woman*, p. 4.

11. Ibid., p. 11.

12. Ibid., p. 16.

13. Ibid., p. 17.

14. Ibid., p. 18.

15. Ibid.

16. Ibid., p. 20.

17. Bureau du Populaire, Paris, 1843.

18. For an interesting account of some of these proposals, see Dolores Hayden, *The grand domestic revolution: a history of feminist designs for American homes, neighborhoods and cities* (MIT Press, Cambridge, 1982).

19. *Vindication of the rights of women* (Walter Scott, London, 1792), p. 342.

20. A good description of Goldman's early life can be found in her autobiography, *Living my life* (A. Knopf, New York, 1931), and also in Alix Shulman's introduction to *The traffic in women and other essays on feminism* (Times Change Press, Washington/New Jersey, 1970).

21. Maruani, *Les syndicats à l'épreuve du féminisme* (Syros, Paris, 1979).

22. Even the great Marxist theorist, Rosa Luxemburg, when she arrived in Germany in 1898 to take over the editorship of a Social Democratic paper, was not considered fit by her male subordinates to take on as much authority as her male predecessor. See Raya Dunayevskaya, *Rosa Luxemburg, women's liberation and Marx's philosophy of revolution* (Humanities Press, New Jersey, 1982), p. 90. See, also A.M. Sohn's description of women's struggles in the Social Democratic Party in that author's preface to Bebel's *La femme dans le passé, le présent, et l'avenir* (Ressources, Paris, 1979). Also in France Marie-Hélène Zylberberg-Hocquard's *Féminisme et syndicalism en France* (Edition Anthropos, Paris, 1978), and the recent *Women and American socialism* by Mari Jo Buhle (University of Illinois Press, Urbana, Illinois, 1981), documenting a similar silencing of women in America.

23. Lawrence and Wishart, London, 1972.

24. Ibid., p. 71.

25. Engels's comment on views such as Mill's and Taylor's are that they are a hold-over from the eighteenth-century enlightenment (*Origin of the family*, p. 113). Certainly one could go further and say that the view that other cultures were brutish was a necessary justification for the reciprocal brutality of colonialism. If, as Rosa Luxemburg argued in *The accumulation of capital* (Routledge and Kegan Paul, London, 1951), capitalism was incapable of operating as an economic system without the invasion of primitive economies, such a justification/obfuscation was necessary for the survival of capitalism.

26. Ibid., p. 120.

27. Ibid., pp. 121–2.

28. This is one of the contradictions in marriage for Engels. It preserves the old sexual freedom of matrilineal society in the form of prostitution and affairs for men; for men the old group marriage is still in effect — p. 128.

29. *Communist Manifesto*, ed. Samuel H. Beer (Appleton-Century Crofts, New York, 1955), p. 29. An example, involving this time also the European attitude towards non-Western women who many times become the repositories for sexuality denied to the decent European women, can be found in the famous *Voyage en orient* of Gerard de Nérval, an 1851 account of his life among 'les Femmes du Caire'. Told by his neighbours in Cairo that he must not live in their vicinity as a bachelor, he describes for hundreds of pages the thousands of women served up for him to buy. Ranging in colour and consequently in price, they parade, veiled, adorned, nude; they are made to sing, talk in Italian, show their buttocks or breasts, even their teeth. Nérval, never shocked, only somewhat careful of his pocketbook, a concern in conflict with his distaste for the cheaper, darker colours, and fearful that any woman he buys may have been already 'used', feels only anxiety that he will not make the best possible bargain. It is this staggering blindness to women's situation that

Marxism claimed it would cure.

30. Engels, *The origin of the family*, p. 136.

31. Ibid.

32. Marx, *Capital*. Trans. from 3rd German edition, ed. by Samuel Moore and Edward Aveling, vol. I (London, 1957), p. 495ff.

33. Labor News Press, New York, 1904.

34. *The traffic in women*, p. 38.

35. Reprinted in *The traffic in women*. Nor, for radical feminists, is the vote the only fetishism. A particular law can take the place of the vote or, as for American feminists with the ERA, a constitutional amendment.

36. Emma Goldman was not the only one to predict the conservative effect of women's suffrage. See also Rosa Luxemburg, 'Women's suffrage and class struggle' in Dick Howard (ed.), *Selected political writings*, (Monthly Review Press, New York, 1971), pp. 219-20.

37. *The traffic in women*, p. 57.

38. Reprinted in *Batailles pour les femmes*, trans. under the direction of Gilbert Badia (Editions Sociale, Paris, 1980).

39. These ideas are worked out in Kollontai's 'The social bases of the women question' and in later articles, some of which are collected in *Marxisme et révolution sexuelle* (François Maspero, Paris, 1975), and in *The selected works of Alexandra Kollontai*, ed. Alix Holt (W.W. Norton & Co., New York, 1977). For a description of her struggles for women in the Russian Revolution and also of Clara Zetkin's work with the German Social Democrats, see Sheila Rowbotham's *Women, resistance, and revolution* (Penguin, Harmondsworth, 1972), Chapter 6; and Richard Stites, *The women's liberation movement in Russia* (Princeton University Press, Princeton, NJ, 1978); and especially Beatrice Farnsworth, *Aleksandra Kollontai: socialism, feminism and the Bolshevik revolution* (Stanford University Press, Stanford, 1980).

40. For current statistics showing a still depressing balance, see D. Atkinson, A. Dallin and G.W. Lapidus, *Women in Russian* (Stanford University Press, Stanford, CA, 1977), who conclude that though the number of women in interesting and challenging professions is greater than in any non-socialist country, women are still clustered at low levels of status where they seldom have authority over men — pp. 224 and 280.

41. This is Lenin's explanation for the retreat from socialist principles necessary to prepare the way for true communism. See Lenin, *State and Revolution*, esp. Chapter V (Foreign Language Press, Peking, 1976).

42. See Batya Weinbaum, *The curious courtship of women's liberation and socialism* (South End Press, Boston, 1980), as well as her *Pictures of patriarchy* (South End Press, Boston, 1983) especially Part III, 'Kin categories in the economy', for an analysis of kinship roles, such as father, brother, daughter, which structure both capitalist and socialist work relations.

43. Engels, *Origin of the family*, p. 145.

44. 'The social bases', reprinted in *Marxisme et révolution sexuelle*, p. 89.

45. *Origin of the family*, p. 144. Engels makes no argument for this essential exclusivity, or for why it is that men would become monogamous rather than women non-monogamous.

46. Bebel, *Woman in socialism*, p. 347. Certainly Zetkin, Bebel's disciple, would have needed patience with this complacent waving aside of

women's heavy responsibilities in the home onto babysitters, teachers, friends conscripted to help, and mechanical aids. Nothing describes so well the continued plight of the working woman as she depends on such unreliable and inexpert supports for her professional survival. One must note that there is in Bebel no suggestion that the father might help or that the friends conscripted were anything but female.

47. Ibid., p. 347.

48. An account of these conversations is in Zetkin's 'Entretien avec Lenine sur les femmes, l'amour, et la révolution' reprinted in *Batailles pour les femmes*, p. 185; English version, 'My recollection of Lenin', Appendix to Lenin's *The Emancipation of Women* (International Publishers, New York, 1966).

49. This brushing aside of Freud is notable, given Freud's later importance in feminist theory, see Chapter V, below.

50. See 'Ce que les femmes doivent à Lenine', reprinted in *Batailles pour les femmes*.

51. Stites, *Women's liberation movement*, p. 106.

52. 'The social bases', in *Selected writings*, p. 58ff.

53. See the various proclamations collected in his *The emancipation of women*.

54. For example, in his interview with Zetkin (p. 191), Lenin argued that sex was not like drinking, the simple satisfaction of a need — though, he adds prudishly, even when drinking there are some rules of hygiene. Sex, unlike drinking, is social because it involves two people.

55. In her later 'Make way for winged Eros' (1923), reprinted in *Selected writings* (p. 276), Kollontai, whether under puritanical Stalinist pressure or because of change in conviction, proposed a different ethic much closer to Lenin's. There, she deplores the youth who thinks too much of sex and who commits excesses. Casual sex may have been necessary in the chaotic first years of revolution; now, however, with the revolution instituted and needing everyone's hard work, romance must take a back seat. This will be a 'winged Eros' and not 'an Eros without wings', which will be focused less on sexuality *per se* than on comradeship and collective interest.

56. See 'The new woman' in *Autobiography of a sexually emancipated woman* (London, 1972).

57. See also Kollontai's stories, some of which are included in *Selected writings*.

58. Goldman, *La tragedie de l'émancipation feminine* (Syros, Paris, undated), pp. 54–8.

59. *Traffic in women*, p. 40.

60. For Kollontai these norms are necessary to encourage healthy reproduction and beneficial sentiments, and have just as much a place in socialist as in capitalist society. The proletariat must give all for the collectivity; and even individual sex satisfaction must be subordinated. Is this not a new prison; a new wing clipping? Yes, Kollontai answers, but each era has its own rules ('Make way for winged Eros', *Selected writings*).

61. See Kollantai's interesting discussion of 'possessiveness' in 'Sexual relations and the class struggle' in *Selected writings*, p. 242ff. Transformation of socio-economic structures may be a necessary condition for sexual

liberation but it cannot automatically guarantee a new sexual morality. In addition, the personal individualism of men who see wives as possessions must be corrected.

62. 'The social basis', in *Selected writings*, p. 69. Before any idealistic pronouncements on free love can be realised, it is necessary to have a 'fundamental reform of all social relationships between people'.

63. That a feminist perspective is privileged on the grounds of the different nature of women's work is also argued by Nancy Hardstock, 'The feminist standpoint: developing the ground for a specifically feminist historical materialism' in Sandra Harding and Merrill Hintikka (eds), *Discovering reality* (Reidel, London, 1983).

64. See especially 'Give way to winged Eros', *Selected writings*.

65. Emma Goldman, *La tragedie de l'émancipation feminine* (Syros, Paris), p. 41.

66. L.D. Easton and K.H. Guddat (eds.) *Writings of the young Marx*, (Anchor Books, New York, 1966), p. 303.

67. 'The change in an historical epoch can always be determined by the progress of women towards freedom, because in the relation of woman to man, of the weak to the strong, the victory of human nature over brutality is most evident. The degree of emancipation of women is the natural measure of general emancipation'. Charles Fourier, *Théorie des quatre mouvements*, p. 195.

68. See Susan Griffin, *Woman and nature* (Harper Calaphone Books, New York, 1980), for a fascinating exploration of how deep this identification of women and nature has been in the history of philosophical and political thought.

69. Marx distinguished between 'crude communism' where a state takeover does not result in the change in relationships necessary for real collectivisation, and true communism. Easton and Guddat (eds.), *Writings of the young Marx*, p. 302.

70. Goldman is an interesting exception here, just because she died before the struggle over authoritarianism fully developed. One would have to think that, given her general intractability on matters of principle and her anarchistic commitments, long in conflict with Marxist communists, that she would have been an outspoken critic of Stalinism. Her silence, even in the early days of the Revolution after she had been deported to Russia, shows how excited, how hopeful feminists were for the new glorious Revolution.

71. Reprinted, *Selected writings*, p. 159. On the other hand, Kollontai did not support Trotsky in his struggle with Stalin. The reasons are not clear. See Introduction to Kollontai's *L'opposition ouvrière*, trans. by Pierre Pascal (Ed. du Seuil, Paris, 1974) for possible explanations. In any case, by that time Kollontai seems to have reached some understanding with Stalin, and peacefully played a minor, unprovocative role in Soviet affairs until her death.

72. Ibid.

73. Even contemporary Marxists lapse into restoration of the family: see, for example, Reimut Reiche, *Sexuality and class relations* (New Left Books, London, 1974), arguing against the sexual revolution of the 1960s.

74. M. Dalla Costa and S. James, *The power of women and the subordination*

of the community (Falling Wall Press, Bristol, 1975) argued that housework is 'productive' in the Marxian sense of the term. W. Seccombe, 'The housewife and her labour under capitalism', *New Left Review*, no. 83 (1974), pp. 3–24 argued that although housework was not productive (did not produce surplus value), it did produce value. Less technical treatments of the issue, such as Alison Jaggar's in her defence of socialist feminism in *Feminist politics and human nature* (Rowman and Allanheld, Totowa, NJ, 1983), claimed that Marxist productive activity should be widened to include 'procreative and sexual work that is done by women in the home' (p. 303). See also Christine Delphy's argument that there is no relevant difference between production on farms for self-consumption, which *is* treated as wealth in state accounting of gross national product, and housework, which is not: 'The main enemy', *Close to home: a materialist analysis of women's oppression*, trans. by Diana Leonard (Hutchinson, London, 1984).

75. Arguments in support of this view: S. Himmelweit and S. Mohun, 'Domestic labour and capital', *Cambridge Journal of Economics*, vol. 1 (1977); J. Gardiner, S. Himmelweit, M. Mackintosh, 'Women's domestic labour', *Bulletin of the Conference of Socialist Economists*, vol. 4, no. 2 (1975).

76. J. Gardiner, 'Women's domestic labour', *New Left Review*, no. 89 (1975), pp. 47-72.

77. The claim that sex constitutes labour (e.g. Jaggar, *Feminist politics*, p. 131) shows how vacuous the concept of labour can become. The Marxist position was made clear by Lenin: even prostitution is non-productive although the proceeds may enrich a capitalist pimp. In the case of the sex industry, Marxist analysis may produce an antimony. Marxism can explain non-productive clerical and sales work by its function in passing on surplus value; but although pornography, strip joints, and massage parlours may be heavily capitalised, there seems to be *no* connection with Marxist value.

78. See Veronica Beechey, 'Women and production: a critical analysis of some sociological theories of women's work' in A. Kuhn and A. Wolpe (eds), *Feminism and materialism* (Routledge and Kegan Paul, London, 1978), pp. 181-95.

79. Jaggar, *Feminist politics*, p. 318.

80. Ibid., p. 319.

81. See Michele Barrett in *Women's oppression today: problems in Marxist feminist analysis* (Villiers Publications, London, 1980), who also points out that there are many kinds of sexual oppression which cannot be accounted for economically e.g. of homosexuals. Her solution is attractive. Although gender relations are now in fact embedded in capitalist productive relations and cannot be changed without an overthrow of capitalism, women's oppression (1) was not a necessary element of capitalist relations, (2) pre-dates capitalism, and (3) cannot be expected to disappear automatically with capitalism.

82. This is essentially the argument of Ann Foreman in *Femininity and alienation: women and the family in Marxism and psychoanalysis* (Pluto Press, London, 1977). She concludes that in consciousness-raising groups, where women discuss divorce, abortion, and child-care, women can begin to undermine repressive family relationships.

83. *Women's estate* (Penguin, Baltimore, Md., 1971).

84. 'The maintenance and the reproduction of the working class remains a necessary condition for the reproduction of capital. But the capitalist may safely leave this to the workers' drives for self-preservation and propagation.' Marx, *Capital*, vol. I., p. 572.

85. Mitchell, *Women's estate*, p. 162.

86. See Schulamith Firestone's attempt to develop a materialist feminism based on the new possibilities opened by contraception and artificial reproduction. Firestone argued that such techniques made the family unnecessary for reproduction, but she gave no explanation of how people could be persuaded to make the radical changes in their reproductive lives that she proposed in *The dialectic of sex* (Bantam Books, New York, 1971).

87. *Psychoanalysis and feminism* (Penguin, Harmondsworth, 1975).

88. The seminal article is 'Ideology and ideological state apparatuses' in *Lenin and philosophy* (Monthly Review Press, New York, 1971). Althusser, obviously under the influence of the post-structural Lacan, increasingly fashionable in modish Paris (see Chapter 5), argued that ideology functions in separate systems and that these systems are supported by their own material 'apparatuses'. Not only are there state institutions, there are also family, church, and — for Althusser the most important — educational institutions. An analysis of productive relations is, therefore, insufficient, without a separate analysis of how the consciousnesss of the labourer is reproduced in the family and especially in education.

89. *m/f*, no. 1 (1978), pp. 7–24.

90. See, for example, Coward, *Female desires* (Grove Press, New York, 1985).

91. This change from ideology and representation to discourse represents an epistemological shift more fully discussed in Chapter 5. Representation, as well as Marx's definition of ideology, the argument goes, requires a subject/object split between a representation and what it represents. 'Discourse' suggests the new insight borrowed from post-structuralist French thought, that there can be no independent 'represented' object and that one must examine the signifying chain to find meaning.

92. This is in general the view of A. Cutler, B. Hindess, P. Hirst, A. Hussain in *Marx's Capital and capitalism today* (Routledge and Kegan Paul, London, vol. 1, 1977; vol. 2, 1978), a massive rethinking of Marxism that attempts to develop a non-economist Marxism to correct failures of the British Labour party. The authors substitute an amorphous 'conditions of existence of the means of production' for the unitary 'mode of production' in order to validate a pluralistic analysis of ideological and cultural systems and legitimise practices that aim at their transformation. See Coward's review 'Rethinking Marxism', *m/f*, no. 2 (1978), p. 85, which points out that even for Cutler *et al.*, economics is still central and feminist political action is ignored. See also Paul Hirst, 'Althusser and the theory of ideology', *Economy and Society*, vol. 5, no. 4 (1976), p. 385, for a shorter, if not more accessible, discussion of the argument and its relation to Althusser.

93. See the articles collected in Delphy, *Close to home*.

94. See the articles in L. Sargent (ed.) *Women and revolution: a discussion of the unhappy marriage of Marxism and feminism* (South End Press, Boston, 1982), and Z. Eisenstein, *Capitalist patriarchy and the case for a socialist feminism* (Monthly Review Press, New York, 1979).

95. David McLellan, *Marx's Grundrisse* (Macmillan, London, 1971), p. 18.

96. Ibid., p. 21.

97. Engels, *Origin of the family*, p. 218.

98. Ibid., p. 220.

99. See, for an extended argument, Beverly Brown, 'Natural and social division of labour: Engels and the domestic labour debate', *m/f*, no. 1 (1978), pp. 25–47. See also Marx *Capital*, vol. I, 'The process of capitalist production' (International Publishers, New York, 1967), p. 351, where Marx argued that in the family there is a 'natural' division of labour based on sex or age with a purely 'physiological foundation'.

100. This is implicitly suggested by Marx when he claims that industrial mechanisation, which makes muscle unnecessary, *allows* women to enter the workforce.

4

A World Without Women:
The Existentialist Feminism of
Simone de Beauvoir

The existentialist critique of Marxism

Though unremarked and seemingly insignificant compared with the impressive machinery of Marxist explanation and prediction, there is a blindspot in Engels's description of the moment when the female race was overthrown. It is property relations that were to have been the culprit, but if property is not to be a simple *demon-ex-machina*, one must also explain why property relations would have been instituted against the community in the first place and why they were uniquely instituted between men. Without such explanations the connection between sexism and productive relations does not hold and production takes on an automatic precedence which guarantees the correction of sexism regardless of the actual situation of women. Not having explained sexism, Marxism is unable to come up with an adequate programme for women's liberation.

As the twentieth century proceeded, this disappointment was part of a general disappointment with visionary politics. Marx's vision seemed to a Europe exhausted and numbed by the battle with Fascism, to have been transformed, just like Hegel's perfectly integrated German state, into an oppressive totalitarianism where domination and submission were the style of all social relationships. After the war, feminists shared with men a world irrevocably changed. Nazism had altered the terms of existence by proving that there was no limit to the evil that could be contemplated and accomplished. With the 'unthinkableness' of absolute evil came the 'unthinkableness' of infinite destruction through the atom bomb. Especially in countries like France which had been occupied by the Germans, ethics, or the sense of any sure conviction of what one should do, had been stretched to breaking point. In the unbearable situations that the German occupation had generated, there no longer seemed any possible guide to right and wrong.[1]

After the German defeat came the disappointment in communism. Communism had been the antidote to Fascism, but under Stalin, Soviet oppression and brutality made the Marxist experiment a sham. It was no longer possible to embrace socialism as did Kollontai and Zetkin without agonised self-questioning and endless reservation. Socialism, instead of a great adventure into the future, had begun to have the feel of an unhealthily closed room in which one remained out of loyalty and commitment or, in the end, perhaps only because there was nowhere else to go.[2] The belief that social justice could prevail became at best a token automatic allegiance, and at worst an absolute despair. Meanwhile the Cold War went on between the two new world powers, the United States and the Soviet Union, resulting in a further feeling of impotence for Europeans. The only political alternative was a choice between two equally unpalatable alternatives, and, in the end, the acceptance of a very slightly lesser evil.[3]

It is from this perspective that Simone de Beauvoir attempted to rethink the terms of feminine existence in a revised mid-twentieth century context. There were no absolutes left, no certainties. God had been dethroned by scientific reason; now religion no longer had even a subjective validity in a world in which there were death chambers and the mutilations of atomic war. All hope and certainty had been called into question. Still, as life and action required hope, conviction would have to be regenerated if only out of that emptiness itself where once there had been some absolute truth. In this atmosphere of dissolution, shock, emptiness, and disillusion, Beauvoir, prompted by Sartre to explain what it was to be a woman, began work on *The second sex*, a comprehensive examination of the situation of women.

There had been a certain strengthening of the position of women after the war. The battle for legal equality had been largely won; women voted, could hold property, were legally equal in marriage, and civil society seemed to have accepted them as functioning members. More importantly, by the thousands they had been enlisted in war work, had proved themselves capable of running the factories and doing the work of men. In Germany, with so many men killed, they continued to work and to be needed. Just as industrialisation, with its requirement for cheap labour and its exploitation of the poor, forced women into the workforce and gave rise to Kollontai's new women, so war work and the sensation of managing alone, along with disgust at the male world of war, made women less inclined to return to traditional roles. Unfortunately, the men who were returning home had different expectations, creating conflicts that are reflected in the extended discussion of the female role that went on in the following decades as individuals and governments tried to reconstruct families whose affective and economic ties had been severed by the war.[4]

But where in the ruin of socialism were feminists to find an ideology to shape their demands? A return to democratic theory seemed no better, as democracies increasingly showed themselves to be compromised and shallow, willing to support authoritarianism when it was anti-communist and economically committed to colonial regimes which flaunted principles of self-determination and human dignity. Beauvoir's existentialism was an attempt to locate the dynamics of an oppression that was not specific to either socialism or capitalism. In so doing, she returned to themes prominent in Marxist feminists' disputes with communist orthodoxy. Firstly, there had been Kollontai's analysis of male resistance to change in sexual matters. We are all alone, Kollontai said, whether capitalist or socialist. Men have solved this problem in a certain way, by appropriating a woman as their security object, an appropriation which they may have no motivation to abandon. Secondly, there was Goldman's unsocialist focusing on the question of personal relationships. The big question, she suggested, was not, after all, who owns the means of production, but how one could live with others and still remain oneself. Feminists had made the mistake of focusing on the vote, on conquering external enemies when the real enemies were in their own minds: the prejudgemental blocks, the fears, that kept them from living fully. The feminist had better look to herself and not so much to the immorality of others. It is with these questions that Beauvoir's existentialism begins, the questions unaskable and so unanswerable in Marxist theory.

Firstly, Beauvoir exposed the illusions on which Marxism was based. There are no absolutes: there is no final classless society which will end human conflict, and there is no absolutely infallible universal class. Such absolutes can only lead to dictatorship and totalitarianism. Examples came readily for Beauvoir: the Jew sacrificed to the pure absolute Aryan race, the Siberian peasants crushed for the survival of communism, Japanese children sacrificed for a tidy end to the war. Each time, the absolute rightness of a goal had justified an action that was at best morally ambiguous, and at worst horrifyingly evil. Marxist absolutism, Beauvoir argued, was a holdover from Marx's predecessor, Hegel.[5] Hegel began admirably enough with his description of the dynamic interaction between self and other but then allowed absolutism to intercede in the guise of a World Spirit working its absolutely right progress toward complete self-realisation. This may theoretically guarantee a problematic reconciliation between conflicting interests, but as an imposed resolution from 'on top',[6] it easily becomes a justification for the absolute oppressive power of the state. Marxism substitutes for the ideal subjective dialectic of the World Spirit the materialist, objective dialectic of productive relations, but keeps the absolutism of a final goal, not now metaphysical and pre-existing as in utopian socialism, but generated quasi-automatically in class action. Such an absolute may be reassuring, just as Hegel's grand vision was reassuring to Beauvoir, reading in the deceptive calm of the Bibliotheque Nationale in 1940.[7] Even then, however, it only took a walk in the street to convince her that such reassurance was illusory. Marx's absolute, as Hegel's, must become the absolute of unreflective power masquerading as objective necessity. Then, as was made clear in Stalinist policy, the masquerade must be preserved so that no reflection or self-consciousness seem to mediate the absolute rightness of state action. The repression of thought and speech in communist countries becomes a necessary corollary of Marxist absolutism.

What has been omitted, Beauvoir argued, what always is crushed by any absolutism, is the individual. Individuals are subordinated to the unity of state or collectivity. Certainly Beauvoir could have used the frustration of Soviet feminists as an example. The interests of women and their need for support services would be served only when the good of the whole society was not in question. When the state was threatened, individuals, whether women or men, must be sacrificed. Individual action was not responsible, Marxism argued, for the revolution which had to do with larger structural dynamics; nor was individual action responsible for the institution of socialist society. It could not be so, because individual action was a function of greater forces or movements beyond individual will and intention. This leads not only to the oppression of individuals, Beauvoir argued, but it is also metaphysically incoherent.

Firstly, no Marxist is consistent. Marxism, as revolutionary philosophy, preaches actions, drastic actions. In addition, regardless of its theoretical position that morality is simply a reflection of class consciousness, it misses no chance to chastise the enemy in moral, even crudely moral, terms.[8] It is always necessary to arouse the slothful proletariat who might, as Beauvoir noted, 'sleep on in dull comfort'.[9] Furthermore, once the revolution had occurred, leaders must continue to rally individuals to the cause, goading them to further sacrifice.[10] This is because, no matter what Marxist theory might assert, we are separate consciousnesses and, as Kollontai said, alone. This was, in fact, the problem with which Hegel, Marx's predecessor, began. If we are all particulars, how can we ever become a community?[11] One cannot solve this problem by doing away with it, by refusing to accept the fact of our essential separation from each other. We start as consciousnesses — that is, thinking things set off from other thinking things and in conflict with each other. Therefore, it is with an analysis of consciousness that a study of the human condition and of the female condition must begin.

A conscious individual is first and foremost not a thing; he is not an object whose movements can be equated with the movements of billiard balls. Instead, he is a subjectivity. Marxism gives no account of subjectivity. Marxist 'objectivity' means that it treats people as objects, but in fact people do not and cannot experience themselves or be understood in this way. To be completely objective is to miss the condition of being human. Thus, a communist state becomes dehumanised. The masses of people behave as 'sub-men' and the leaders, not much better, act unreflectively beyond all moral accountability. However, even in a totalitarian state, the human cannot be completely suppressed: more and more there is a malaise, a deadness, a dull misery. Humans do not accept the status of 'thing' comfortably or happily. In some way they must assert their subjectivity, if only by a painful submission; beyond, there is always the possibility of revolt and the responding violence of the repressive state.

Neglect of the individual and of subjectivity, Beauvoir continued, has some important additional implications. If individuals are not theoretically important, then relations between individuals are not either. The relation of man to woman becomes significant only as a symbol of the progressiveness of a society. What happens between a specific man and woman is irrelevant because control is invested in larger forces within which any interaction is structured. The real dynamics of interpersonal power cannot therefore be discussed in Marxist theory. Consequently, in a socialist economy, power relations remain or are re-established — between manager and worker, administrator and private citizen, party member and non-party member, husband and wife. Because these relations were automatically to lose their oppressiveness in socialism, any oppressiveness that remains can be ignored or reinterpreted and so flourishes in a way it could not in a democracy assuming inequality. In democratic theory, where the struggle between men for ascendancy is taken for granted as primary and inevitable, power is accommodated and controlled in institutions constructed to limit and balance power.[12] Hierarchy and inequality, of course, exist, but being acknowledged they are regulated. Not existing by definition in a socialist society, power is not controlled.

Consequently, there is in Marxism no useful discussion of two concepts of fundamental importance to women: oppression and liberation. Women have been oppressed, but this, if it is to have pragmatic weight beyond simple passive suffering, must have some content. The complementary term to oppression is liberation but when oppression is not defined, liberation is correspondingly empty. For existentialists like Beauvoir, Marx's definition of oppression as economic oppression was simplistic and consequently the liberation offered was illusory. No adequate definition of either oppression or liberation can be given until people are seen, not as objects, but as subjects, because it is in respect to their subjectivity that oppression operates. Likewise, it is only in relation to their subjectivity that freedom or liberation can have meaning.

By 1972 it was clear to Beauvoir that women's situations had not substantially changed under either capitalism or socialism.[13] The legal reformism of feminists in democratic countries had failed, but so had the socialist feminism of Kollontai and Zetkin. Reporting on her visits to the USSR she noted that the expectation that women will work did not prevent women's clustering in low-status jobs and retaining responsibility for the home and children. The exception of medicine only proved the rule. In Russia where doctoring had become a woman's profession, the status of doctors was consequently lower than doctors in Western countries. Russian doctors, unlike their Western counterparts, were poorly paid and overworked. It was clear then that socialist as well as democratic theory was inadequate. The question remained as to the possible theoretical basis for renewed woman's struggle.

Such a new approach was presented by Beauvoir in *The second sex*, written 23 years before her actual entrance into feminist politics. This time the ideological base was not to be economics or politics, but — what was more profound — philosophy. Existentialism, Beauvoir argued in her introduction, will be the perspective out of which she will be able to understand women's situation. Existentialism will fill the gaps in socialist theory, because it deals with human individuals, not dumb collectivities, and deals with them as subjective. An existentialist feminism can therefore offer an analysis of both women's oppression and of their freedom.

The existential nature of subjectivity

Beauvoir began from the existential description of consciousness given by Sartre, her life-long lover and partner, in his monumental *Being and nothingness*. In that work, Sartre claimed to begin at the philosophical beginning, and the beginning was not, as Marx thought, economic. Simple survival hardly raises the human above the animal level. The important human question is not what to eat, but what to be. A human being, Sartre argued, is characterised not by its inert characteristics, not by being something in the way that a stone is something, but by a lack of being. The difference is between an 'in-itself' (e.g. a stone) and a 'for-itself' (a person). A man becomes what he chooses to be, and what he becomes does not follow automatically from heredity, environment, pre-established personality traits, or social structure. What he becomes depends upon his freely made decisions to act and to think in a certain way. These decisions constitute his substance, a substance never absolutely fixed but always revisible in a new decision. Here was the rejection of the absolutism that paralysed Marxist praxis. There are no absolutes where humans are concerned, no absolute future good, no absolute necessity of any kind, whether physical or metaphysical. When one focuses on subjectivity, what appears is a self in process into which is built no final goal or essence. Man is necessarily free, free to choose his own actions, his own project in the world, choices that he must make without guides. No God, no moral law, no political party,[14] no external authority can make them for him.

This acknowledgement of our absolute responsibility for our actions is almost unbearably painful. The moral law, God, the class struggle, is gone; nothing can be blamed on moral necessity, on the commands of God, or even on one's human emotions.[15] Whatever one does is one's own choice and therefore one's own responsibility. Much of human life, according to Sartre, is concerned with an infinite variety of strategems for avoiding this responsibility, stratagems which he labels with the generic term bad faith ('mauvais foi'). Bad faith is always the attempt to draw back from responsibility into one's posited thingness, to make oneself inert and passive, to claim that one *must* do what one does, whether by embracing a religion and accepting its tenets, by becoming a communist and following the party line, by claiming one has a given nationality or personality or sex or race, or by claiming an absolute allegiance to moral principle. As Beauvoir put it, even if you rise above the level of the sub-men — the masses who simply act reactively and passively, and achieve a sense of yourself as a free agent — you still become the 'serious' man, the man committed to a cause of an ideal.[16]

These philosophical foundations had, for Beauvoir, important implications for those human relations seemingly so resistant to feminist reform. Goldman's question as to the relations between self and others is immediately raised. I am, as an autonomous subject, separate from physical things, and also from other consciousnesses. Furthermore, my relations with other subjectivities must be quite different from my relations with things. Sartre, in his many examples, showed himself to be an acute analyst of human relations. We must succeed in being-for ourselves by creating our own being in our projects in the world, but we must also have being-for-others — that is, we must be recognised by those other consciousnesses who are in our world attempting to carry out projects often opposed to our own. In Sartre's description of this confrontation between competing consciousnesses, Beauvoir found an explanation for the persistent inequality in relations between men and women.

The original position of a Sartrean consciousness is alone and confronted only by a physical world which consciousness experiences, knows, and tries to appropriate. Although the existence of this physical world is necessary so that there will be something of which consciousness can be conscious, the existence of other consciousnesses is a contingent feature of human existence. We can imagine, Sartre said, a consciousness who never encountered another consciousness. It is with surprise and dismay that Sartre's subject suddenly becomes aware that it is not alone in the world. When another human being appears before me, or 'surges up', as Sartre puts it, I am suddenly vulnerable, fearful, threatened. The danger that the other poses for me is expressed in 'the Look'. When another consciousness looks at me, he radically disturbs the ordering of objects in the world around the centre of my consciousness; he represents, as a consciousness, another perspective that I can sense but never grasp. Most threatening of all, he turns me into an object for his gaze, jeopardising my very being as a subject. My only recourse is to attempt to assert my subjectivity, dominate his gaze, and in turn reduce him to an object. In *Being and nothingness*, the recurring paradigm for human encounters is the chance meeting of two enemy soldiers, each threatening the other's life, each trying to subdue the other.[17]

This paradigm continues to be the model for Sartre's description of intimate relations between lovers and friends and eventually for all human relationships. Love between consciousnesses is clearly impossible. We are doomed as consciousness to separation — that is, to our own view of things which must always, no matter how we try to accommodate ourselves to another's wishes or desires, come between us. Another human being, just because he has a view of me, must be a threat to my existence as a free subject. Sartre described in detail the various attitudes possible between consciousnesses. The sadist asserts himself as subject and becomes his object. The masochist submits to the other subject and becomes his object. Indifference can be feigned, but given the threat the other poses, I can only pretend not to care. In sexual desire I can attempt a fleeting moment of physical possession that entraps the free subjectivity of the loved one in the flesh.[18] When sexual desire is exhausted, as it must be with orgasm, we are immediately returned to solitude and hostility. The only remaining attitude is hatred, the wish that there be no one on Earth at all. However, even removing all other consciousnesses cannot satisfy a Sartrean subject. Others, in fact, are necessary. It is only by way of their view of me that I can know who I am, only from them that I can get an external view of myself.

This dependence on others' view of me is a further source of conflict. My dependence puts my 'being' seemingly out of my own control. Somehow I must both control the other, and at the same time preserve his independence. If I control him too much, the other becomes a thing, and no use to me; if I control him too little, I suffer a painful insecurity. This painful ambivalence can never be resolved. We can only play out a futile masquerade as in turn we adopt the role of sadistic master or masochist object, as we feign indifference or hatred. Sartre offers an explanation for Kollontai's painful realisation that relations between men and women in socialism soon reverted to domination and submission. Submission and domination are not contingent features of particular kinds of economic relations; they are the only possible attitudes human beings can have towards each other.

The second sex: an existentialist feminism

In Beauvoir's *The second sex*, there is always palpably present in each chapter — whether on a woman's sex life, her professional life, her religiosity, her household duties — the framing metaphysics of the human condition as laid out by Sartre. In her introduction, Beauvoir explicitly positioned herself not as a woman or as a feminist, but as an existentialist. She had, she said, escaped by a lucky chance the limitations of being a woman. She had never felt herself discriminated against, had always considered herself the equal of men. This gives her a chance to be impartial, to look at women's condition objectively, especially since it is clear from her liberated perspective that so many other problems are more pressing and more important.

She is not, for all that, completely objective. Any examination involves a stance and hers is existentialism. Each human being is a subject reaching towards transcendence and there is no other justification for existence than this movement towards an empty future. The worse evil is to fall into objectness or to inflict such a fate on someone else. It is in these terms that Beauvoir proposed to understand the situation of woman. Men have denied her transcendence, have made her a thing; Engels's economic analysis ignored this deeper confrontation between individuals.

For Beauvoir, the class struggle is not by itself explanatory; instead, the male appropriation of private property is only intelligible as an individual's project of self-assertion and transcendence. The 'otherness' of women is prior to property relations and is needed to understand why property relations take the forms they do. Thus, to intervene only at the level of property or economics is not to change the self/other dialectic from which these relations are generated, but merely to force it into other institutional expressions.[19]

From her existentialist perspective, Beauvoir can now give an alternative account of sexism's origins that answers the question why it was not women who asserted property rights. This is not, she argued, because of any feminine essence, but because of their situation. Woman's situation is radically different from men's. She must give birth, she must endure the bodily upset, distortion and pain which accompany reproduction. Even worse than the pain and the inconvenience, however, is the fact that she is passive in reproduction, a prey to natural forces, not a creator or manufacturer imposing her design on the world. This involvement with reproduction kept the primitive woman back in two ways: firstly, she was physically unable to go on hunts or to work steadily; and secondly, she naturally saw herself as passive and not active. This is the reason why she does not assert herself as men did when they discovered tools and realised that it was possible to dominate and master nature, the reason why she was not included when men set themselves against the primitive community. It was men who competed, who killed, who risked their lives, who dared, and although woman 'finds in the heart of her being the confirmation of masculine pretensions', her situation forbids active participation. 'The superiority is given not to the sex which gives birth but to the sex that kills.'[20] It is this risk of murder, Beauvoir agreed with Hegel, that allows one to grow, to become a subject, to become a free human being.

Women never in fact asserted themselves, and so were never 'overthrown' as Engels speculated. The primitive matriarchies celebrated by some utopians, even to some extent by Engels himself, did not, Beauvoir argued, exist. Although descent may have been matrilineal, women did not have active power.[21] Beauvoir cited her old classmate, the anthropologist Levi-Strauss. Women were never a social force set against men; instead, men exchanged women, and parental structures were only alternative ways of effecting that exchange.[22] In an agricultural society woman becomes a goddess, but this does not indicate her superior status: on the contrary, it indicates a further reification of her otherness. As Goddess, Nature, Earth, she was the other on which men were dependent and their awe only expressed their own powerlessness. When men began to feel their power and the possibility of transcendence and mastery, female gods were overcome. This change to a masculine god was, Beauvoir argued, a necessary stage in human development. God must change from the 'Other' ungovernable nature to man's true 'semblance', a powerful, designing, chastising god, expressing the male principle of 'light, intelligence, order'. As long as female gods were worshipped, humanity remained stuck in immanence.[23]

Not only does failure at transcendence explain the first eclipsing of the female by men; it also explains her present degraded situation. Again, her inferiority is not given, either physiologically or psychologically. A woman has no essence, no more than any human being has. In her free choice, she makes herself what she is. At the same time the description of her different situation occupies most of the 1000 or so pages of *The second sex*. In fact, women behave and think very differently from men. Beauvoir, like Wollstonecraft, spared women nothing; they are deceitful, weak, excessive, illogical, conservative, hysterical, simplistic, and much else that is not admirable, but this is because their situation denies them the normal expression of humanness. Mankind must remodel the face of the Earth, he must create new instruments; he invents, he shapes the future.[24] He must appropriate the world, make it his, put his mark on it. Women's oppression is — as any oppression — that they are denied this self-assertion.[25] A million links bind a woman to the Earth. Men close off her possibility for action, refuse to allow her to participate, relegate her to marking time, 'maintaining herself', doing mechanical tasks.

The oppression of women is even more powerful in that it is masked behind nature, behind the belief that it is women's destiny to be passive. One cannot rebel against nature. Consequently, women do not see the world as theirs, take no responsibility for it, and allow their energies to turn to futile substitutes like narcissism, excessive romanticism, or religion. Because transcendence is refused, women are denied access to the highest human values — heroism, revolt, detachment, invention, creation. Whether it occurs in the kitchen, job, bed or university, Beauvoir always analysed women's oppression in the same way as a thwarting of the human project of self-assertion and self-creation. If women are passive, hysterical, depressed, it is because the world does not appear to them, as it must to any full existentially existing being, as an 'ensemble d'utensils',[26] but only as a dumb and indomitable resistance.

Why then, the question must be asked, have women accepted this oppression? If they are free because a human subject must be free, why is it that they live such restricted lives? Beauvoir's answer was to invoke Sartre's notion of bad faith in all its many forms. Humans are free but can avoid that freedom and, unfortunately, a woman's situation allows her more and better ways to deceive herself than other oppressed groups. Firstly, woman is trapped in the bad faith of men. Men want her to be an object, an inferior, a will-less being. They encourage her weakness, punish her self-assertion, make her dependent, tantalise her with the 'barbed hook' of courtesy or adoration. This is, Beauvoir argued, the worst crime — so to tempt another human being away from her humanity.

The bad faith of others, however, can never by itself account for women's lack of freedom; the complicity of the victim is also needed. Here Beauvoir struck a new note. In Marxism and in democratic theory, women are seen as victims, victims of either the economic structure of society or of an illegitimate discrimination. Existentialist freedom implies that victims are always accomplices in their own enslavement.[27] If women are treated like children then they have chosen to be children, and there are many other strategies which a woman may choose to justify her abject status. A wide variety of descriptions from religion to psychology are available to substantiate woman's passivity and confirm her feminine role. She may even make an idol out of the man, out of her very oppressor, submerging all of her own ambition in his. In this way her bad faith and the man's may nicely mesh. In their struggles with each other, each can project onto the other his or her repudiated self and so each can avoid the ambiguity of the human condition. Both *The second sex* and Beauvoir's novels are rich in the many forms bad faith in love can take, and the precarious balance couples can achieve in their mutual self-deception. A 'vicious circle' results. Each has their own unrealizable dream, the woman of submission, the man of identification; each looks to the other to solve their internal conflict; each may blame the other when this strategy, as it must, fails.[28]

Always evident in the many examples used by Beauvoir of reciprocal bad faith is the Sartrean scenario of sadist and masochist, only now with the explicit understanding that in this confrontation women have traditionally been given only one of the roles. Beauvoir accepted Sartre's account of the relations between consciousnesses; she accepted both the initial inevitable clash and the necessary capitulation by one side, but it is always, she argued, the woman who surrenders to the man and agrees to carry out his projects instead of her own. It is the woman who makes herself an object so as to comfort and assuage the anxiety of the masculine subject who needs her reflection of himself but is terrified of her independence.

The antidote is obvious. The woman must rise up, must reverse the roles, must assert herself against the oppressor. When she does this the oppressor becomes the 'thing' that blocks freedom and she the subject, refusing the limits set by men, taking a fling herself at the sky which is no longer the seat of the transcendental ideas, masculine and feminine. The liberated woman merges into the light of transcendence, learns to be 'l'Homme'. Furthermore, it is only she herself who can take this step towards liberation. With such inspiring language, Beauvoir urged that women take over the initiatives previously reserved for men.

This is not to say that bad faith can be easily avoided, and much of *The second sex* described in often numbing detail the difficulties women face. Of foremost importance for a woman, Beauvoir maintained, is a profession in which she can assert herself as a man. Work is, as it was for Hegel's slave, the place where one's mark is made, where one's designs are projected onto the world. Denied this expression, women will always be 'sub-men'. Women should therefore, avoid marriage, never have children, escape the trap of home and family, and take their place in the world among men. Unfortunately, however, there are many checks on women's ambition, from early family training to outright discrimination. Even more damaging than these social barriers is another much more serious conflict that the professional woman faces. A man from his early days feels that his 'vocation as human being' does not contradict 'his destiny as male'.[29] His sexuality is congruent with his transcendence. It is not so for a woman. It is not only maternity that compromises her subjectivity, but also her very sexual being.

For Beauvoir, as for Sartre, the sexual relation is the locus where conflict between self and other is played out most intensely. Sartre's account of being-for-others in *Being and nothingness*, even when it is not explicitly sexual, carries this suggestion of sexual intimacy where the encounter between self and others is unavoidable. Non-sexual relations can often be regulated by strategies of protection and distance which insulate each combatant from confrontation. In sex, such regulation though present, often fails, or at least is inadequate, given the intensity of the experience and the physical nakedness revealed for the look of the other. In the relation between man and woman, Marx said, one can see how far his natural condition has become a human condition. In Sartre, this natural condition is man's embarrassing body, embarrassing because it encumbers the conscious subject with physicality. Sexual experience is confrontational not only because there is another subjectivity involved, but because what is in question is the very part of oneself that is a thing. Unlike Lenin, who found discussion of sex an unnecessary distraction, Sartre established sexuality as a central philosophical issue. If sex is not a primitive instinct that must be appeased, neither is it a simple reflection of economic relations. Instead, sexuality predates sexual organs and economics as the most immediate way to live out the conflict between self and others.

Beauvoir, in her equally open treatment of sexuality, agreed with Sartre that physical desire is not a simple physiological response. Desire comes first and the physical manifestation of desire later. Sex cannot be seen as a simple subjective pleasure, like scratching an itch or drinking a glass of water. When the physical 'essence' of sexuality, supposedly revealed by biologists or physiologists, is dissolved, then silence on sexual matters, protected first by bourgeois prudery and then by Marxist discipline, can be broken. Sexuality is no longer a physical function outside politics, appropriately discussed by scientists; it is the very heart of the philosophical because it is the place where individuals most narrowly intersect, where they confront most painfully the distance and conflict that divides them from others.

Unfortunately, in that encounter, as in so many others, the woman's subjectivity is compromised. The sex act, Beauvoir argued, forces a woman into a particular role, that of passive object. Furthermore, this disability may then infect all her other non-sexual dealings with the world. A woman is put in the position of making a choice: either she will be aggressive and successful or she will be sexually attractive; the two are not compatible. At her job she must not dress provocatively, she must be as forceful as the men. She must devote herself to her work and not to endless shopping for clothes. She will then be allowed to work with the men but at the expense of her sexuality because the same men will not find her behaviour sexually attractive.

One possibility is to attempt to lead a double life, be tough in her profession and then transform in the evening into someone sweet, yielding. Both vocations suffer: she forgets to be yielding at home, she is weak and cries at work. Alternatively, she may try to play the male role. Becoming rich and powerful, she would like to support a man, but she can find no man who could tolerate her superiority. She may give up the attempt to have a permanent relationship, but then she, unlike men, has no means of casual release with prostitutes or pick-ups. There are few male prostitutes and to pick someone up for her is too dangerous. When she attempts the role of seducer or conqueror, even if she wins it is never her success. She has fallen and the man has scored another conquest.

This incompatibility between woman's sexual being and her professional life goes deeper than socialisation; Beauvoir located it in the sex act itself. In the sex act the man presents himself as a conqueror, as a dominator.[30] There is in the act always a passivity on woman's part, she is penetrated while the man plays the active role. Therefore, a woman in sex must always feel herself a thing, an object, and in conflict with her professional assertive self. She must choose either a sexless professional life or a passive passionate one. No wonder that many women make love their profession and give up on professional advancement; to give up sexuality seems too high a price to pay even for humanness. To succeed at work is not enough, anymore than imposing one's will on the physical world was enough for Sartre. Women must, like men, have being for others — that is, they must in relationships, and especially in the sexual relation, be able to realise themselves as subjects. Therefore, the disability in women's sexual life is even more crippling than her reproductive role, which could always be refused.

In order to offer some hope for the woman, always a sexual object, Beauvoir tried to establish a fragile reciprocity between Sartrean lovers. Those lovers, however, had already been placed by Sartre in a particular kind of situation. Sexual desire, for Sartre, is a response to the self/other stand-off. It occurs after a subject has subjected the other and made her an object. The question then arises what to do with her. She is no good as object because she cannot give back the reflection that is necessary if one is to exist for others. It is at this point, according to Sartre, that 'I make myself desire'.[31] The other as object is purely flesh, and now via desire a sexual object. By the caress, by awakening desire, the lover tries to make the spirit surface and bring this dead body back to life, a life which he controls. Sexuality is a kind of bad faith, the mirage of a possible solution to an irreconcilable contradiction. In the sex act, Sartre's conscious subject continues his search for the illusive object of desire, someone under his control and yet independent, not there as other and yet still providing a freely generated external view. Sexuality will always be a series of failures for such a subject, as the lover makes himself believe one more time that the caress can bring about the impossible fusion of two consciousnesses, only to fall back again into alienation. Paradoxically, the inevitable climax of orgasm itself must bring the lover back to his own sensations and is 'the death and failure of desire'.[32]

Sartre's subject-in-love is easily recognisable in Beauvoir's male who comes to the sex act as master, the condition of his desire that his partner has become an object. As a woman, however, Beauvoir approached sexuality from another point of view. The man comes as a subject, as used to 'transcendence' but embarrassed by this bodily involvement in which his transcendence is compromised. He must come to terms with the fact that he is a body, an uncontrollable physicality. The woman, on the other hand, comes to the sex act as immanence, as flesh, not only because this is the way the man sees her but also because of her role in reproduction. Since she already must suffer the immanence of reproduction, she must struggle even harder for her dignity. The man, on the other hand, used to autonomy and control, will be the initiator. Every woman, Beauvoir asserted, must remember her first 'deflowering' which must always be a kind of rape of her body.[33] Given the anatomy of the sex act, given the fact of male penetration, women will always have to play a more passive role, if not suffer a kind of defilement or pollution. Women are always the sex object. Beauvoir, in example after example, showed the man in sex playing the part of sadist and the woman the part of masochist.

The only possible answer was a reciprocity seemingly impossible on existentialist principle. Sartre had left open only the possibility of an alternation of roles; each lover could have his or her turn at being subject. Beauvoir tried to describe a more satisfying kind of equality. The man can desire the flesh of the woman, she argued, while recognising the woman's freedom. The woman though passive, may consent freely to her submission. 'Each may have a pleasure whose source is in each other; the words receive and give exchange their sense, joy is gratitude, pleasure tenderness.'[34] Beauvoir's sex act was very different from Sartre's manipulative, faintly disgusted play with female flesh. She maintained the unbridgeable existentialist distance between lovers — it is not that the woman feels she is the man or the man the woman — but the two are no longer hostile. The man sees his pleasure as coming from the woman, and is therefore dependent; the woman gives herself as a gift and is therefore active and keeps her dignity. Both accept their situation but transcend it.

The woman's 'active' submission can, at the same time, be distinguished from masochism, the bad faith of becoming an object for someone else's pleasure, because the woman is passive not for someone else's pleasure but for her own. Beauvoir's woman must transcend the Sartrean caress, the proprietary male hand, and the penetration of the active male sex act, 'towards her own pleasure'.[35] She gives herself for herself; she will also be active. For this to happen, however, the man must see the woman as his 'semblable'. Once the woman is seen as 'like' a man — that is, as a subject — then reciprocity in the sex act is possible. Two equal subjects now confront each other, give to each other, enjoy each other.

The 'semblable'

The idea of the equality and similarity of all human beings was essential to Beauvoir's feminism. It is women's human status, their 'semblance' of humanity that will allow reciprocity. Therefore — and it is this which divided Beauvoir from both conservatives protective of women's role and radical feminists who support separatism — Beauvoir was always explicit on two issues: that there is no feminine specificity, and that one must not reject male models. To understand her position one must take into account the conservative view of woman's nature and destiny which she rejected, and which, after the publication of *The second sex*, vociferously reasserted itself.

Typical are two books by Catholic women, published in 1956, Edith Stein's *La femme et sa destinée*,[36] where as nun and teacher Stein addressed in particular the question of the proper education of women, and Firkel's *La destin de la femme*,[37] also written from a Catholic perspective. Both authors began from the premiss that women are different from men, and, although worthy of respect, have different values, virtues, and roles to play in the world. The human species, Stein argued, is a double species, male and female. Everything about the female half is different from the male half. A woman's internal economy is different: her physical life, the rapport between soul and body, between spirit and sensibility. Different spiritual symbols apply to the sexes: for a woman, the closed circle of physical and spiritual, symbolising a harmonious deployment of forces; for men, the accumulation of power. These different natures have a theological expression: the human species is to dominate the earth and to give it form as the creator. In this work the man creates and the woman helps. In birth the roles are reversed.

According to their different roles, women and men have different virtues. A woman has the ability to 'penetrate another soul, to make their goals hers'. She is 'sensitive' to others, she can grasp 'concrete beings in their particularity and proper value and take a position in respect to them'.[38] Love, not sex, dominates her life. On the other hand, a man's virtue is to be strong, forceful and masterful. Correspondingly, the sins of the two sexes differ. Man can become domineering and brutal or a slave to his work. Woman can become a slave to man, mired down in her sensuous life. Because of these differences men and women will play different roles in life and so require different educations. Man must be prepared to dominate and master the earth: 'he aspires, by pure knowledge, to subject the world and make it his spiritual property, to conquer it as a possession with all the joys it offers, finally by a personal action, to make it his creation'.[39] Woman, on the other hand, will learn to help and support the man in this activity.

Firkel supplemented this difference with an analysis of the story of Adam and Eve. Adam and Eve are not just two human beings; they are the two types of humanity — masculine and feminine. Adam's punishment is the male destiny of labour and creation and Eve's is suffering in childbirth. Firkel traced this dichotomy in theology. Christ is the active male principle, and the Church the female. The male priest is to give the sacrament that mediates between the male God and earth. Mary is, instead, the receptive and giving interceder. Like Mary,

> the woman welcomes in her breast the semen of the man, carries a child that she has nourished with her own substance and gives it to the world; she knows how to act similarly in all domains where she gives what she has received augmented with her own substance.[40]

Male Catholics agreed, provoked by heretical notions, such as Beauvoir's, of feminine equality. Marcel Clément in *La femme et sa vocation*[41] asked the masculine question, 'What is a woman?'.

Even women, he maintained, do not know. The question is asked because women *are* different — in body, in role, in attitudes of dependence and collaboration, and in their responsiveness. Clément cited the authority of the Pope who proclaimed in 1943 that social structure based on equality is based on a false assumption. Men and women have equal dignity, and value, but they are not equal in everything. Women have different gifts from men, not just superficially caused contingent differences, but 'qualities with essential repercussions in the life of the family and in the community'.[42] Such an assertion of women's irreducible specificity did not necessarily rule out a kind of feminism. For Firkel, women's influence was badly needed. Men had a tendency to treat other beings like machines, especially in this technological age. Women could intervene, and to do this they must enlarge their role past the family, they must take part in public activities, always consistent, of course, with their own feminine nature. Women must not attempt masculine professions in which they would lose themselves; instead they should devote themselves to causes such as human dignity, rights of man, defence of the family, cultural exchange, and peace. This kind of feminism, as Firkel noted, hardly means 'the reign of women', only that women must intervene to help man dominate a technology that threatens to get out of his control.

Even more insistent on the necessity of feminine difference and feminine intervention was the Jungean Elisabeth Huguenin. In *La femme à la récherche de son ame (The woman recovering her soul)*,[43] she criticised views like Beauvoir's that would equate the masculine and the feminine. When women are educated, treated like, and consider themselves the same as, men, women become 'masculinised' and thereby lose their feminine souls. They become cold, competitive and reduce sex and love to straightforward lust. She cited in particular 'socialists' like Kollontai[44] who make of woman only a comrade of men and encourage promiscuity, serial affairs, and easy divorce.

It is because of such failures of femininity, Huguenin argued, that there is a modern crisis. Marriages fall apart, there are no spiritual or moral values, children are uncared for. The war encouraged women to forget their femininity; they went to work in the factories, they hardened themselves, they adapted themselves to male values. The consequence is that women, as women, disappear, as does their feminine influence with them. The inclusion of women in the workforce is only a further deformation of their nature. Instead of the women's work of cooking, embroidering, housekeeping, tasks into which they would put their hearts, women find themselves operating a senseless machine that repeats the same operation over and over again and may at any moment cut off their hand. In fact, the inhumanity of factory work can perhaps only be grasped by women to whom it is so unnatural. It is therefore no achievement for women to have adapted to such work and to have been absorbed into the workforce.

Before, women created a world apart that was still part of the masculine world. Now, with the family gone, there is no sensitivity, warmth, or communality left. All is cold and hard because women have withdrawn their influence. The feminine becomes the superficial 'l'air féminine', a matter of seduction and clothes, and at the same time there is a one-sided exaggeration of male principles of organisation, hierarchy and technology. Communism, with its socialisation, organising, and hierarchical structuring of the functions formerly performed by the feminine family, is just a further extension of this male principle. Certainly the war had shown what a world dominated by masculine values without women might be like; now women, as specifically feminine, will be its only salvation. It is women who, returning to their natural roles, will make the world inhabitable again.

Many of Huguenin's proposals for women are similar to those of the Catholic Firkel's. Women's work, housework, education of children, child-care — all must be revalued. These activities, where mechanical production is inappropriate, bring grace to life and without grace life would be a disparate, cold nightmare of impersonality and ugliness. Furthermore, as Firkel also argued, women should also move out of the house into the world, where they could express their proper femininity in professions such as teaching, social work or charity. Huguenin also supported such liberal goals as equal pay for equal work, maternity leave, and flexible hours for mothers that make outside work possible and desirable for women.

If this is feminism of a sort, it is very different from Beauvoir's. It was precisely the redeeming female nature and role that Beauvoir rejected. In the social work, charity and homemaking of Firkel and Huguenin's women, in the ongoing attempts to return women to the home in the post-war period, Beauvoir saw all of the limitations that had closed off the sphere of masculine accomplishment to women. Women must see themselves not as one-half of the race but as men.[45] As for the passivity, meditativeness and

spirituality which Firkel, Stein and Huguenin praise, they are all
bad faith ways for women to escape being human. Beauvoir's
independent woman wants to be active and knowing, refusing the
passivity that men impose upon her. The independent woman
accepts male values: she pushes herself to think, act and create in
the same way as males. She does not denigrate male accomplishment which is 'far superior to that of women'.[46]

Beauvoir had nothing but contempt for the woman who denies
the masculine, who accuses 'Cartesianism', who criticises male
philosophers' views on knowledge and metaphysics, who would
like to substitute feminine neo-Platonism for reason, spiritualism
for materialism, who looks for that living harmony, described by
Huguenin as feminine, in which the woman places herself 'just in
so far as she is a living thing'.[47] Such an identification with
nature duplicates the crippling bonds that tie women to the earth.
The human project is instead detachment and mastery, the assertion of the human spirit over and against mere physical stuff. For
Beauvoir, any retreat into the grace of a moment of spiritual union
with nature is an inadequate substitute for authenticating male
activity. Moments of spiritual grace or union are no consolation
for not being free. What Huguenin criticised as 'masculinisation'
is really humanisation, according to Beauvoir. There is just one
human enterprise, which women miss out on, and any argument
that makes an activity non-feminine is an argument for continued
subjection. The feminine activities cited by Firkel and Huguenin
were in fact the same few either low-status or gratuitous services
traditionally reserved for women, away from the seats of power
and away from challenging responsibilities. Beauvoir did not deny
the existence of the 'masculine' and the 'feminine' or their institu-
tionalisation in the family or in the organisation of work. The
acceptance of such categories is what perpetuated women's
inferiority, but liberation will only be accomplished when women
overcome stereotypes. Beauvoir saw herself as a proof of the
possibility of such transcendence. Had she not lived with and
worked with men, been accepted as their equal?

The question that remained is how transcendence was to be
possible for women other than the exceptional Beauvoir. By its
very terms, an existentialist liberation was individual, a matter of
individual will and choice. Anyone liberated by anyone else,
would only fall victim to a new tyranny; any adherence to a pre-
established revolutionary goal was equivalent to bad faith. What
then could be done for women who were firmly fixed in the lives

described by Firkel and Huguenin as feminine? Beauvoir's prescription for women was always the same. Women must work and, in order to be successful, refuse marriage and certainly children. If a woman was already married with children, then it had to be acknowledged that there might simply be nothing that could be done. For the masses of women who did have children and were already compromised by a feminine life, such lack of concern was, to say the least, bracing.[48] By its very terms, existentialist feminism had nothing else to propose.

Radical feminism and the battle of the sexes

Beauvoir's insight that women are always the slaves and that men always the masters was inherited by several generations of British and American feminists. A name was coined to denote the universal domination of women by men — patriarchy.[49] The breadth of subjects treated in *The second sex* prepared the way for radical feminist claims that: patriarchy is the universal constant in all political and economic systems, that sexism dates from the beginning of history, that society is a repertoire of manoeuvres in which male subjects establish power over female objects. Rape, pornography, prostitution, marriage, heterosexuality — all are impositions of male power over women, it was claimed. Women's acquiescence is a bad faith unwillingness to face their own lack of power.

The practical experience of women in the American Civil Rights movement, Vietnam War protests, and the student revolts of the 1960s confirmed Beauvoir's critique of Marxism. The male left accepted women into their organisations but not as initiators or leaders, nor were they interested in women's issues. Women again found themselves holding coats and making coffee. 'Sex class' seemed to go deeper than economic or social class. If leftist men envisioned a classless society, it was not to be a genderless society. As Beauvoir observed in *The second sex*, women, not the proletariat, are the original 'other' against whom male subjects, whether capitalist, feudal, or socialist, assert themselves.

After the ground breaking of *The second sex*, feminists continued to map out the many ways in which male power is exercised. In the *Female eunuch*,[50] Germaine Greer concentrated on women's sexuality. Women, she argued, have been castrated; the active expression of their sexuality has been repressed. Instead, they are objects for men, playing their role in male sado-masochistic fantasies. The result is a heightening of male aggressivity and a passive acting out of feminine resentment. With such partners, relations between the sexes must always be conflictual, if not hostile. The answer proposed by Greer was a version of Beauvoir's reciprocity. Women must assert themselves sexually, discover their own pleasure and their own right to sexual expression. The goal is parity, mutuality, exchange in sexual relations. Greer's sexually active woman need not be content with an active passive giving of herself; she may also take the more aggressive role in her own right.

Kate Millett found patriarchal relations in literature. In Henry Miller's, Norman Mailer's, and Genet's portrayals of the sex act, Millett discovered the Sartrean relation between sadistic subject and masochistic object. Coitus, Millett argued, is not just a physical act, but must be set in the larger context of human relations. Millett claimed to discover a *sexual* 'politics', where politics means 'power structured relationships, arrangements by which one person is controlled by another'.[51] The relations between the sexes in the works of Miller, Mailer, and Genet are a matter of dominance of men and subordination of women — the essence of patriarchy. Such power politics, Millett argued, is not peculiar to twentieth-century literature or any particular political institution but is deeply embedded in social life, immune to superficial change in government or economics.

Millett went on to examine the ways in which patriarchy is kept in place. All power, she agreed with Sartre and Beauvoir, requires consent on the part of the oppressed. Women's consent is gained by socialisation. Women are not always governed by force. The masculine will that women take a subordinate role is masked in theories of a female 'nature'. Institutions of socialisation, especially the family, ensure that this 'nature' reappears in each generation by mediating between individual and social structure. Sometimes, on the other hand, brute force is used — in laws that make abortion illegal, or in wife-beating and rape. Titillating descriptions of violence against women in the media, pornography, and misogynous jokes all are ways of using violence to assert male power.

The assertion of patriarchal power involves an extensive repertoire of strategies and attitudes. Some of the attitudes were examined by Eva Figes in *Patriarchal attitudes*. It is not, she argued with reference to anthropology and psychology, a question of natural facts. Women do not have a nature, nor men a natural response.

It is social structure that shapes the way men feel about love, women, marriage and the family. Men in power have created 'woman' in order to ensure that power: 'In a patriarchal society, male dominance must be maintained at all cost because the person who dominates cannot conceive of any alternative but to be dominated in turn'.[52] Men assert their power in all areas. In the sex act they assume the 'natural' most advantageous position for male pleasure. In religion they co-opt the priesthood and make the gods masculine, leaving women as passive onlookers. In economic life they confine women to bourgeois marriage and make a cult of the housewife. Different eras develop different patriarchal institutions according to need, and so the symbols and images of male power may change while the power relations of master to mastered remain in place.

Ti'Grace Atkinson in *Amazon odyssey* argued that women must name the patriarchal enemy. Again using the terms of Sartrean power relations, she noted that a 'master' will tolerate no reform that threatens his role as master, and that women have been 'massacred' in human history. The answer, Atkinson maintained, is to fight back, to cease futile diplomatic manoeuvring and to force the aggressor to stop. The 'battle of the sexes' must be fought in earnest and women must realise that they are attacked as a social class [53] — that is, as a 'grouping' subjugated to male 'will'. Certainly their masters will never accept willingly any abolition of women's slavery unless they get a recompense in 'power'; therefore, men must be forced to stop enslaving women.

In this new confrontational tone, Susan Brownmiller and Andrea Dworkin continued to use power relations to explain violence against women. Brownmiller, in her influential *Against our will*, placed rape at the threshold of human history as an exercise of male power over women. Although Brownmiller gave a detailed account of the history of rape and showed how rape laws conceptualised women as property and spoils of war, she located rape's deep source ahistorically, in the male sex drive and male anatomy. The male sex urge is not dependent on female receptivity as it is in other animals; a man's genital anatomy means that he *can* rape; when men discovered they could rape, they did rape; when men saw that women were afraid of their penis, they were able to institute a 'conscious process of intimidation by which all men keep all women in a state of fear'.[54] The result is that culture is a rape culture; all men are implicated in rape because all men profit from the fear which actual rapists induce in women.

Dworkin's *Pornography: men possessing women* analysed pornography as the ideology of male domination. The power of men, Dworkin states in her first line, is 'a metaphysical assertion of self';[55] it is '*a priori*' and only ratified by political and economic institutions. It is '*a priori*' both historically and in the history of an individual. The boy child feeds off his mother, he uses her up. A little boy has a 'choice' — to remain loyal to his degraded mother or to ally himself with his father.[56] Inevitably he chooses the latter, emulating his father and 'dissociating himself from powerlessness'.[57] With this exposure of male violence, Beauvoir's hope that women could compete with men becomes naive. Either they will be forced to submit or be tolerated condescendingly in token positions.

Like Brownmiller, Dworkin saw male sexuality as inherently violent. Men are the killers and women the Jews in Nazi prison camps, socialised into docility by masculinist ideology. Even Dworkin's infant male subjects assert themselves as masters against female victims. This rigid distinction between a dangerous aggressive male sexuality and benign passive female sexuality worried some radical feminists. Beauvoir's observation that in society women were 'the other' seemed to have turned into necessary truth. If sexuality, as Sartre argued, was inherently sado-masochistic, women as well as men should be allowed their turn to fantasise, act out, and experience the role of sadist. To posit an essentially gentle innocent female sexuality was to deny women the full range of human expression. Women should be allowed their turn as subject.[58]

Radical lesbian theorists added a further element to patriarchal power politics. Adrienne Rich, in 'Compulsory heterosexuality and lesbian existence',[59] argued that heterosexuality is not natural but imposed on women by men. As with men, women's primary tie is to their mothers, and heterosexuality 'wrenches' them away from that first love.[60] Marriage, gynecology and rape are institutions that allow men to repress female homosexuality and force women into bed. Enforced heterosexuality is the deep source of female oppression. Lesbian feminist theory added further detail to Brownmiller's and Dworkin's primal rape scene. Men had to force themselves on women who are not naturally inclined to experience sexual desire for the opposite sex. Males force sex on women because men want children, or, as Rita Mae Brown seems to imply in her novel, *Rubyfruit jungle*,[61] because men are such incompetent lovers no woman would want to have sex with them. Men are the aggressors because they desire women who do not naturally desire them, therefore a forceful taking of a woman is necessary. In Atkinson's battle of the sexes, women who give aid and comfort to the 'enemy' and engage in heterosexual sex support sexist society. The heterosexual act must always be carried out against the woman's consent or pleasure, is always an imposition of male power, no matter how many survival techniques a woman may devise to protect her sexual identity.[62]

Motherhood also, Rich argued, is forced on women by men. Although motherhood can be a valuable experience for a woman, as an institution it is under male control. Denial of abortion and contraception are ways of forcing women into pregnancy. Gynecology and male experts on child-rearing keep women's mothering under the control of men. The patrilineal family, with economically dependent female and male head, ensures that the mother's child remains the property of the male. The unavailability of child-care keeps her on the job as its caretaker.[63]

The description of male power over women reached its apotheosis in Mary Daly's *Gyn/Ecology*.[64] Patriarchy is total, all powerful, universal, and crushes women everywhere and at all times in history. Men are murderous, sadistic, and assert their power over women in violent ways. Daly cited the practices of Chinese foot binding, Indian suttee, African genital mutilation,[65] witch burning, and nineteenth-century gynecological cures, to illustrate the tortures that men inflict on women. Men are not just power-hungry, they are lovers of death: their desire is to reduce women to helpless corpses. Daly pointed to the death symbols in Christianity; the cross and crucifixion becomes the highest expression of spirituality in patriarchal culture. History, for Daly, is a killing field of murderous necrophiliac men and prostrate women.

These works and others articulated for American and British readers, in non-philosophical and popular terms, the mechanisms of patriarchal power and the strategies by which conscious male subjects managed to subjugate female consciousnesses, not only in economic arrangements or in restrictive laws, but also in family and sexual relationships. Everywhere the violent assertion of male power was cited, in wife-beating, date rape, child abuse, homophobia, pornography, and heterosexuality itself. Beauvoir's realisation that the subject/master is characteristically masculine, and the object/slave is characteristically feminine, hardened into universal fact. Women were seen everywhere and in every age as oppressed, not only by laws or by economic arrangements, but by violent men prone to sexual assault, maiming, even murder.

Although this exposure of male power and of the ways women are kept in their place sparked feminist anger, at the same time it was not clear from radical feminist theory what could be done about it. The theory of patriarchy itself proclaimed the universality of male dominance deeply rooted in male consciousness. The most logical possibility — that women declare war and assert themselves as ruthlessly and as aggressively as men — was almost never taken seriously.[66] Instead, radical feminists returned to the old liberal remedies of legal reform. Brownmiller — inconsistent with her biological interpretation of rape — proposed sweeping changes in rape laws which would reconceptualise rape as a violent assault against a victim rather than the theft of a male's property. In several states which passed rape laws consistent with Brownmiller's recommendations, there was better treatment of rape victims, but no appreciable decrease in the number of rapes. Dworkin and others proposed a revision of civil rights legislation which added pornography as discriminatory. When enacted by local ordinance, however, such laws were declared unconstitutional[67] by a United States appelate court. In the meantime, women struggled for funding for shelters for battered women and counselling for rape and incest victims, while statistics showed an increase in cases of violence against women.

Radical feminism inherits from Beauvoir a weakness in theory that makes inevitable this weakness in practice. In the first place, power, whether seen as the metaphysical form of relations between subjects or as the universal form of relations between men and women, is too crude a theoretical device to explain the complexity of human interaction. Even if it were true that men, as Atkinson charged, *need* to play the role of oppressor, the social and ideological sources of that need must be examined. To posit an innate male viciousness provides a villain against which anger and frustration may be vented, but avoids the deeper question. This is not to say that men have not committed atrocities or that they are not responsible for those atrocities; but male original sin is no more useful than female original sin as an explanatory principle.

Radical feminist theory cannot satisfactorily explain why it is that from the earliest days of existentialist history or radical feminist history it was men who asserted themselves. Beauvoir, in the move typical of radical feminism, inevitably reverted to biological determinism: women must give birth and so are disadvantaged. Atkinson and others followed, citing women's reproductive capacity as the weakness that men have the 'wits' to exploit. Other radical feminists agree, such as Schulamith Firestone[68] who saw in reproduction the material conditions of a woman's subjugation. Male anatomy was also claimed as a biological determinant. Beauvoir suggested that in the natural sex act, the penetrating man is anatomically in the superior position; Brownmiller speculated about an anatomical component in early man's rape of women. However, whether the biological determinant is found in female reproductive organs or in male genitals, the outcome is the same: there is little hope that any non-visionary solution is possible.[69] Beauvoir imagined a reciprocity impossible by the very terms of her existentialist perspective. Firestone, facing squarely the implications of biological determinism, proposed a futuristic brave new world in which all reproduction is artificial and women are once and for all relieved of the burden of pregnancy. Other than the equally visionary mass castration of males, no other remedy seems possible.

Given that most radical feminists are not willing to declare outright war against men, and given the superficiality of political or economic change, the only remaining alternative is separatism. This is especially appealing to lesbian feminists who need not thereby renounce their sexuality. Separatists attempt to escape the ubiquitous male aggressor by forming their own separate communities. In such communities, women will associate only with other women, away from the masters. In *Gyn/Ecology* Mary Daly imagined a visionary women's spiritual circle that would 'spark' and 'spin' its way free of masculinist thinking, leaving the masses of 'fem-bot' and 'token' women behind.[70] Such a group, however, with no material base, no footing in any religious establishment and no economic foundation, was unlikely to be more than a temporary alternative to church on Sunday, always subject to women's other economic and social commitments in patriarchal society. The full realisation of a separatist community would have to be fictional. In utopian portrayals of separatist communities, some magical device was found to protect the community from invasion. Charlotte Perkins Gilman in *Herland* imagined a geographical barrier which would hardly stand up against modern technology; Monique Wittig, in *Lesbian body*, tried a safer, but even more visionary, retreat to a prehistoric and imaginary past on Greek islands inhabited only by women.

Any real lesbian community, on the other hand, remains

economically dependent and subject to the laws of the larger 'patriarchal' community. As a result, relations in actual separatist communities must be narrowly personal with none of the concrete specificity of relations grounded in economic relations or in social institutions. Lesbian communities are ephemeral and vulnerable, often amounting to little more than a decision to be room-mates, or a contract to set up a small business. Even in an established community the unavoidable fact of stigmatisation can create an oppressive atmosphere where pressures to conform are high. In the stigmatised group there may operate a 'fascist' levelling of difference.[71]

Even if a lesbian community could insulate itself from male dominated society, radical feminism provides little in the way of guidance for the establishment of non-alienated relationships. Individuals might avoid falling back on stereotypical Sartrean butch/femme role playing, but there is no theoretical basis for the development of other kinds of relationships. Lesbians, as well as heterosexuals, learn to relate in a family before they are capable of conscious choice. Lesbians, as well as heterosexuals, form their conceptualisations and scenarios for love out of the pornographic images of mass culture. Radical feminists, having theorised a world of warring wills, cannot so easily escape their own theory. If power politics is everywhere in human affairs — in economics, sexuality, popular culture — what hope is there that lesbian relationships will escape power politics or that new power relations will not be established between masterful lesbian feminists and 'fem-bot' collaborators?

Radical feminist condemnation of 'token' women, or male-identified women, or straight women, glosses over the formation of feminine identity in family and ideology. Early radical feminists catalogued in detail the 'socialisation' of women, but socialisation did not excuse women's capitulation. Socialisation implies an intact female self which may be influenced but which also can refuse to accept the rewards of collaboration and courageously accept the pain of non-conformity. Gender identity and the choice of sexual object, however may not be accessible to conscious change. If it is not clear that a male child makes a 'choice' to abandon his mother and ally himself with his father, it is also uncertain whether women consciously and voluntarily take on their feminine roles.

Nor is there any positive prognosis in radical feminist theory for a woman's refusal to be a fellow traveller. Women can fight back against rape in self-defence courses; they can assert themselves in business and scholarship, as Beauvoir hoped; they may even force new equal rights or pornography laws, but there can be only these final outcomes: either a precarious stand-off between the armed camps of still vicious men and now militant women, or an imposition of an oppressive rule of women, or a cloistered and dependent women's community marginally surviving on the edge of male-dominated culture. In each case, feminist theory and practice continues to operate within the space of Sartrean metaphysics, in a world in which warring subjects can find mutuality only in the sharing of object status. This metaphysics, one that continues to shape radical feminist theory, is inadequate to feminist practice. Even in *Being and nothingness*, it failed to make intelligible our relations with others.

The 'nothingness' of subjectivity

The conscious subject which was Beauvoir's starting point in *The second sex* has been the hero of 'modern philosophy'. In the seventeenth century, Descartes established the subject's 'necessary' existence with his famous 'cogito' — 'I think, therefore I am.' Descartes went on to prove that a supreme male god also exists. Relying on the goodness of that god and his own 'god-given' reasoning powers, he called men to the task of constructing an objective, mathematically grounded science. Although the exact terms of this science would be reworked in the subsequent history of philosophy, the identification of the subject as knower remained. Locke's subject, for example, was the owner of a mental storehouse of ideas which he compared, sorted and generalised, to develop an empirical knowledge firmly supported by his own experience. Husserl's subject refused all but the given of his own experience, bracketed the existence of the physical world and other people, and took a transcendental stance that allowed him to claim to apprehend the necessary structures of all experience. Sartre's subject departed from tradition and admitted his clay feet. For there to be perception, and therefore knowledge, Sartre argued, a subject must perceive from a particular embodied perspective. However, Sartre's subject admitted his dependence on a body only to reassert his independence. The body may thirst or hunger; it may position the subject in a particular family, class or culture but these are only 'givens' for the subject to 'surpass'.[72]

For a subject, whether Descartes', Locke's, Husserl's or Sartre's, the 'other' must always be problematic. The starting point of subjectivity immediately raises the question of the existence of other consciousnesses, and the problem of other minds constantly recurs in modern philosophy. The existence of others is something to be *proven* in precarious arguments from analogy or empathy, an inference that comes after, and is subsidiary to, the primary existence of the knowing subject. Sartre, attempting to avoid the solipsism that inevitably results when these inferences fail, posited the other as a 'surging up' that suddenly confronts the subject working his own projects on the physical world. This primal Sartrean moment is replayed in radical feminism as primitive man surges up to subjugate primitive woman.

When the independent existence of others is admitted, however, the autonomy of the subject is immediately threatened. Having excised the substance from Descartes' subject imprinted with god's ideas, from Locke's subject filled with impressions, from Husserl's transcendental subject, Sartre was left with a consciousness who had an identity only in another's view of him. This admission makes incoherent the existentialist prescription to assert ourselves and live authentically, aware of our absolute responsibility for all our actions and attitudes. If our very identity is constructed by others, it is not clear how we can have such a freedom or take on such a responsibility. If women are the other, looked at and objectified by men, any assertion of their subjectivity can only be against the view that men have of them. Therefore the feminine object that they are for men must haunt any attempt they make as subjects to assert their freedom. They can consciously assume their femininity and proclaim it as a value, or deny it and adopt an unfeminine 'butch' identity, but they can in no way escape femininity.[73] Neither of these alternatives, characteristic of two schools of radical feminism, escapes the masculine and the feminine, either as roles or categories.

Subjectivity projects, however, an illusion of autonomy; either the presence of others is myopically ignored or they are subjugated in a move which compromises the freedom of the master as much as the freedom of the slave. This illustration has a particular place in philosophical history. If Descartes invented the *cogito*, he also made it clear why its invention was necessary. Mathematical science, the new science of the seventeenth century, had to be put on a firm foundation. The *cogito* is the necessarily true starting point from which that can be done. Once the conscious subject is separate from the world he is to know, philosophers can work to show how intercourse is to be set up between knower and world. The subject must not become just another thing in the world and so incapable of knowledge; and alternatively, the world must not dissolve into an insubstantial projection of the subject's thoughts. This is necessary so that knowledge is possible. At stake is Descartes' and other men's dreams of an objective, unified, universal science which will result in technical mastery of the physical world.

The creation of a subject is the key move in the realisation of this project. The 'ekstasis', as Sartre called it — or drawing back of the subject from the world — creates the world to be known by such a science and guarantees that the distorting viewpoint of an actual person positioned in the world is removed from view. The only substance of Sartrean consciousness is 'negation', the putting of the self back and apart from the world. Sartre, in his attempt to overcome the duality of non-communicating physical and mental substances, denudes subjectivity of all protective covering, revealing it as an act of pure will or choice. The 'ekstasis' of the subject is not an inescapable human separation from the physical world and from others; it is instead the wilful assertion of the 'for-himself's' difference and detachment from his physical environ-ment and human relationships, necessary for a certain kind of knowledge. The mastery of the other, which such a subject must also attempt, does not occur at the dawn of history but is an historical creation conceived at that point in time, and in the lives of individual men, when the project of a universal science is conceived. Sartre's discussion of knowledge in *Being and nothingness* described in detail what such a creation entails.

The subject, Sartre maintained, asserts himself as a totality against the totality of Being. At this point the world consists of only 'me' and 'what is not me'. This construction out of nothing allows there to be a physical world to know: 'This nothingness *is not* anything except human reality apprehending itself as excluded from being and perpetually beyond being, in common with nothing.' (original emphasis)[74] The subject is a vantage point from which reality can be known and manipulated. The knowing subject then continues by further negation to separate out 'this' from what is 'not this', to establish quantitative relations between 'this's', and to construct an abstract empirical science. Knowledge, Sartre admitted, leaves reality exactly as it is; it adds nothing and subtracts nothing. To say 'this is not that' is to think 'nothing'.

> This determination is a *nothing* which does not belong as an
> internal structure either to the thing or to consciousness, but
> its being is *to-be-summoned* by the for-itself across a system of
> internal negations in which the for-itself is revealed in its
> indifference to all that is not itself. (original emphases)[75]

For Sartre, the 'determination' of reality by the knowing subject
is connected with instrumentality. The subject sees the negations
it hollows out in the world as 'tasks', as instrumentalities which
the for-himself projects into the future.[76] His project is based on
no pre-set goal or value, but merely on the assertion of his will to
appropriate and mark nature.[77] The subject is the creation of a
nothing out of nothing, necessary for the foundation of male-
defined science.

  This is not to say that knowledge is the exclusive province of
men. It is, however, to acknowledge that a woman may find it
difficult to become a 'for-himself' and participate in producing
and theorising certain kinds of knowledge. The fact that women
have been under-represented in the physical sciences and
mathematics reflects a deep, and often unconceptualisable,
dissatisfaction with the way in which these disciplines are
theorised and the unexamined methodological assumptions with
which they are practised by male subjects. A mathematics which
is pure instrumentality, set apart from its actual application in
weaponry and nuclear energy, may hold little interest for a woman
with an affective concern for human life; physics focused on quantitative prediction of mathematical irregularities that ignores
qualitative change may seem a futile intellectual exercise; biology
that gives a mechanistic account of organic processes may not
yield the practical results that would motivate a woman scientist.[78] In the social sciences, women researchers may refuse to
treat the people they study as 'objects' and so fail to achieve
'reliable' results. Other paradigms, which do not involve the
'ekstatic' Sartrean subject, have been developed in feminist
theories of knowledge — such as respect for and co-operation with
nature, or empathetic understanding through participation.[79]

  Sartre's tortured but revealing descriptions of the intellectual
acrobatics necessary to remove the subject from his physical-social
environment are an improvement on the sleight of hand practised
by his predecessors. His account exposes the fragile identity of
such a subject and the illusory movement of withdrawal necessary
to establish his autonomy. Once the metaphysical necessity of

such a withdrawal is rejected, new kinds of questions can be asked about its individual and social purpose. Men may indeed be wilful, assertive, even violent 'subjects', but that subjectivity has a history, both an ideological history and a familial and social history in the lives of individual men. Rape in our era may be the action of male subjects who see women as the other-nature on which they must establish their mastery, but that subjectivity need not be taken as a biological given.[80] Rape in other eras may have another economy and another ontology.

Radical feminists, on the other hand, accepted subjectivity at face value. Male subjects subjugated women; women must become subjects in turn. The only alternative would be to attempt, by an act of feminist will, to step beyond the metaphysics of the subject and establish a community apart from men. This, however, does nothing about the concrete existence of male subjects who continue to threaten the existence of such a community. More importantly, because the familial-ideological roots of subjects' alienated relations are covered by the fiction of an original position, whether human or male, those roots can always continue to generate in the separatist community, or between the separatist community and others, the destructive dynamics of subject and other.

Again radical feminist theory intervenes after the decisive step has been taken, after the masculine consciousness has already established its fragile identity in conflict with others. Theorists then can only explore the moves by which subjects can avoid killing each other. Hegel reassures himself that the World Spirit will realise itself in the perfectly ordered state; the early Sartre resigns himself to the seesaw of sado-masochism broken only by moments of illusory sexual union; the late Sartre posits a group of subjects-in-fusion that can temporarily rise up against domination;[81] Daly imagines a separatist community of 'others'. But Beauvoir and radical feminists were mistaken in thinking they could find a woman in the 'other' of existential theory. Sartre may arouse the passive body he caresses to live, but the actual woman to whom he attempts to make love is most probably somewhere else, thinking in tragically different terms about their relationship. When Beauvoir is drawn into the war of subjectivities, she is drawn into a masculine fantasy, a way of rationalising and validating masculine interactions in which all that is left of a concrete living man is a will in competition with other wills, making his mark on the alien material of the world.

Radical feminism accepts Sartre's description of himself, but to accept men's description of their subjectivity may be equally dangerous as accepting their description of their social contract or of their production relations. In each case, theorising begins from a masculine problematic. To adopt the problematic of warring consciousness is to be party to male self-deception, as well as to limit feminist response to resignation or emulation. Although reciprocal assertion and/or violence is the only conceivable response in the master/slave scenario, feminism in practice cannot accept such a retaliation. This refusal leaves radical feminism with no praxis at all.

Again the same pattern emerges. Women, attempting to understand the causes and the mechanisms of women's oppression and to envision strategies for change, borrow from a theory of Man: political man, productive man, man the subject. In each case theory begins from pre-suppositions which are eventually proven to be inconsistent with feminist practice. Women do not do well in the alienated competition of the capitalist market place, stepping up over the suffering of their sisters doomed by the feminisation of poverty. Women do not do well in the modern totalitarian state, dedicated to the systematic stamping of the image of man on nature. Women do not do well in an alienated war of wills. Each time, feminist practice must either accept the limitations of its ideological commitments, and with it tokenism or marginality, or expand its theory. Psychoanalysis and post-structuralist theory of language provided such opportunities: to explore the familial history of the aggressive male and passive female, and to map out the conceptual structures in which they find their gender identities.

Notes

1. Some examples, all from Beauvoir's *Ethics of ambiguity*, trans. by Bernard Frechtman (Philosophical Library, New York, 1948), p. 114: officers who must send their men on missions where they will most certainly be killed; political leaders in concentration camps who are asked to choose the next victims of the gas chambers; mayors of occupied towns who are asked to give up resistance fighters for civilian lives. See also pp. 8–9 for other examples.

2. French intellectuals struggled with the problem of Stalinism, with a range of results, from Louis Aragon's absolute fidelity, to Merleau-Ponty's painful acceptance, to Camus' refusal, to Sartre's provisional

support, to Beauvoir's reserve. Sartre's history illustrates the inconsistency and wavering that the discovery of Stalinist oppression could provoke. After an attempt at neutrality with the independent non-party RDR founded in 1947 (see Sartre, *Entretiens sur la politique* (Gallimard, Paris, 1949) for a description of his hope for Europe's role as mediator between the US and Russia), in 1952 Sartre decided that the communists were the only real choice — only to break with them again in 1956 over the invasion of Hungary.

3. *The ethics of ambiguity*, p. 139.

4. See Juliet Mitchell, *Psychoanalysis and feminism* (Vintage Books, New York, 1975), pp. 227–31, for a discussion of British attempts to reinstate the family. Also, Dinnerstein, *The mermaid and the minataur* (Harper and Row, New York 1976), for a discussion of the link between the break-up of families as a result of war and the 1960s resurgence of feminist radicalism.

5. This discussion can be found in *Ethics of ambiguity*, pp. 17–22.

6. Marx himself warned of the danger of such an imposition in his *Theses on Feuerbach* (3) where materialism is described as 'dividing society with two parts — one of which towers above'. L.D. Easton and K.H. Gudat (eds.), *Writings of the young Marx on philosophy and society* (Anchor Books, New York, 1966), p. 401.

7. *The ethics of ambiguity*, p. 158.

8. Perhaps the simplistic nature of so much communist moralising can be traced to the problematic status of ethics within Marxism. If morality is only bourgeois ideology, then one does not dare to dwell on it for too long or to refine it too carefully. See my 'On the alleged freedom of the moral agent', *Journal of Value Inquiry*, no. 17 (1983), pp. 17–32, for a discussion of what a Marxist morality might look like.

9. The reference is to the American proletariat, bought off by gadgets, TV, cars (*Ethics of ambiguity*, p. 20). See also Beauvoir's reference to Flora Tristan's difficult task waking the European proletariat, ibid., p. 86.

10. Ibid., p. 103. Again, the reference to Hitler's totalitarianism where public spirit was to be constantly roused in rallies and parades.

11. The question comes out clearly in Hegel's early theological work, before the absolutism of the World Spirit is firmly established. In that work, the early Christian community provides the model for a very different 'reconciled' ethical totality.

12. For example, Bentham's democratic theory where the power of legislators must be tempered by the device of recall and reflection, or the US Constitution which establishes a 'balance of powers'.

13. 'La femme révoltée', *Nouvel Observateur*, no. 379, Du 14 au 20 Fev. (1972) p. 47, the interview in which Beauvoir explained her entrance into feminist politics.

14. The difference here can clearly be seen between Sartre and such loyal Communist Party members as Louis Aragon who consistently supported Party decisions. Sartre, on the other hand, roused nothing but contempt in communist circles for the ease with which, by a new 'decision', he changed political hats from liberal, to communist, to libertarian, to socialist, to Maoist, to post-structuralist textualism.

15. All three excuses were commonly given for the morally ambiguous decisions of wartime — for example, the priest in Camus's *The plague* who sees suffering as God's will, or the Kantian who cannot tell a lie and turns in a neighbour, or the collaborating mayors who turned in resistance fighters out of love for their people.

16. *The ethics of ambiguity*, p. 46ff.

17. This account can be found in *Being and nothingness*, Part III, Chapter 1, IV, 'The look'. Sartre, in his later writings, commenting on the paranoid tone of the examples in *Being and nothingness*, blamed the atmosphere in which he had written it — the German occupation of Paris in which the French lived under the hostile eye of the Germans. In his later work, faced with the problem of justifying social responsibility and collective action, Sartre considerably revised the account of human relationships in *Being and nothingness*, trans. by H. Barnes (Washington Square Press, New York, 1966). Beauvoir did not write a corresponding revision of *The second sex*, trans. H.M. Parshley (Vintage Books, New York, 1974), except to remark occasionally that she should have given a more materialist (i.e. Marxist) account of women's subjugation. She did not, however, make clear how such a materialist analysis could be squared with the powerful critique of Marxism in *The second sex* and in *The ethics of ambiguity*. Sartre's later Marxist existentialism, developed in his *Critique of dialectical reason*, attempted an explanation.

18. *Being and nothingness*, Part III, Chapter III, 'Concrete relations with others', Sartre's graphic dissection of the 'project' of sexual desire.

19. *The second sex*, Part I, Chapter III. 'The point of view of historical materialism'.

20. Ibid., p. 72.

21. 'The actual condition of women has not been affected by the type of filiation (mode of tracing descent) . . . she is always under the guardianship of the males.' Ibid., p. 80.

22. Levi-Strauss's interpretation of his structural models for exogomous kingship relations in *The elementary structures of kinship* (Beacon Press, Boston, 1969) as exhibiting the universal exchange of women, is now controversial. Not only does he impose on native customs concepts meaningful only in industrialised commercial societies, such as 'exchange', 'purchase' and 'mortgage', but he does so against the self-descriptions of the participants themselves. Thus, for example, brideprice, which to Levi-Strauss illustrates the purchase of women, to the bride herself is instead a propitiatory gift from a lowly suitor. (See Robert Briffault's interesting discussion of this and other customs as proving the enduring claims of an older matrilineal, matrilocal tradition in *The mothers*, abridged by G.R. Taylor (Atheneum, New York, 1977), p. 198ff).

After the early, anxiety-ridden *Tristes tropiques* (Plon, Paris, 1955), Levi-Strauss did almost no field work, but concentrated instead on showing how kinship relations could be reduced to semiotic structure. Leaving aside what a psychoanalysis of such a retreat into formalism might reveal, the empirical basis for even the claim that the Amazon Indians, which are the subject of *Tristes tropiques*, exchange women is still not established. Some contemporary women researchers find that in such tribes women play a leading role in all decision making, including the making of marriages.

23. *The second sex* ('History', Part II, Chapter V, 'Early tillers of the soil'). Beauvoir's discussion of Goddess worship is clearly deficient. Subsequent research into its intricate metaphysical and ethical implications showed that Goddess worship cannot simply be dismissed as a confession of male impotence. See, for example, Merlin Stone, *When God was woman* (Harcourt, Brace, Jovanovich, New York, 1976); Mary Daly, *Gyn/Ecology* (Beacon Press, Boston, 1978); Jaquetta Hawkes, *The dawn of the gods* (Random House, New York, 1968). It is her existentialist presuppositions that forced Beauvoir to this unreflecting rejection of the different values inherent in early agricultural societies. Because these values do not correspond to existentialist self-assertion, Beauvoir had no other recourse but to relegate them to the passive, the imminent, the animal, the nothuman. On the specific point of whether the image of the Goddess was a product of male impotence, cf. Jones Millaart, *Catal Huyuk, a Neolithic town in Anatolia* (McGraw-Hill, New York, 1967) for a description of very early paintings, figures and chapels seemingly created by women.

24. *The second sex*, p. 72.

25. See *The ethics of ambiguity*, p. 83, for a generic analysis of this sort of oppression.

26. Heidegger's phrase quoted by Beauvoir, *The second sex*, p. 665.

27. See also *The ethics of ambiguity*, where the tyrant cannot completely make subjects objects but must rally them, woo them, inspire them — p. 103.

28. *The second sex*, pp. 779–80. In *She came to stay*, published in the same year as Sartre's *Being and nothingness*, Beauvoir described a similar destructive triangle in which each person has designs on the other and in which there is no recourse but to the Sartrean strategies of indifference, masochism and sadism. Françoise, the woman who like Beauvoir thought herself liberated, remains trapped in her own jealous dependence and ends by murdering the 'other woman', the ultimate suppression of the other.

29. *The second sex*, p. 758.

30. Ibid., p. 418. Beauvoir's description of the physiology of the sex act in which the woman must be to some extent passive, as well as her description of the physical horror of maternity (*The second sex*, p. 553) are in conflict with her assertion that women's subjection is not a biological given. Beauvoir is not alone in locating oppression in the sex act itself. Compare, for example, Ti'Grace Atkinson, 'The institution of sexual intercourse', in her *Amazon odyssey* (Links Books, New York, 1974).

31. *Being and nothingness*, p. 511.

32. Ibid., p. 515. This account is reflected in Sartre's fictional presentations of sexuality where there are no lasting relations between men and women, only casual encounters.

33. *The second sex*, p. 428. Beauvoir later attempts to repudiate this comment in *Tout compte fait* (Gallimard, Paris, 1972), p. 507. Even with a virgin, she says, there can be an exchange.

34. *The second sex*, p. 448. One must compare Sartre's assertion that respect for the freedom of another is only empty words.

35. Ibid., p. 446.

36. Amiot-Dummont, Paris, 1956.

37. Mame, Paris, 1956.

38. Stein, *La femme*, p. 44.

39. Ibid., p. 166.

40. Firkel, *La destin*, p. 24. St. Thomas Aquinas's view of woman's role in reproduction as the empty receptacle/body is supplemented here with an astonishing cannibalising of the woman eaten away by the other's demands.

41. Nouvelle Editions, Paris, 1959.

42. Pope Pius XII, Allo de 24 Avril 1943, cited by Clément, *La femme*, p. 16.

43. Editions de la Baconnière, Neuchatel, 1949.

44. Ibid., pp.37–9.

45. In fact, Beauvoir's early religiosity tends in exactly the opposite direction to Huguenin's. In *Simone de Beauvoir l'enterprise de vivre* (du Seuil, Paris, 1966, p.257), she tells Jeanson that it was in fact her early experiences in the church which gave her the conviction that all souls must be alike. Compare, however, *The second sex*, p. 691, where Beauvoir claims that religion justifies a delusive equality.

46. *The second sex*, p. 698.

47. Ibid., p. 690.

48. *Nouvel Observateur*, no. 379, Du 14 au 20 Fev. (1972). Some of their reaction can be seen in the follow-up interview: 'Response à quelques femmes et à un homme', *Nouvel Observateur*, no. 382, Du 6 au 12 Mars (1972), p. 382, where Beauvoir acknowledged letters from women in response to her article, letters defensive of the value of the family and marriage. Beauvoir spent most of the interview, however, arguing with the more theoretical objections of the male intellectual Clavel.

49. In anthropology, 'patriarch' has a precise referent not at all congruent with its use by radical feminists: an historically specific system of social organisation, nomadic, pastoral, tribal, and centred around an extended family with a male 'patriarch' at its head. In radical feminism it became the more vacuous universal set of institutions that legitimise and perpetuate male power and aggression.

50. Germain Greer, *The female eunuch* (Boston Books, New York, 1971).

51. Kate Millett, *Sexual politics* (Doubleday, New York, 1970), p. 22.

52. Eva Figes, *Patriarchal attitudes* (Faber and Faber, London, 1970), p. 50.

53. Atkinson's co-option of the Marxist concept of economic class is typical of radical feminism. Atkinson says that women are a biological classification that is turned into a political classification. In the process, 'class' loses much of its meaning. Atkinson's tangled formula: 'individuals grouped together by other individuals as a function of the grouping individuals, depriving these grouped individuals of their human status'. *Amazon odyssey* (Link Books, New York, 1974), p. 172.

54. Susan Brownmiller, *Against our will: men, women and rape* (Simon and Schuster, New York, 1975), pp. 13–17.

55. Andrea Dworkin, *Pornography: men possessing women* (Perigee Books, New York, 1981), p. 13.

56. Ibid., p. 49.

57. Ibid., p. 50.

58. Essays debating the pros and cons of this question, much discussed

in the 1980s, are collected in Carol Vance (ed.), *Pleasure and danger. Exploring female sexuality* (Routledge and Kegan Paul, Boston, 1984).

59. *Signs*, vol. 5, no. 4 (Summer 1980), pp. 631–60.

60. Ibid., pp. 637–8.

61. Daughters Inc., Plainfield, VT, 1973.

62. Ti'Grace Atkinson, 'Vaginal orgasm as a mass hysterical survival response', in her *Amazon odyssey*, p. 5.

63. Rich develops this argument in *Of woman born: motherhood as experience and institution* (W.W. Norton, New York, 1976).

64. Mary Daly, *Gyn/Ecology: the metaethics of radical feminism* (Beacon Press, Boston, 1978).

65. Daly's interpretation of these practices has often been criticised as ethnocentric, especially by non-Western women. Daly was more interested, they claim, in proving her thesis that the male will to harm is universal than she was in understanding practices from the standpoint of the women who engaged in them.

66. Monique Wittig is one exception with her *Les guérillères* (Viking Press, New York, 1971), a visionary evocation of women warriors who win the world from men in violent rebellion. Accordingly, some radical feminists engaged in urban terrorism, spray-painting offensive advertisements, denting cars with sexist bumper plates, and so on.

67. On 27 August 1985, a three-judge panel of the US Court of Appeals for the Seventh Circuit declared the Indianapolis Ordinance to be unconstitutional. The ruling was upheld by the Supreme Court in February 1986. A similar ordinance had previously been introduced in Minneapolis (1983) as an addition to an existing Civil Rights Ordinance, had been passed by the City Council, and then vetoed by the mayor on the grounds that it was unconstitutional.

68. *The dialectic of sex* (Bantam Books, New York, 1971).

69. See Alison Jaggar's detailed account and criticism of radical feminism's biological determinism in *Feminist politics and human nature* (Rowman and Allanheld, Totowa, NJ, 1983), pp. 106–13.

70. Two epithets Daly often aimed at women 'collaborators'. 'Fembot' women made themselves into the objects of men's desire and so became robots; 'token' women accepted positions in Women's Studies or were otherwise co-opted by the male system.

71. See Susan Krieger's sensitive discussion of pressures to conform in a lesbian community and difficulties individuals have in developing a sense of identity. *The mirror dance: identity in a woman's community* (Temple University Press, Philadelphia, 1983).

72. Sartre is not arguing that we *can* on some occasions overcome handicaps. As subjects conscious of our situation we *necessarily* decide how to live our situation. *Being and nothingness*, Part IV, Chapters I, II, 'The situation'.

73. Sartre left it to Beauvoir to apply this insight to sexism. His primary interest was in racism. His essay *Anti-Semite and Jew*, trans. G.J. Becker (Schoken Books, New York, 1948) describes the plight of the stigmatised Jew who has two choices: either to accept a stigmatised Jewishness or to renounce his Jewishness, satisfy his liberal defenders, and become a 'citizen'.

74. *Being and nothingness*, p. 251.

75. Ibid., pp. 25–7.

76. Ibid., p. 274.

77. At this point Sartre's later alliance with Marxism becomes predictable; the existentialist subject has much in common with productive Marxist man.

78. See Evelyn Fox Keller, *A feeling for the organism: the life and work of Barbara McClintock* (Freeman, New York, 1983) or *Reflections on science and gender* (Yale University Press, New Haven, 1985).

79. See the essays collected in S. Harding and M. Hintikka, *Discovering reality* (D. Reidel, Boston, 1983).

80. Susan Griffin explores the complicated nexus between violence against women, and the scientific mastery of nature in *Pornography and silence: culture's revenge against nature* (Harper and Row, New York, 1981).

81. Aware of the inadequacies of a metaphysics that make common cause and social responsibility impossible, Sartre supplemented the phenomenological ontology of *Being and nothingness* with a social ontology in the later *Critique of dialectical reason*, trans. by A. Sheridan-Smith (New Left Books, London, 1976). The autonomous subject, however, remains able in his freedom to assert himself against institutions and oppressive social structures.

5

The Analysis of Patriarchy

The feminist critique of Freud

Sexism proved as resistant to its philosophical exposure as it had to economic reorganisation. The ensemble of strategies, behaviour and attitudes so meticulously described in *The second sex* seemed indelibly inscribed on the male and female psyches, passed on from one generation to another, inaccessible to either political or economic change. Women could not so simply will themselves to be childless, to be unmarried, not do housework, not to be 'feminine'. The existential self from which this exercise of the will was to come was a point of not only theoretical but also practical weakness if it was the case that the assertion of a free, autonomous, self-willing subject deceptively masked whole areas of feminine and masculine experience. When male/female relations are analysed only as power relations between consciousness, the concrete psychological reality in which women live is ignored. Women do not struggle against an anonymous other male, but against fathers, brothers, mothers, husbands. Any theory that posits original autonomous selves must in the end present women's failure at self-assertion as weakness of will and bad faith, if it does not revert to real biological disadvantage. Neither result offers much in the way of hope. A woman cannot change her anatomy, nor, perhaps, can she will to be wilful.

Instead the situations in which women struggle have a history, a familial history both social and individual, and their reactions are shaped in that history. Furthermore, this shaping of the female self, of the female personality, is accomplished in a dependent childhood in which it is senseless to talk of will or understanding. Personality is formed in the family, for better or for worse, beyond choice, and often beyond memory. With a prodigious act of will, one may change surface behaviour, but if these changes skim over deep childhood sources of emotion, they will be increasingly difficult to sustain. A woman may soon lapse back into the dependence, the vulnerability, the deference to men, the insecurity for which her formation as female has prepared her. The assumption of an original, autonomous self assumes a primal egalitarianism which does not acknowledge the real extent of feminine disadvantage in the master/slave dialectic. It is not that the woman is a subject like any other subject; she *is* a slave. Her serfdom is no assumable role but is written into her very feminine identity.

For an account of that feminine identity, feminists, disappointed with the superficial gains of post-war feminism, turned back to Freud. Psychoanalytic studies of feminine sexuality and female character had already provoked in feminists a lively, if highly critical, interest, but Juliet Mitchell's *Psychoanalysis and feminism* provided a fresh, less reactive re-evaluation of Freudian theory. Freud, Mitchell argued, was not prescribing but describing, and if the patriarchal world he described was not ideal, perhaps he located some of the mechanisms that kept it in place, If, as radical feminism had so well documented, patriarchy with all its myths had survived intact from one generation to another, in psychoanalysis could be discovered the mechanism of its transfer, not in bad faith, or in conscious male assertion or manipulation, but in the family in which every self, male or female, is formed. To overlook the family is, as Mitchell puts it, to overlook 'the place in which the inferiorized psychology of femininity is produced and the social and economic exploitation of women . . . legitimated.'[1]

Mitchell's Freud provided a different kind of corrective to Marxism. Existentialism had tried to show that individuals did not act automatically in the interest of their class, but were free self-choosing consciousnesses. Freud showed how the male and female personality, apparently so resistant to socialist engineering, was formed in the family.[2] In the familial context of reproductive relations, surviving from capitalism to socialism, a female achieved her femininity, and perhaps also her submissiveness. Existentialist feminism had made it seem as though the power of patriarchy was imposed on the female self; what feminists re-reading Freud would discover was more troubling. The enemy is within, implicated in the very self that seeks liberation. In order to be a self, to emerge as an independent person, it is necessary that the relations of patriarchy, whether economic, political, or reproductive, be internalised. A woman only becomes a woman as she works through conflicts and finds her place in a particular structure of social relations. Only in the context of those relations can any kind of feminine ego be established. The defective female subjectivity exposed by Beauvoir becomes essential for 'normal' development.

It is, therefore, not surprising to find Freud passionately rejected by radical feminists. On a first reading no one seems less likely to be a feminist hero. A woman, Freud argued, bore the marks of her upbringing. Her narcissism, her passivity, her lack of creativity, her inferior sociability, her vanity, and moral weakness, are all a result, a necessary result, of her formation as a woman.[3] This is not flattering. Freud had argued, it seemed, that women *are* inferior, and that this inferiority leads to an obsession with physical appearance, pettiness, vindictiveness, and incapacity for moral judgment. These claims, taken outside the theory of psychoanalysis, seemed like nothing more than the usual insults that male chauvinists aim at women.[4] Indeed, not infrequently, Freudian catchwords were actually used as insults by those ignorant of theory but current on popularised jargon who accused 'women's libbers' of 'penis envy' or cited their lack of a 'super-ego' as the refutation of their claims for equality.[5] Freud's judgment on woman's crippled spirit, however, came only after a complex description of the sad inevitability of that result.

To make the situation worse, Freud was available to American and British readers only through a particular translation of his concepts and through a corresponding adaptation of psychoanalytic therapy. Freud's work, riddled with questionings, false starts, revisions, and reworkings, lent itself to varying interpretation. In this spirit of adaptation and development, Anglo-American psychoanalysis emphasised some dicta of the master over others. Unfortunately, these adaptations often worked to the detriment of women.

Firstly there was the increasing biologism of American psychoanalysis. Freud's ambiguous comment, 'anatomy is destiny', was taken seriously and both his anatomical analogies and his ambivalent references to a woman's 'constitution'[6] were accepted without the hesitancy which almost always accompanied such citations in Freud. His distrust of the theory of instincts as quasi-physical drives was forgotten. The 'it', that part of us which we do not avow, became the 'id', a pool of primitive sexual drives, to be controlled by the 'ego', and the biologico-chemical basis of these processes was emphasised in the requirement that psychoanalysts be medical doctors. The goal of analysis became in its American version a strong ego which could control the rebellious impulses of the id, and the discovery of a reality principle that would allow the patient to deal successfully with the external world. The result for women was a ratification of traditional values. Traditionally vulnerable to the charge of biological specificity, their inferiority, whether normal or pathological, could now be blamed on anatomy. They were hysterical because of hormone changes, depressed because they had a womb; their docility and receptivity were correlates of their open genitals. Ego psychology with its goal of adaptation to reality pressed women back into traditional behaviour. They were encouraged to transcend their infantile 'penis envy' and become normal women with interests focused on home and children. They were encouraged to give up their hostility to men and become loving helpmates.

The vehement objections of feminists like Beauvoir, Millett, or Freidan were not solely to this particular pernicious practice, or malpractice, of psychoanalysis, however. There were also theoretical objections, objections deeply rooted in existentialist voluntarist feminism. This can be seen clearly in Beauvoir's chapter on Freud in *The second sex* in which it is by no means Freud on femininity alone that is rejected but also Freud's conception of the human mind.[7] Beauvoir had already, at the very starting point of her enquiry, postulated conscious autonomy. The self-conscious ego comes first; sexuality is a later formation, a variant of the subject's attempt to realise itself. Freud's most shocking discovery, however, was infantile sexuality, certainly not a sexuality that could be seen as the 'project' of a transcendental subject, but a polymorphous confusion of impulses and images. Out of this diversity, this shifting and sliding of sexual energy, by way of the mediation of the family, would ultimately emerge a sexed human being whose selfhood was closely linked with sexual identity. To this Beauvoir opposed 'an existential fact': 'The anxiety that (the subject's) liberty induces in the subject leads him to search for himself in things, which is a kind of flight from himself.'[8]

This anxiety, she argued, leads the male child in bad faith to overvalue his genitals, and the female, in reaction, to feel inferior. Beauvoir could tolerantly admit some of the Freudian concepts that explained these responses. Penis envy, castration fear and Oedipal complex might name some actual childish thoughts, but for Beauvoir they can only be possible, and rather silly, traps of deception into which a woman can fall. Given the always adult consciousness she assumes, she can dismiss these deceptions as bizarre, unlikely, or at least, easily exposed. Freud's emphasis on them can, in turn, be dismissed as 'masculine bias'. It is men who are afraid of castration, who can only understand female genitals as deprivation, who can only see female sexuality in terms of their own masculine project. Freud's fixation on the penis as the centre of value, Beauvoir argued, is a kind of masculine pathology that involves the alienation of the self in an object and a fascination with images, mirrors, and how others see one. Beauvoir rejected what she saw as Freud's mechanical production of personality. Freud made it seem, she maintained, as if the unconscious, together with a mysterious group mind, automatically produced the female personality. He made it seem as though the unconscious symbolism that analyses reveal is imposed on the spirit. Freud missed here, Beauvoir argued, the fact that symbolisation is the result of a prior project of a self who practises his mastery of the world. It is this self, ignored by Freud, that chooses, no matter what external restraints may be put on that choice.

It was indeed this rational power of conscious choice that Freud denied. If it were so easy to be rational, he would not have had so many patients nor would their behaviour have been so interesting. The self that chooses is the ego, but that ego is already a product, the product of the split between id and ego, between conscious and unconscious. At that split the very possibility of willing or choosing is established. The self is already formed by its ability to choose, and whatever is to be done about neurosis or hysteria, or even about normal crippling femininity, it is not the autonomous decision of a free subject. Instead, analysis suggested a much more difficult and complicated process in which psychoanalytic history would be relived, restructured, and a new self formed.

This sort of cure would have to be rejected by theorists like Freidan who argued that the problem was not in the female self but in what the self must rebel against, i.e. the patriarchal family. To blame the self is misplaced if it is socialisation which is at fault. In the Victorian family women were repressed, submitted to sexual deprivation and abused. The self, no matter how

119

ontologically free, could be oppressed by circumstance; but both times and the family had changed and there was no reason why, with the new freedoms, feminine psychology should approach in any way the psychoanalytic description. Freudian explanation was dated, Freidan argued, and could be discarded — if anything, merely an interested attempt to preserve male hegemony.

Like Beauvoir, Freidan rejected the primacy of sexuality. It only seemed so important, she argued, to a repressed Victorian like Freud. Instead, she proposed the more basic, and more rational, need to grow: 'When the teeth grow, the mouth can bite as well as suck; the child becomes capable of control, mastery, and understanding'.[9] Again, appearing first and already formed is the self looking for mastery and control. Sexuality can then be seen as a secondary extension of that mastery. If the function of the family is to repress this self-expressing subject, then the function of the family can change to leave the subject more free to engage in her own projects.

Kate Millett continued this line of argument. Instead of the mysterious concept of penis envy, repugnant to rational thought, the little girl is confronted with a given social reality. Men have penises and men have power. She will never have that power and so must content herself with substitute satisfactions. The emphasis should be on the external social order that gives men all the power, and not on sexuality or on the unconscious sources of sexuality. Fear of castration is the realistic rational fear of rape in a patriarchal society; penis envy is the desire for male privilege. Millett's 'eminently sensible little girls', as Mitchell calls them, already are, as of course they must be, the transcendental selves who choose their own inferior course among the inferior alternatives offered by society. They are selves that are subjected to various socio-economic realities, and when Freud pretends to dismantle this self his motives can only be patriarchal. He was sexually deprived, culture bound, and an apologist for male power.

In this feminist rejection of Freud there is a continuing logic. If Freud rejects the transcendental self then he must instead be a determinist. He must fall back on the anatomy of instinctive drives, or allow the individual to be swallowed up in mechanisms of socialisation or of the unconscious. As determinist, Freud is then seen to close the door on a feminist praxis which can make no headway against the necessity of constitution or social structure. What is most interesting about Freud, however, is the way in which his argument for the universality of patriarchy falls outside such dualistic categories, outside the philosophical model of an essentially free consciousness confronting an external reality which operates according to natural law. There is no simple opposition between individual self and social reality. The structure of the self is at the same time the structure of the human world, the world in which we live. This change in focus places patriarchy in a completely new light. It does not consist of the will to power of men, claiming their subjecthood; it is not the reciprocal bad faith of women; instead, it is the very shape of the social, the conditions by which human life is perpetuated. The conclusion — perhaps not initially promising for women, but inevitable — is that women also, if they are to have any identity at all, if they are to be selves, if they are not to lapse into hysteria or psychosis, will have to find themselves somewhere within patriarchy.

Here again Freud's conclusions were rejected by feminists like Figes, who specifically considered Freud's sociological work. In *Moses and monotheism* and in *Totem and taboo's* speculative extensions of analytic theory, Freud explored the subtle liaison between what is social and what is individual. How are values passed on from one generation to another? How is the behaviour of sexed individuals perpetuated? Figes did not just question the sufficiency of Freud's particular explanation — the never forgotten and foundational murder of the primal father and the resulting pact between brothers. She questioned the very idea of a socio-individual inheritance. Progress could never be made, she argued, through fear of castration; instead 'the original mind has to break away from the values of the preceding generation'.[10] Such a magical leap was indeed the only praxis which existential feminism could offer. It was also the possibility that the feminist critique of Freud was determined to keep open.

The motives behind feminist rejections of Freud went deeper than a simple defence of female honour against Freudian insult. If patriarchy is a power play, a conscious accessible strategy of men, then two outcomes remain possible: firstly, men may be persuaded to stop, and secondly, women may be persuaded to resist. If Freud was right, however, the mechanisms of sexism are not accessible to either male or female choice in any direct way, and perhaps not at all. Thus, existential feminism, by rejecting Freud, retained at least the illusion of hope, the hope that with sufficient pressure, men and women could be persuaded to change. It was the illusory nature of this hope that turned feminist theorists back to Freud. Perhaps, after all, it was best to know the worst. To ignore the psychic structures that supported and perpetuated patriarchy would be to limit oneself to a praxis without real efficacy, a purely surface protest that would always end by adapting itself to the perpetuation of male privilege. Instead feminists like Juliet Mitchell, or Julia Kristeva and Luce Irigaray in France, taking Freud as the key to the concrete continuing and functioning of patriarchy, hoped to find a new depth of understanding and of feminist practice. Marxism, in its analysis of economic structures, developed the praxis of materially based revolution: perhaps in an equally non-utopian way, Freudian analysis could lead to a praxis of the spirit, a praxis which went to the source of communal symbolisation in order to revise the very notion of sexual difference.

The engendering of a female self

In Freudian analysis there is no primal unitary self or subject. Instead the point of analysis is to undo and remake the self, to rediscover the structuring and destructuring that leads to psychic function and dysfunction. Nor is there any primal identity, sexual or other. Identity is produced in society and that production can easily miscarry, as Freud's neurotics and borderlines illustrated. The assertion of selfhood or subjectivity is not given; it is an achievement and a precarious one. As an achievement it has a history and it is that history which psychoanalysis is to reopen, undo, or redo. For both masculine and feminine sexuality the analytic task is the same: to show how polymorphous fragmentary infantile sexual excitations are transformed to fit narrow perimeters of normal genital expression focused on acceptable sexual objects.

Freud's major discovery of the Oedipal complex, the primary structure of the psyche, came out of his own self-analysis. The boy, whose original love object was his mother, must give her up because of the father's prior claim and superior strength, symbolised in the boy's fear of castration. The successful resolution of this Oedipus complex is achieved in the boy's acceptance of his father's authority and his willingness to wait until he has a woman of his own. However, although most of Freud's early patients were women, he had considerably more difficulty accounting for female development. After an early attempt to give a symmetrical account and much complaining about the 'dark continent' of femininity, Freud sketched late in his life a very different female progress toward sexual identity.[11]

The girl begins with the same 'bisexuality'[12] as the boy; and also, like the boy, her first choice is the mother. She, however, suffers a significant disadvantage. Firstly, in so far as she desires her mother, her genitals are inadequate, in fact, non-existent. As a consequence she cannot hope for another woman as a substitute object, but must, from the very beginning, live with an absolute deprivation in her sex life completely unlike the mediated transfer of the boy's affection onto a similar object. This disappointment, if not despair, is symbolised by her 'penis envy'. Secondly, and even more difficult, she must actually change the organ of her sexual satisfaction from the masculine clitoris to the up-to-now-insensitive female vagina. She must find a substitute pleasure in the genitals of her husband and eventually in the having of his child. To this end the girl's masculinity — that is, her sexuality — must be repressed, and it is this repression, Freud observed, which is 'the chief determinant of the greater proneness of women to neurosis and especially to hysteria'. Inevitably, 'a considerable portion of her sexual trends in general is permanently damaged'.[13] She will probably never completely overcome her Oedipal longings and will necessarily suffer some degree of frigidity.[14] Her masculine sexuality may always disturb her precarious femininity. These differences in development mark women much more deeply than any socially imposed inferiority. A woman's very invulnerability to the threat of castration, because she is already castrated, prevents her from questioning authority and developing an internalised set of values and from achieving independence. Instead, even when married, she remains protected and childlike in the family.

To say of such an account, as feminist critics did, that Freud has missed the social is to miss the point. The structuring of the personality that goes on in the family *is* social; it is also individual. Each family history is different but at the same time the same. There is always a father, mother, a child. What is social, what is general, however, is not the aggregate of their rational wills, which in any case would only result in an atomism that is not social at all. Society is not 'they' who manipulate 'us' intact individuals. Instead, it is what defines us as someone, as someone in relation to someone else. Since there is no original self to which one could return that could predate the beginning of social life, there is no way one can, by will, neutralise the effects of socialisation. There is no self outside of society to which one could return, except the impotent, insane, or psychotic, which constitutes only a fragmented, objectless failure to be anything at all. Any self carries the mark of its genesis from the beginning. Furthermore, what is outside is not a manipulatable ensemble but a reality that is also a social construction unalterable without a corresponding adjustment in self. In analysis there is no brute reality to be discovered but only the various complex forms — both individual and social — taken by our thoughts.

What is therefore at issue is not a causal determinism, as radical feminists claimed, in which female anatomy leads to inferiority. In fact such a determinism, often reverted to by radical feminists themselves, never left feminists without hope. It was always open to argue with Mill and Taylor that physical strength should no longer be the basis of right, or with Firestone that technology could remove the burden of reproduction. Instead of a causal mechanism that always might suggest a manipulative handle, Freud's analysis seemed to leave no point of entry at all for feminist action. Women could act, but action, if it was to be meaningful, must remain within the only meaningful matrix of familial relations. Women could, in conscious or unconscious protest, keep their attachment to the mother and become homosexuals, or express their penis envy in male projects, but these reactions were as much formed by those relations, as much lived out under their law, as normal femininity. Neither course of action would significantly disturb family functioning. Feminism, itself, was quite possible as a reaction to the shame of castration, but not any less the product of a male dominated society.

The first critical comment on this grim analysis of the concrete psychological disadvantages of femininity came from women analysts like Karen Horney and Melanie Klein. In fact it had been their challenging observations and discoveries which led Freud late in life to reconsider the problem of femininity. Eventually controversy settled around that Freudian motor of female development, penis envy, the concept that was to be so repugnant to feminists like Beauvoir, Freidan and Millett.

There were, on one side of the controversy, orthodox analysts, such as Helene Deutsch and Marie Bonaparte, who supported and developed Freud's account. Deutsch, in her classic *The psychology of women*, changing from Freud's description to prescription, expanded on the normal development which was for a woman the only alternative to hysteria and neurosis. Much less hesitantly than Freud, she pointed out the actual inferiority of feminine sexual organs. The clitoris is small and not so sensitive as the penis; furthermore, the reproductive function leaves women at an additional disadvantage. To be normal women must manage to outgrow their masculinity, to become passive, dependent, and resigned to a life of nurturance not active creativity. Freud's description of the results of women's difficult role in the Oedipal drama becomes the discovery of what is constitutionally proper for women.

Meanwhile, in response to this orthodox view, an opposition made itself heard centring around the work of Karen Horney and Ernest Jones. Freud was, Horney argued, a man, and it showed. From a male point of view, female organs are deficient both because men see them only in comparison with their own, and because men may be envious of a woman's capacity to give birth. To insist that girls have penis envy, then, is wishful thinking. This is not to say that there is no penis envy. Horney agreed that it was there and operative in the psychic development of girls. However, it does not, she contended, come from the fear of castration. It has instead two sources; one is the physical fact of the actual inferiority of feminine genitals, which Horney agreed was to some extent less visible and less available to masturbation. In addition and even more important, however, is the social fact of the male's superior position and authority. The castration complex only comes later, as a result of an actual event in the little girl's life. Her father flirts with her and seduces her and then at a certain point rejects her. Castration fear in women is a realistic fear of an actual danger, the danger of rape and the danger of rejection. In answer to Deutsch, Horney made her charge explicit. Psychoanalytic theory is a male fantasy. Men find women threatening and powerful, and so in analytic theory find them a safe inferior place in a world of masculine values.[15]

Both sides in this dispute emphasised a certain inescapable brute reality. Firstly, there was the supposed physical fact of a woman's genital inferiority. For Deutsch the woman must be resigned to the inferior sensitivity of the vagina; for Horney there is the real disadvantage of her invisible genitals. To compensate, however, for Horney, there is another physical fact; the fact of a woman's reproductive power: or, as suggested by Horney and later elaborated by Melanie Klein, the supposedly insensitive vagina may be sensitive after all, producing a specifically feminine and 'natural' attraction to the opposite sex that is oral and receptive. In addition, in Horney's case, as for Deutsch, there is the ratifying influence of social forces. It is a social fact that men have power, that women are expected to play a submissive role. The difference is in the conclusion drawn: Deutsch believed women must play the role allotted to them, Horney that they have a legitimate 'protest'. Here Horney could, as analyst, introduce new strategies. Instead of Deutschean adaptation to anatomical handicap and social reality, there was room left in analysis for a pride in reproductive capacity and a legitimate protest against male prerogatives and male failure to control sexual impulses. 'Penis envy', a theoretical construct which is retained to explain certain clinical facts, is supplemented with the reproach 'it isn't fair'. At the same time, an alienated female subject still confronts an obdurate social order, and has again had to find a compensating satisfaction in motherhood.

Another, more promising, response was to return to that area of feminine psychology where Freud confessed himself particularly unsure: the pre-Oedipal attachment of the child to the mother. Freud focused on his great discovery, the Oedipal drama, but the necessary precursor of those events is in the love for the mother that initiates Oedipal conflict and rivalry. For the woman, with her incomplete transfer of love to the father and her immunity to castration, the importance of this phase is obvious; she, unlike the man, never quite escapes her primary attachment to the mother. Furthermore, this is an attachment that Freud admitted he did not fully understand; there seemed to operate, he said, 'an especially inexorable repression' of the relation with the mother.[16] Still, by the writing of 'Femininity' Freud was beginning to sense the possibility of surprising discoveries.[17] In the life of the girl, the mother retained a great importance; many times her relations to her husband seemed nothing more than a repetition, with its attendant love-hate, of her relation with her mother. Freud was able to trace even her supposed fantasy of seduction by the father back to her earlier seduction by her mother.

Nothing in Marxist economics or in existential philosophy had touched deeply this sensitive area of feminine experience. Motherhood was neither production nor was it an assertion of mastery and control; as such it could not be explained in either Marxist or existentialist theory; most radical feminist theorists choose to avoid the supposed female burden of reproduction. The inadequacy of philosophical and political thought in respect to feminine relationships, especially the mother-daughter relationship, drew feminist philosophers to psychoanalysis. The strong women's movement of the 1950s and 1960s had begun to splinter, to dissipate into unresolvable hostilities between lesbians and straight women, authority figures and workers, black and white women. There seemed indeed to be an unexplored feminine experience whose mysterious workings could erupt and subvert feminist politics. Feminist Jane Flax, in reaction to these painful schisms, became a therapist, determined to explore this 'continent', to watch gender identity develop through 'preverbal and non-rational experiences'.[18] The key subject here was not the neurotic, already trapped in Oedipal tangles, but the psychotic, or borderline, whose more serious troubles were believed to originate in the pre-Oedipal and specifically in the child's relationship with her mother.

This emphasis on the pre-Oedipal allowed Flax a further insight into feminine inferiority. Because of her different relation with the mother, Flax argued, the girl comes out of this stage already deficient in 'core identity'. The love for the mother is resolved differently for the girl and boy: the boy, fearing his father, acknowledges the father's superior claim, while unfortunately the girl has no such incentive to separate from her mother. Caught, then, in a relationship that is, Flax agreed with Freud, ambivalently both loving and hostile, the girl has no chance of escape. The father standing outside the mother-child symbiosis is no help: he represents a masculine independence and success which the girl cannot emulate. She can remain with her passive, mutilated mother or she can try to act like a man. Because the latter is inevitably impossible, there is, as Freud would have agreed, 'an endless chain of women tied ambivalently to their mothers, who replicate their relation with their daughters'.[19]

Unlike Freud, however, Flax carried this analysis one step further. What underlies the process that results in the female's lack of identity is the structure of the family. Women exclusively care for children in the home, which means that the mother is the only object of the child's affection. That women do so under the rule of the father means that rationality and worldly success are separated and cut off from nurturing and affection. Because of this split,[20] girls grow up to be dependent women, and boys to be men contemptuous of the female. As long as such a family exists, Flax argued, 'difference will inevitably be translated into relations of dominance and submission, superiority and inferiority'.[21]

This replication of female inferiority always occurs under the shadow of the male head of the family who, even when he substitutes at some motherly task, is at the same time always present symbolically as a contrast to the physical presence of the mother. At this point, Flax argued, there is an alternative to Freudian conservatism. Freud himself admitted that relations with the mother are unexplored; in these relations it may be possible to find the inspiration for a different family structure. Freud, she maintained, placed his psychology only after women have been dominated, after women have become slaves to the male family head who establishes his authority by separating their sphere from his. Freud assumed that women will have exclusive care of children under male command and that the male will have the privileged access to the public world. If, on the other hand, there is a sharing of child-care, if the mother, as well as the father, can show a way out of the family to an independent existence, then the impossible dilemma of the little girl is removed. Her first love need not be an unrealisable object and she may identify with a member of her own sex as a successful independent figure.

Other analysts also saw in Freud's pre-Oedipal a possible remedy for women's subordination. In *Les enfants de Jocaste: l'empreinte de la mère*,[22] (*Jocasta's children: the imprint of the mother*), the French Christine Olivier suggested a new myth that, instead of focusing on the Oedipal father/son, has the mother as central figure. Unlike Flax, she argued that it is not that mother/daughter relationships are too close, but that the girl is treated differently by the mother. The mother is sexually attracted to her son as a member of the opposite sex. They have between them a kind of love relation from which the girl is always excluded. At the same time the girl cannot turn to her father, because he is not there. The result is that the girl feels alienated, distant, and rejected. These female complaints continue into later life, whereas men, threatened by closeness of the mother, complain of the opposite claustrophobia and restriction. This difference is reflected in male and female language, Olivier argued. A woman as speaker seems always to attempt to establish a lost connection with mother; the male seems always to attempt to maintain distance and objectivity.[23] The determining factor is again the family in which it is the woman who is the only custodian of the young child. One-sided parenting alienates the girl and gives the boy no escape from his mother's affection. The absent father cannot give the girl her sexual identity or the boy a role model. The obvious answer is again that women must give up their exclusive control of child-rearing.

Another more extensive examination of the effects of early exclusive attachment to the mother was Nancy Chodorow's *Reproduction of mothering*.[24] Chodorow's description of the mother-daughter relation was more complex than either Flax's inability to separate, or Olivier's alienated resentment. What is involved is not just a child's relation to father and mother but his or her relation to any object at all. Consequently, it is also a question of his or her existence as a self, that is as a being separate from other beings. What is involved in the pre-Oedipal stage, Chodorow argued, is more primary than sexual identification or role modelling which are typical of the Oedipal stages of development. The child's ability to think of itself as a subject and to form the idea of stable objects outside the self must be accomplished through the mother-child relation. Chodorow began with the Freudian concept of primary narcissism. The child at first does not distinguish between self and anything outside. There is no self and no perception of self. The establishment of 'ego boundaries' is, however, essential for the later health of the personality, and because it is the mother who is custodian of the child, it is in the relationship with the mother that these boundaries must be established.

Chodorow argued that because Freud neglected this crucial stage in development, the phenomenon of penis envy, admittedly traumatic, is not sufficiently explained. If he had examined the pre-Oedipal stage more carefully, Freud would have found a reversal of his hypothesis of an obvious female inferiority. There, because of the exclusive attachment to the mother, someone with whom the male can never identify, the male core identity, not the female's, is conflictual. Like the girl, the boy experiences an early non-verbal oneness with the mother, a sense of identity with her, and consequently a femaleness. His later maleness must always be asserted against the challenge of that primary identification. He must learn in a difficult fashion to be not feminine, and the mother must, because of his maleness, treat the boy differently. Whether or not a sexual attraction exists, he is not, in the end, like her and so is left out of the female world she creates with her daughters. Given the precarious, insubstantial status of his masculinity, the male must work hard to create an identity, establishing rigid and stereotypical differences between what is male and what is female. He must create differences and distances, must constantly alienate himself, not, as Olivier suggested, to escape the mother's sexual designs, but to establish against her positive identity a precarious maleness.

Girls, on the other hand, are more fortunate at the pre-Oedipal stage. They have the secure sense of being female like their mother and need not defend themselves as 'not something'. The identity problems that will come later for them and that revolve around the Oedipus complex are a reversal of this early security. The gender female by this time is negatively valued by males who are desperately attempting to establish something non-female, and it is only at this point, after a male reaction to insecurity has made rigid divisions between male and female and has devalued all that is feminine including mothering, female genitals and female symbols, that penis envy is comprehensible. The emptiness of masculinity becomes the denigration of women, as if this negation could take on positivity by a double negation. Thus, sexual difference is itself a production, a production of a male reaction to a primary insecurity. This is the 'reproduction of mothering'. Girls and boys develop different relational capabilities and are prepared for their different roles — girls as mothers, boys as functional in an alienated capitalist environment of work.[25]

Again, shared parenting is the antidote, but Chodorow's analysis went one step further in proposing not only shared parenting, but also a change in the quality of that parenting. It is necessary to return to the difficult establishment of boundaries between self and other, of 'object-relations'. Already in the special interest of Anglo-American psychoanalysis in children, this crucial phase of development had been investigated, especially by the developmental psychologist Winnicott. In the beginning, he argued, the child is completely dependent on the mother, and so subject to an unbearable fear. In order that the very young child be secure the mother must be adequate to the situation. She must give the child her complete attention, must merge her interests with those of the child in a way that is almost pathological: in fact, she must give the child the illusion of omnipotence, the illusion that he can create objects, can create his world.[26] Then, and only then, she will, as the child matures, little by little allow him to become independent. Meanwhile the child must find himself in the other, find his image in her reflection of his needs and only in that way can a secure ego be established.[27] This 'good-enough' mother devotes her life to the child, feeds his image back and allows him freedom only when he is ready for it. Even in her eventual retreat there is a devotion to and incorporation of the interests of the child. Problems in child development can be traced back to deficiencies in the mother, who is the one to be analysed and questioned.[28]

It is this account of good mothering, so close to the traditional view of women's sacrificial role, that Chodorow proposed to review. It is true enough that the child's strong ego depends on object relations established early in its development, but the style of this differentiation as well as the sex of the parent is responsible for rigid, alienating distinctions between what is male and what is female. Again the pivotal point is the mother-child relation. In Winnicott's interpretation, the essence of good mothering is the mother's non-existence. She echoes and reflects the design of the child; nothing intrudes between his wishes and hers. Still, there is never perfection, the mother can never be invariably present and the child must learn to be independent. However, the child's development should not stop with the perception of separation and an answering self-sufficiency. There is another step to be made, the recognition of the other's subjectivity, of the fact that the mother has needs and desires of her own. The 'good enough' mother, protecting the child from this realisation, may actually stand between the child and emotional growth. As a result, the mother is seen by the child not as a subject but as an object, and mother-blaming becomes a convenient recourse in cases of deviance.

In the meantime the child has never learned the lesson of inter-subjectivity but must always be locked into his own subjectivity looking out at a collection of 'instruments' for his happiness which in their distance from him will never be really satisfying. This isolation is intensified for the boy by the additional fact of his difference from the mother; for him she must become irrevocably an object and all the women he later meets are expected to duplicate this mirror he has come to need and expect. On the other hand, the girl soon finds that there is no one who will be *her* mother, especially as she is usually expected to help the mother in anticipating and fulfilling the needs of male members of the family. The male is allowed to perpetuate his illusion of omnipotence. In continuing to create his world, he strengthens it in alienated institutions, excessive theorising, regulated exchanges, and especially in the articulation and maintenance of gender differences.[29]

The assertive male subjects of radical feminism are mother's sons. The good mother produces lonely, manipulating, hostile individuals who escape anxiety in obsessive behaviour. For Chodorow there is another possibility, another style of mothering that would show to the child 'that the mother is a separate being with separate interests and activities that do not always coincide with just what the infant wants at the time'.[30] Such a personality would develop not at the expense of others but in relation to them. The necessary correlate to such a self-assertive mothering is a change in the structure of the family that would allow a woman the freedom to develop and maintain interests outside the family.

Different though the specifics of the analysis of the mother-child reaction may be, from Flax's no-escape intimacy, to Olivier's rejection, to Chodorow's object relations, there is one antidote that is suggested. If the mother were not the only custodian of the child in the early years, the dynamics of male-female development would be different. There would be a choice of identification and a choice of love objects. The male could establish an identity with the father and so avoid the necessity of a defensive, negatively defined masculinity that would inevitably collapse into hostility or violence against women. Men would not refuse to recognise the subjectivity of their mothers and go on to treat all women as projections of themselves. If, as Freud had shown, the patriarchal family produces females or males whose core identity must be unstable or destructive then the family must be changed. Once this is done, deficiencies in both male and female personality can be corrected. The male will not need to assert his power over women, and the woman will not masochistically accept victimisation. Such a remedy, however, requires a deeper revision of Freudian theory. Mother and father, separated by their seemingly irreducible difference, may not, in fact, be interchangeable. For Freud the family triangle of father/mother/child was immutable.

The primal father and the origins of society

Equal parenting, if it is not to be a superficial, impermanent sharing of household tasks, must interrupt the structure of family relations. It must challenge the father's position as head of the family, and the woman's position as domestic labourer. If not, feminist demands for 'help' may be met, but just barely, and a thanks required that places help as gift and not duty. Certainly, in liberated families eager to try shared parenting, such attitudes often prevail. The father participates in child-care and housework, but only while maintaining at the same time a stubborn and often unconscious resistance which shows that the structure of the family remains intact. Sexual difference, already present in the relations of the small child with sexed parents, stubbornly subverts the very rational reforms proposed by Flax, Olivier, and Chodorow.

Logically, there is no reason why the father should make the law and be the authority in the family. Logically, it would seem that authority could be shared or be maternal.. It is at the same time a fact, Freud asserted, that everywhere in human history it has been the father who has been the head of the family. Freud offered an explanation for this, an explanation that rooted patriarchy not in biology or in will to power but in a complex of thought and symbol inherent, not only in the individual mind, but also in society itself. These are structures, largely unconscious, that cannot be changed at will no matter how reasonable the argument. In fact human behaviour is for the most part not governed by reasonable arguments, and no consideration of the weakness of the female ego or the failure of the male to acknowledge others can make any difference. In response to initiatives for change, patriarchy will always find new ways to perpetuate itself.

It was with the determination to understand this longevity in the face of feminist protest that Juliet Mitchell reconsidered Freud in *Psychoanalysis and feminism*. She would 'locate this oppression that courses through the mental and emotional bloodstream'.[31] Is the family an institution particular to capitalism, or to Western society?; or does it, as Freud argued, coincide with history, with culture itself? To take Freud seriously is to see that in the construction of each psyche similar symbols are involved which relate that individual to a given family structure: a family in which the young child is cared for exclusively by the mother under the direction of the father, a family in which the father intervenes to rupture the child/mother relationship, a family which directs a son out into the world and gives a daughter to another man. It is this family whose structure dictates Oedipal and pre-Oedipal relations and that ensures that the child's first attachment to the mother will be forbidden by the authority of the father and diverted elsewhere.

Freud argued not only that the Oedipal triangle was the nucleus of all neurosis, but that it also accounted for the beginnings of religion, morals, society and art.[32] The patriarchal family was, in fact, the source of the shared symbols and significance that create a human community. Freud thought that he could show in a study of primitive practices and kinship systems that this 'single concrete point' of man's ambivalent relationship with his father was the focus around which culture has its origin and development. He considered in detail several phenomena typical of primitive culture: the universal horror of incest, taboos that seem to have no rational justification, and systems of exogamy that centre around the identification of a group with a totem. What is striking, Freud pointed out, is the similarity between these phenomena and the unconscious thought of the child as revealed in psychoanalysis. The horror of incest 'reveals a striking agreement with the mental life of neurotic patients', patients who had failed to free themselves from incestuous fixations. The complex of behaviour surrounding taboos is similar to the behaviour of obsessional neurotics; the totemic system of exogamy could be considered a precursor of our Oedipal family where the name of the father determines the identity of family members who may not then intermarry. It would appear that there is a kind of phylogenetic correlation between the infancy of an individual, an infancy that neurotics have not transcended, and the infancy of civilisation. Each individual, in a sense, repeats in his own development the history of human development, a development that is dominated by one particular problem: the regulation of sexual instincts in a stable social order where access to women is subject to patriarchal control.

Freud, however, went even further. The mysterious practices of totem and taboo as well as the insane fixations of neurotics can be understood by positing a primal event that reveals their mythic underpinning.[33] At some point in prehistory there was no human society, and instead an old male controlled a group of females. At some stage there was a revolt and the dominant male was killed by a coalition of his sons. At the animal level the dominance of one male is simply reasserted and a new 'patriarch' takes over; but in order to avoid this struggle-to-the-death that would leave only one male the victor, the sons make a pact: each will abstain from sexual relations with his own female relations. In this way the very possibility of a society is created on the basis of a horror of incest and a system of exogamy. The law of the father is instituted, both in reparation for the guilt of the murderous sons, and to monitor the alliance in one authority. There is nothing essentially horrible about incest; what is horrible is the possible relapse back into

134

animal existence. The memory of their murder of the father haunts the sons. The primal father is dead but must live on and be respected; only in that way can the community be preserved and murder prevented.[34]

The radical implications of such an analysis took Freud far beyond the rational choices of free subjects. Not only is each individual shaped in ways he or she cannot control or even remember, but that shaping is not a coercion from the free 'subjectiveness' of parents and guardians. How they relate to the child also has a history:

> The sense of a guilt for an action has persisted for many thousands of years and has remained operative in generations which can have no knowledge of that action. I have supposed that an emotional process, such as might have developed in generations of sons who were ill-treated by their father, has extended to new generations which were exempt from such treatment.[35]

Such a 'collective mind' in fact must exist, Freud argued, if there is to be an explanation of how psychic processes are continued from generation to generation. For this explanation, 'direct communication and tradition' are not adequate. Instead, even if unconsciously, 'everyone possesses an apparatus which enables him to interpret other's reactions, that is to undo the distortions which other people have imposed on the expression of their feelings'.[36] It is such an unconscious understanding of the original relation to the father that makes the nucleus of the Oedipal family invulnerable to social change. Each child inherits the guilt and with it the necessity of the institutions that mediate that guilt. Thus Freud may conclude that, although the family may take various forms, it is always patriarchal, always based on the rule of the father.

Women are not active participants in this drama. They are hardly mentioned in Freud's account. At the same time, they are essential because it is by way of women that the alliance between the men is established. It is women who are a value, or better, *the* value, whose exchange establishes social relations. Men can only live in peace when they renounce their own daughters and give them to someone else, thus establishing the social ties on which any community is based. The family cannot therefore be expected to wither away with capitalism, or because it oppresses individuals, or because it leads to the inferiorisation of women. To do away with it would be to do away with human society altogether. Without the taboos of patriarchal law, without the strict regulation of the ownership of women, men would supposedly revert to a bloody anarchy in which one tyrant would emerge only to be eventually replaced by another.

Not completely convincingly, Mitchell argued that the situation is not hopeless. Admitting that the family is the beginning of society does not mean that it must be the end. The family changes even as it remains subject to patriarchal law, from complex systems of primitive exogamy through many stages to the very different nuclear family of capitalism. In that claustrophobic setting Mitchell saw new possibilities. It is not by accident that psychoanalysis is contemporaneous with capitalism and with the nuclear family. In such a family, closed in on itself, Oedipal tensions are magnified. The dysfunction that results is the dysfunction for which Freud thought he had discovered a cure. However, what is sick is not just the patients; it is the family, not because it oppresses — indeed, oppressive institutions can be healthy — but because the nuclear family, as a system of social organisation and exchange, is subject to intolerable strain. With civil society, with socialised labour, it is no longer necessary that identity be established via a family affiliation. Therefore Mitchell's suggestion was not a revised family in which men and women share responsibility, but no family at all. There must be some other device found for the entry into culture than the exchange of women.

The limits of the thinkable: Lacan's symbolic

In order to assess the possibility for such a break with the past, it is necessary to probe in greater depth the extraordinary Freudian hypotheses on which Mitchell's recommendation was based. In the history of each individual, as well as in the history of society, religions and cultures, the same set of events is repeated over and over again: resentment of the father's authority, guilt of the son, alliances and rivalry between men, the exchange of women. Why, after all, would human beings, supposedly capable of considering a situation freshly and devising an original response, find themselves enmeshed in such a pattern, find themselves captive to this myth that even now, when they pride themselves on scientific objectivity, guides the large part of their behaviour? At this point, another interpretation of Freud is possible, one which changes the terms in which the Oedipal conflict is understood and, at the same time, explains its supra-historical status. It was by way of this different interpretation of Freud that French feminists, coming from the French phenomenological-rationalist rather than positivistic tradition, returned to Freud. They did so through the mediation of another translation, another reading, of Freud, that of Jacques Lacan, the mysterious and extravagant 'French Freud'.[37]

Lacan told the Freudian story of the achievement of masculinity and femininity in a different way. What is in question is not a development in historical time but a structuring and destructuring of identity. Gone from Lacan's account is any regressive reference to anatomy or to instinct. In its place is how we think about physical fact and about ourselves. The child, as he or she works through the anal to the genital stage, is not undergoing a process of development, but is, just like the analyst, trying to make sense of and structure his experience. Nor does the subject in analysis remember what happened as a child; instead it is the always-present structure of thought that is investigated and it is in that thought, not in the past, that his problem must be solved. This immediately puts the problem of femininity in a new light. There can be no manipulation of events, no simple corrections. One will not be able to engineer changes in the family. There is no way out of thought and language, and therefore no way around the analytic discovery that the feminine has a specific function in that thought. As for real women and men, they must place themselves on one side or another, on either the masculine side or on the feminine, which itself shows how little any physical reality is determinant. Masculinity and femininity are, for Lacan, a by-product of the split in subjectivity that establishes a self.

To simplify Lacan's intricate and sometimes inscrutable account: in the beginning a child has no self. This does not mean that nothing happens or that he (Lacan's subject is always masculine) is not aware of anything, but that at this stage he is not yet a thinking self. Instead he is locked into an animal-like symbiosis with his mother. The founding moment of the self occurs at what Lacan called the 'mirror stage'. The child sees his image in a mirror, and the alienating fiction is created of a discrete being. The first division, before speech, before the child can even walk, prepares the way for the child's social identity.[38] Lacan explicitly denied the existentialist's autonomous self. Such a self would only be 'a liberty locked in a prison', a 'pratique that can surmount no situation'.[39] Instead, for Lacan, since the self is in the very beginning 'other', otherness does not rise up surprisingly as it does for a Sartrean subject. The fundamental alienation which makes us always construct our discourse for another, or like another's and so always leaves us ready to be exposed by another, is not a function of a confrontation with any other person but with otherness in ourselves. Thus, the Lacanian self has a never remediable fragility, a self-identity that is always challengeable and so continually defensively defended as the ideal 'I' of the mirror stage and the precursor of an ego always undermined by something else, a 'me' who can never be the ideal but stands apart.

Of course, there is more in the child's world than himself and the mirror. There is also his mother, or more properly his need for his mother, because she cannot exist yet for him as an object. His need is not an object but a natural state. The crucial movement here will be from need to demand. This transition from unreflective feeling to articulated demand can only be accomplished after the internal division of the mirror stage. The discovery of the mirror image by the child suggests a certain strategy in dealing with his need for others which is carried out in the demand. To demand is to separate from one's need, to hold it off, to be a 'je' in conflict with a 'moi'. Consequently, in the demand much is left behind, unarticulatable and unsatisfiable. One can never demand what one really wants. We have already removed pleasure from ourselves, focused it on an imaginary object, and so made it impossible. Felt satisfaction is no longer at issue. What is 'left over' from the demand as impossible of fulfilment becomes the unobtainable 'object of desire', so important in the relations between men and women.[40]

In order to master these difficult moves toward the human, the child learns a new game, Freud's Fort/Da game so often cited by Lacan. The infant plays peek-a-boo; he learns to make himself and, at the same time, his mother, disappear. By reproducing in his game the mother's absence and his own absence to his mother, he takes control of the situation. He in fact transplants it to another level where he is not subject to his mother's painful disappearance. With this new faculty, with this removal of the problem to the symbolic, he transcends the puzzling riddles of imaginary desire, and establishes himself as independent, as a wielder of a universe of symbols.

This universe cannot remain, if it ever was, of his own personal devising. Even the peek-a-boo is learned, and in mastering these beginning representations he makes the crucial step toward learning a common language, the language that will return him from the solitude of the mirror and the peek-a-boo game to the social. In this common language infinitely more complex games can be played, and, because the game is known by all, can be played with others. The point, however, of linguistic representation remains the same — the mastery, in an alienated medium, of the confusing dependencies of childhood. Each step removes the child from his pleasure and pain, from animal intersubjectivity,[41] and at the same time creates the new gratifications of the imaginary and the symbolic.

Sexual relations will be the articulation *par excellence* for this alienated symbolic and imaginary existence. Lacan claimed that sexuality has nothing to do with sexual need or instinct. Just as the rudimentary Fort/Da game symbolised the presence and absence of the mother, so, as the child enters into adulthood or into the Oedipal period, he is introduced to another symbolisation of presence and absence: the phallus. This is the symbol that will structure the whole field of sexual relations. Here, in his account of the castration complex, Lacan showed how far he had come from biology. The castration complex for girls or for boys is not based on any physical organ or any anatomical fact: instead, it derives from a myth — that is to say from a meaning-bearing symbolic construction. In the play of symbolisation, mostly unconscious,[42] in the metaphors and metonymies that make up the signifying chain, there must be a master signifier, one signifier which symbolises representation or presence itself and which allows the subject to have a place. Thus the Phallus, the master signifier, becomes the symbol of desire.[43] The correlate of this master signifier in language is the name of the father. Even before a child is born, his identity is already fixed in a language that incorporates the rules of kinship and determines his paternal name.

The result for women is as Freud diagnosed. Women are at a disadvantage.[44] Their subjecthood is always in question because they will have to find the signifier of their desire not in themselves but in the body of someone else. Therefore, women, Lacan asserted in the Freudian manner, tolerate frigidity better, do not have as pressing a desire. The girl has no phallus, nor is she but transitorily the owner of the father's name. She has a name, as

139

she has a penis, only through a man, only second hand. Therefore, there is much more to her feminine situation than the immediate refusal of certain rights or privileges. Access to the very language in which those rights are expressed is denied her. Without a phallus, without a name, the female subject will always be in question, always have to find its identity in something else, will always hover on the edge of non-existence.

Again the subjection of women is placed at a deeper, more seemingly inaccessible, level. It is not that certain family events have produced contingent personality traits that could be removed with proper parenting. Nor is it that the remembered experience of the community has imposed on human institutions a particular form: 'This tradition [i.e. language], well before the historical drama is inscribed there, founds the elementary structures of culture and these structures reveal an "ordination" of exchanges which, be it unconscious, is inconceivable outside the permutations which language authorizes'.[45] Prior to either the individual's history or experience, or society's history or experience, is language. Without language, without the transition from animal to human there can be no history and no experience. Furthermore, in this linguistic founding of the human much has already been decided. For Lacan, there can be no question of the elimination of elementary kinship structures as proposed by Mitchell, and no question of the replacement of the phallus and the name of the father, because without these symbolisations there would be no language and therefore no human life at all. Language is already there at the beginning, authorising and presiding at the first gifts, the first exchanges between men.

It was perhaps only Lacan's personal charm and seductiveness that redeemed his theories for French feminists. Lacan's reading of Freud fixed women's inferior situation ever more securely. He asserted that:

(1) Sexual difference is built into language, into thought, and therefore into culture.
(2) Sexual difference must be structured as feminine lack and masculine presence.
(3) The woman as mother must always be the natural residue left behind as the speaking being enters the symbolic.
(4) The only way out of imaginary illusion is by the law of the father.
(5) Femininity cannot ever be expressed.

(6) Drawing the recalcitrant 'moi' into the 'je's' mastery of language will always be difficult for women because her 'je' will be more unstable and her 'moi' more recalcitrant.

At the same time, just as in Freud, feminists saw in Lacan a realistic description of things as they were, unpleasant or not. No one better expressed the tragedy, the mismatch of sexuality, the way in which men and women miss each other in their inter-actions, the way in which their behaviour is like a phonograph record (Lacan's metaphor) that turns and turns, an automatism, a symbolic that cannot touch actual bodies, emotions, experi-ences, all of which have been left behind. If patriarchy is a symbolic universe, then no one better than Lacan expressed its surreal qualities,[46] the mirrors, the intricate games, the convoluted turnings of always failed relations, where no one ever manages to reach anyone else. No one better described the horror of it.

The result is a more powerful analysis of patriarchal relations. The effect of the Freudian revolution, as interpreted by Lacan, was to situate women's struggle in a new dimension that transcended particular political or economic systems. What was in question was the symbolic construction of society, of Western society, of all society. It is this change in focus that inspired the new generation of women described by Julia Kristeva in 'Women's time'.[47] These women had read Freud and Lacan and had also read extensively in Western philosophy, linguistics and literature. From political activities such as lobbying, legal change and constitutional reform, they turned to an investigation of the symbolic basis of the laws and practices that define women.[48]

Kristeva and a maternal semiotics

With Lacan the last vestiges of biological determinism had dis-appeared. Sexual differences are thought differences, signified differences, and there is no residual female nature outside analysis or outside theory, from which feminist thought can be subverted. However, the source of sexism is even more inaccessibly located in the internal structure of thought itself.

If this is true, feminist theory, if it is to be intelligible, must be expressed in a logic inevitably phallic. It is no longer possible to begin from a discovered truth (e.g. the rights of Man, dialectical materialism, the human subject) and from that centre confidently spin out, by deduction or analogy, a feminist programme. If, as Lacan seemed to show, the only possible structure of meaning is around phallic presence and the only source of deductive certainty the law of the father, any articulation from any centre will carry sexism along with it. A Lacanian feminist theorist will have to have a new decentred, less straightforward, more conflictual relationship with any non-feminist foundation. The French feminists, Julia Kristeva and Luce Irigaray, admitting the authority of Lacan and acknowledging his irreducible presence in their thought, used Lacanian insights and strategies with a new consciousness of the dangers in such an alliance. On the shifting ground of Lacanian theory, the very uncertainty of a woman's foothold became the only feminist stance.[49] From that unstable vantage point, Kristeva and Irigaray tried to rehabilitate Lacan's banished maternal.

One focal point of Kristeva's agreement and disagreement with Lacan was his theory of desire. Lacan, Kristeva argued, was correct to locate the genesis of the self in negativity and in difference, but he quickly abandoned that negativity. When the Lacanian infant plays the Fort/Da game, he forgets his mother, forgets his pleasure, and enters into a symbolic world of desire divorced from need. This rejection of lived satisfaction allows the unitary existential subject of rational thought and philosophy to reappear. Although Lacan may have described a certain kind of subject, a subject who cuts himself off from his affective life, learns at the expense of his emotions, and is prone to paranoia and totalitarianism, this is not the only way one's relation with language and the pre-linguistic can be negotiated.

Lacan saw the mirror stage as a barrier beyond which nothing can be known or said. This, for Kristeva, meant only that the pre-symbolic had been repressed. Analysis must instead examine the boundary between the imaginary and the symbolic, between the pre-linguistic and the linguistic. Freud's dark continent of femininity became, for Lacan, the even darker pre-symbolic. Once that emptiness is given substance, it becomes clear that language is not a sudden appearing out of nowhere but is prepared for in a pre-symbolic maternal 'semiotics'.[50] Again Kristeva's strategy was to investigate the mother-child relation which remained lost for Freud behind an 'inexorable repression' and for Lacan behind the absolute barrier of nonrepresentibility. The feminine or maternal, Kristeva agreed, is pre-symbolic. In the duality of the primal child-mother relation there is nothing that can be directly represented. This does not mean, however, that the maternal is inaccessible. There is other expression beside linguistic expression. Kristeva in 'Motherhood according to Giovanni Bellini',[51] looked to visual art. In Bellini's paintings of Madonna and child, she saw the absolute barrier of the mirror stage begin to give way to shadows, to images, of mothers and babies, of distance and closeness, of love.

The maternal experience expressed in Bellini's paintings is not reducible to the Freudian desire for a penis. Motherhood seems, Kristeva maintained, to be impelled by a 'non-symbolic, non-parental causality'. There is a union/reunion between bodies, a union in which there is no logical structure but a whirl, a flux of feeling and expression, filled with nuance, and eventually with a peace that has nothing to do with phallic release.[52] As mother, the woman reaches past the limits of language, past the autonomy of subjectivity, to the inscription of biological processes of which she is not the master. This is the language of the body and of the emotions which the symbolic must 'seal off' and 'censure', along with the 'jouissance',[53] or sexual pleasure, of the child-bearing woman. In rational language, her pleasure can only be (mis)represented as phallic, but in art the rejoicing body is expressed in Bellini's intense, emotionally charged interactions between mother and child. Artistic representations of motherhood can also be phallic. Leonardo reproduced the woman's body differently, as an object with the baby-object of her attention. In Bellini's Madonnas, on the other hand, Kristeva saw evoked the very function of the maternal in colour, light, shadow. This fusional nexus between mother and child is not without conflict, conflict between the mother's restricting hands and the child's energy, between the mother's seduction and the child's freedom, between the mother's distance and the child's love, between the child's demands and the mother's independence. Always Bellini's lovely, placid, peasant faces have the transcendent calm of motherhood, a motherhood from which it is the child's business to escape.

The child must eventually break with the mother. For Kristeva, however, this rupture is not from nothing. Even before the child enters Lacan's patriarchal symbolic, its experience is structured. The Oedipal is not the first psychic structure. Before the father appears to complete the Oedipal triangle the mother has a desire for something other than herself, and this desire

points the pre-Oedipal child towards a pre-linguistic ideal identification, not with the stern forbidding Oedipal father (the image
of Freud's chief of the rebel horde), but with an 'imaginary
father'.[54] The result is that the child sees his mother in a new
light. Desiring of something else, the mother reveals herself as a
'pas-tout' or 'not all', as needing something beyond herself.
Although not yet a symbolic object for the child, she becomes
what Kristeva calls 'abject',[55] rejected as unworthy, as even
disgusting. With this abjectifying of the mother, the child makes
the first steps towards Lacan's symbolic and towards a normal,
that is alienated, sex life. Eventually the child will make the
mother an object that can be represented, and thereby establish
his or her identity. The ambivalent love-hate relations of sexual
desire will follow.

In this process, the mother does not play a heroic role, and
here Kristeva's view of the maternal does not mark a sharp break
with Lacanian analysis. The mother, for Kristeva, enters into
language as 'abject' as what must be repressed or put down if the
child is to progress normally. Though the maternal influence
must always be there, it must remain suppressed and denigrated.
The detailed explanation of this structural necessity is in
Kristeva's *Les pouvoirs de l'horreur* (The power of horror),[56] a
reworking of Freud's analysis of society in *Totem and taboo*. If the
mirror stage does not surge out of nothing, nor does its
sociological counterpart, the alliance between brothers and the
exchange of women. If men make the law and exchange women
as countable objects, that social fact has a pre-history. In the
interdiction of the unclean, in taboos and in sin, in the sacred in
general, Kristeva analysed that pre-history.

Following Freud in looking at symptoms like phobias and
primitive practices as structurally similar, she noted the connection between such symbolisations and fear. Freud was interested
in relations between men, relations of guilt, rivalry, and alliance,
but Kristeva saw an underside to these relations, unmentioned
but assumed, a kind of primary hostility and hatred specifically
against women. If women are to be the tokens passed from hand
to hand in order that some sort of binding exchange can be made
between men, they must first be made into objects in order that
exchange be possible, and this, Kristeva agreed, is a process in
itself. The establishment of society is not just *between* men, it is
also *against* women as the maternal bodies which stand in the way
of social identity. Social law by itself is insufficient for this

purpose; the power of the maternal continues to threaten and the constant temptation to regression must be socialised and accommodated in ritual practices which involve the denigration or abjection of women:

> Abjection is co-extensive with the social and symbolic order, with hierarchies both individual and collective. As such, just as the interdiction of incest, abjection is a universal phenomenon one encounters as soon as the symbolic and/or social and human dimension is constituted and in every civilization.[57]

There are differences in ritual practices, different ways in which this rejection of the unclean, the sinful, is articulated,[58] but everywhere it is women who are the subject of interdictions. It is women who must always be the other, evil, dangerous, and fascinating, who must be protected against, whether in the form of women's blood, women's pregnancies, or a child's bodily functions regulated by the mother. There is, in other words, not just one social principle that is patriarchal, but two, one of which, the masculine, continues to claim 'against the other, the feminine, that he is threatened by a power that is asymmetrical, irrational, duplicitous, and uncontrollable'.[59] This irrational underside of culture can never be completely destroyed, because the very existence of culture depends on it: 'If language, or culture, establishes a separation and, by way of discrete elements, enchains an order, it is precisely in repressing this maternal authority and the corporal topology which joins them.'[60] Otherwise, culture becomes a dead letter. The mother must continue to be repressed because she: '. . . constitutes also, in the specific history of each, this abyss that it is necessary to make into an autonomous, and not invading place, an object distinct that is signifiable, if the child is to learn to speak'.[61] The mother is not a Lacanian blank, but an abyss, an invasion, a positive danger to the speaking subject. If he is to speak, she must be abject. This is the power of the horror that is the subject of Kristeva's book: 'The mother and death, abominated, abject, amount to a victimizing and persecuting machine at the price of which I become subject of the Symbolic as the Other of the Abject.'[62]

The nothingness of the unrepresentable pre-symbolic has become the dangerous power of the mother on which adulthood and civilisation rest. Where then, given the necessity of the horror of feminine abjection, should a woman intervene? Kristeva had isolated two pre-symbolic structures outside of patriarchal law for psychoanalytic explanation. She had uncovered the explorable, pre-Oedipal, 'guiltless' maternity chosen not just for the penis-child but involving a real unique confrontation between self and other. In 'L'abject d'amour', she described the archaic father, object of an ideal love outside of the rigidity of paternal law but accessible in mystical union. Although recognition of these non-phallic structures might be useful in the psychoanalysis of women, any attempt to live them as an adult would be regressive. The tie between mother and child must give way to the law of the father if the child, whether male or female, is to become a speaking being. The love for the imaginary father can cripple sexual function as the subject fails to find a real object for her ideal love.

Instead Kristeva focused on poetry as the place where the repressed maternal could resurface. There has always been, Kristeva argued in *La révolution du langage poétique*, a residue of maternal emotion that escapes the regulation of patriarchal law and functions outside the social network of meaning. In mystery cults and ecstatic rites of fertility, death and birth, a fusional return to the maternal body is celebrated. Poets are the modern heirs of this alternative expression, especially in advanced, over-populated, industrialised societies where the need for reproduction, and consequently the need for sexual repression, has been weakened. For Kristeva, as for Mitchell, advanced capitalism presents a special opportunity for relative freedom from the structural necessity of kinship systems regulating the exchange of women.[63] Avant-guard poets, such as Mallarmé and Lautréamont, were able to attack the very syntax of traditional bourgeois society.

Women are not the privileged bearers of Kristeva's poetic revolution. Women acquiesce in their victimisation, both because they receive narcissistic pleasure in the compensating mystery with which male society endows them, and because their restriction to the household 'spared them the efforts necessary for professional apprenticeship and assured them the prolongation of their auto-erotic pleasure, united to the child'.[64] However, women also have a special connection to the maternal and are not as likely as men to deny it. Because their entrance into the symbolic is more problematic than the man's, they are less threatened by the gestural, song-like, alogical qualities of poetry.

A woman can hear in poetry her maternal feminine pleasure, fascinated to see that a poetic process can disturb logical structures: but she is more a listener than a creator; her own poetry is self-indulgent rather than revolutionary.[65] She all too easily returns to her traditional role.[66]

Neither poetry nor mysticism can constitute a feminist practice for Kristeva. She offers instead theoretical understanding. What, she asks at the conclusion of *Les pouvoirs de l'horreur*, is the result of such an understanding?

> It is possible to understand, to understand oneself, to build a discourse around this braid of horror and fascination which signals the incompleteness of the speaking being but which, when understood as a narcissistic crisis at the limits of the feminine, clarifies in a cosmic light the religious and political pretensions which try to give sense to the human condition.[67]

Once the great machine of horror, of religious war, of racism, of hatred, of genocide is revealed as a way to exorcise the lingering and feared feminine, all the pretensions of the supposed highest in human thought are exposed as a joke, as laughable. This understanding laugh 'on the edge of the volcano' is, Kristeva hinted, perhaps the only way to escape being abject oneself. A feminine practice is always negative, opposed to what exists, permanently outside of established structures and ideologies and continuing to undermine their stability.[68] According to Kristeva, the structures of patriarchal thought and society must necessarily be reconstituted for there to be any social order at all, but women theorists who recognise the maternal base of culture can prevent them from ossifying into rigid tyrannies.

In *Les pouvoirs de l'horreur*, Kristeva seemed to leave half-open the possibility of a positive source of matriarchal power which inspired the awesome patriarchal defence systems of taboo and sin. Elsewhere she rejected any feminine presence and consistently argued that there is no feminine specificity, no female essence, no ancient matriarchy. Without any such foothold, the feminist theorist is in a difficult position. In 'Women's time', Kristeva discussed the problem of separatism versus reformism. How, faced with an analytic exposure of patriarchy that goes as deep as society itself, can a woman participate? She may work within existing symbolic systems, take advantage of the insights of liberalism, socialism, or existentialism and their very real gains for women, find a place in the patriarchal hierarchy 'as a man'. The problem will then become, especially if she achieves success, how not to be as patriarchal and phallic as men, or even, out of reaction, more so. On Kristeva's terms, the alternative establishment of a countersociety is equally dangerous. Since there is no *Woman*, no *'la femme'* as Lacan put it, no ancient matriarchy, any such countersociety can only be a reversal of existing power structures. This is the route to fetishism and perversion, Kristeva argued.[69] Any society must be based on a symbolic contract, and even a countersociety must be based on sacrifice. A matriarchy that is the opposite of patriarchy will have its own victims and executioners. There can be no *maternal law*. When the countersociety relapses, as it must, into patriarchal politics, the danger, as Kristeva saw it, is that separatism can degenerate into meaningless violence.[70] Even attempts at mothering outside patriarchal law can be dangerous, as in lesbian societies where there is no protective 'mother law' to safeguard children or mothers.[71]

To abandon the patriarchal symbolic is to fall back into marginalism or psychosis. Kristeva's own forbiddingly theoretical style illustrates her conviction that women must not abandon the masculine world of theory, science, and logic. At the same time, women scholars must work to make the system 'budge', as Kristeva put it, constantly to undermine patriarchal order by reviving the abyss of the rejected maternal that threatens any claim to logical certainty. Kristeva's woman becomes if no less a nothing, at least now a necessary nothing and at the same time a threat. Women must achieve respectability by entering and mastering patriarchal thought for there is no other, but at the same time they must constantly expose that thought. The result — a loosened, pluralistic, non-dogmatic patriarchy — is the most that can be hoped for. Other feminist 'daughters'[72] of Lacan were more ambitious and more critical of the 'father'.

A feminine jouissance: Luce Irigaray

If a woman analyst returns to theory, to the self-duplicating structures of signifying practices, then she returns to a world alien to women's experience. Perhaps some old pieces have been rearranged into a new pattern, but she is confined in the straitjacket of logic. Instead Luce Irigaray proposed a more radical questioning of Lacanian theory. With her book *Speculum*, she initiated a new kind of confrontation between the woman reader/thinker and her 'masters'.[73] These masters included Freud and Lacan, as well as the heroes of philosophical thought in whose tradition Lacan placed himself — Descartes, Kant, Hegel, and Plato.[74] Irigaray proposed a new way of reading the texts of patriarchy, one that was less reverent and more sensitive to what is actually being said.

In his opening remarks on 'Femininity', she noted, Freud had already situated his discourse in a certain way; it was to be a masculine discourse between men. Irigaray read on, from the perspective of this exclusion, about the famous Freudian bisexuality. Bisexuality sounds, on the face of it, egalitarian, as if everyone is both male and female, but, as Irigaray unravelled Freud's argument, a different logic was revealed, not of bisexuality but of rigorous unisexuality. Bisexuality in Freud is a concept used to explain feminine, not masculine, psychology. It is only women who are bisexual. But what does this mean? It means that women, like men, begin with an 'active' sexuality; a girl is a 'little man'. There is in fact no libido for Freud except the masculine, 'active', libido. The girl focuses on her clitoris which she uses as a boy uses his penis and desires the mother in the same way as the boy. It is from this bisexuality, or this masculinisation, of the little girl that all her troubled later development flows. The question from then on is how to make a girl out of a little boy, and in the process the girl will inevitably be maimed, her aggressivity turned painfully back on herself. The only substantive presence in this account is masculine sexuality, active, unitary, aggressive, penetrative: the feminine is a simple negative. A person is masculine or not masculine, phallic or not. Freudian sexual theory is a continual reiteration of the 'same', a kind of homosexuality. Women have value, as in Freud's active mothering, only if they are able to mime the masculine. Freud's account of sexuality depends on a 'prior logic' that has already isolated the masculine and made it the presence against which all else shall be measured. This is, as Irigaray's chapter title suggests, 'the blind spot of an old dream of symmetry'.

From this 'homosexuality', Irigaray traced a systematic exclusion of the feminine. The feminine will be from now on only the nothingness, the dark continent, of what is not masculine. Sexual pleasure will be seen as only phallic and the woman's experience inevitably inferior. There is no feminine pleasure *per se*, and women must give up their phallic clitoral pleasure for the substitute phallic pleasure of child-birth. Penis envy programmes all the emotional economy of the girl, just as castration fear does for the man. The woman must reject her mother because the mother is not phallic. The mother is inadequate and so longs for a substitute phallus child. Freud sees even female homosexuality as a 'virility complex' in which the girl unrealistically mimes the aggressive male. The phallus becomes the guarantee of meaning, the ultimate signifier.[75]

Freud acknowledged by the time he wrote his late works on femininity that there is something feminine that escapes analytic theory, something anterior to the male psyche and civilisation as we know it. Notwithstanding this scruple, Freud still returned to the same inadequate conceptual economy to explain the feminine. This failure reflects, for Irigaray, a problem even for women. There is no ready signifying economy for the feminine, no images, representations, that can name her experience. Femininity *is* a kind of 'trou', or hole, which there are no words to express. As analyst, Irigaray did not deny that, given this lack of appropriate symbolic expression, the inferiority of women may indeed be inevitable. The woman will be an object of love, not a loving subject, and she will compensate with vanity and shame. She will have no sense of justice because masculine justice in its very essence denigrates the feminine and any attempt to find a feminine 'measure' must fail. From the very beginning, a woman's needs, her desires, are suppressed, inhibited, converted into self-hate or channelled into the fetishism of religion or mysticism. She is excluded from the very activities in which a sense of justice is evolved. She is not socialised and cannot sublimate because she cannot participate in society, and so remains in a state of infantile dependence to patriarchal authority. She is fixed, immobile at 30, just as Freud pointed out, as against the active, interesting man. What has fixed her is not 'constitution' or even 'social rules' but the 'representation' of femininity which has been prescribed for her. The feminine has place only inside the models and laws prescribed by masculine subjects. Lacan made this eclipse of the feminine worse; not only are women excluded but only the male analyst may speak of that exclusion.[76]

Irigaray, using a complex sequence of metaphors, attempted to show that the woman is not a simple negative even in this patriarchal account. She has a vital function in the male economy, as a blank, but as a blank that, like a mirror, reflects the masculine. The male's sexuality is, as Freud pointed out, aggressive and this 'death drive' is handled, especially in Lacanian Freudianism, by the constitution of the self as a kind of narcissistic monument. The insecurity of such a construction is obvious. Here the woman must serve. Refused any expression of a death drive by her 'constitution' and by 'social rules', she must be a mirror to 'reassure him as to his validity': 'The woman will shore up this specular redoubling, giving back to man "his" image repeating him as the "same", the intervention of an other image of an other mirror signifies always the risk of a mortal crisis.'[77] Even the famous penis envy can be seen as such a 'shoring up'. It is the boy, Freud maintained, who first looks at the little girl and is shocked that she has none. Feminine 'penis' envy then is a reverse of this male anguish; it is that anguish reflected as in a mirror and so reassuring the castration-fearing man with the real 'not having' of the woman. In the girl, the boy is able to see the reflection of his fears and is assured that if she has 'envy' then he must have 'something' after all.

With this metaphor of woman as the mirror-substance reflecting the image of man, Irigaray moved a step beyond Kristeva. A woman analyst's task is not only negative, not only the disruption of patriarchal categories, it is also an uncovering. For this uncovering, it is necessary that there is something to be uncovered — that is, there must be a feminine substance which the words of men have concealed. Irigaray's exposure of Freud and Lacan is not just disruptive; it also clears the way for a new kind of feminist thinking. Once the simple presence/absence of phallic logic is abandoned, the feminine can appear as a value in its own right, opening the way, Irigaray argued, for a real, not sham, sexual difference in which both sexes are valorised.

Consistent with analytic tradition, sexuality, now specifically feminine sexuality, provided the model for Irigaray's new feminine thought. Feminine sexuality was the positive, not just negative, presence on which feminist hopes must rest. Obscured by masculine thought, repressed as improper and sinful, ignored in analysis, a woman's sexuality, Irigaray argued, is very different from a male's. A man's sexuality is instrumental; he must do something to himself. A woman's is auto-erotic; she can 'touch' herself. Because of this self-touching, there will be no sharp break in her thought between touch and touched, between subject and object. A woman is always in contact with herself; she is both one and at the same time two, contrasted with the male logic which takes things one by one. From this anatomical difference, Irigaray derived a feminine specificity, a new kind of heterogeneous feminine pleasure that even men may discover imaginatively. Inherent in femininity is not oneness or sameness but plurality. A woman can accept an other because she is herself other. She will think in ways traditionally rejected by male reason; her thoughts flow, rather than 'mount and dissipate'. This feminine mode of experiencing the world is repressed by masculine logic.[78]

According to Irigaray, such a feminine thought can point the way to a different kind of relation between persons.[79] Consistent with the general repression of what is feminine, relations between women have been unexplored. The relation between mother and daughter is eclipsed by the father/son rivalry to which it is always assimilated by Freud. Another syntax would be needed to express the mother/daughter relation[80] and to express the relation of women 'entre-elles'. Having discovered the feminine, Irigaray's women also discover a substitute for the masculine society based on the exchange of women. Exchanges *between* women will be different, without account, without number — not a matter of commerce, but free.[81] Irigaray also proposed a corresponding change in the function of a woman analyst. She must first and foremost listen, not as a Lacanian analyst for the death of the subject and for the alienated beginnings of logical language, but for another syntax which is not necessarily structured visually.[82] She must not prejudge, identify, classify, or discriminate all operations that are structured by masculine logic. The goal of such an analysis is not the recognition of an imaginary break with any lived satisfaction. It is not the introduction of the subject to the ordering law of the father. The analyst must acknowledge masculine imagery, but at the same time permit other, feminine, imagery to emerge in the new myths, images, metaphors and syntaxes. The female subject, and the male, must be encouraged to think and imagine outside of the masculine symbolic. In this way, either in analysis or alternatively in self-discovery and expression, a woman can come to discover herself as a woman. The preliminary exposure of masculine thought is necessary so that the feminine can emerge.

Irigaray's positive feminine presence promised more than Kristeva's enlivening maternal which could only temporarily disturb symbolic thought. The symbolic contract that sacrifices women is inevitable only if there is no other conceivable way to think or relate to others. Irigaray's femininity opened the possibility of a different founding myth, a different way of ordering reality, different relations, different key metaphors, a different way of life that women among themselves, removed from male influence, might discover. This would require separatism, although a feminine universe would not sacrifice masculinity in the way that masculine society had sacrificed the feminine. Irigaray recognised the danger in separatism. Since the masculine is in fact in power, feminine separatists must be marginal to that power. Furthermore, this feminine universe could become a matriarchy — that is, only another patriarchy. Nevertheless, separation, and therefore marginality, is necessary if women are to be able to think free of the masculine symbolic.[83] That such a rupture is possible, that a symbolic by definition hierarchicalised, ordered and sacrificial, could be transcended — with all that might mean in terms of relations with self and others — is the utopian premiss upon which such a recommendation is based. Women should abandon futile attempts to negotiate in a man's world. They should not attempt to gain political or economic power. Instead, in analysis with feminist therapists, they must discover the repressed female side of sexuality. In separatist groups they should explore new ways of thinking and relating among women.

Attractive as such reopened possibilities may be, for some feminists the price paid by Irigaray was too high. Monique Plaza's critique of Irigaray's feminine essence is an example.[84] Firstly, Plaza argued that Irigaray returned to the biological, the traditional means by which women have been classified as different and inferior. A feminine discourse based on feminine sexual organs again traps women in their sexuality and physicality. Although Irigaray's exposure of male logic is tempting, the alternative of feminine non-sense is dangerous. Women, because of their anatomy, are not to use logic, concepts, theories. They are, in fact, Plaza argued, reduced to babies, babbling incoherently, meaninglessly, contradictorily. Sexual difference is reinstated, but at the price of reinstating with it all the old stereotypes of female incapacity, illogic, physicality.

In the end, Plaza argued, Irigaray accepted too much from Lacan. As a Lacanian analyst, the historical aspects of women's oppression escaped her. She took no account of the actual form that oppression takes, but instead explored a utopian, mythological, unreal future. She did not see the symbolic as a means of masculine oppression, but as the necessary structure of masculine thought. She did not consider the real historical-social context of the philosophical writings which she analysed and so her reading was simplistic. She did not see the violence with which the symbolic world of male/female difference is imposed on women in the family but treated individuals as automatons on which symbolic structures are passively imprinted. She therefore allowed the patriarchal devalorisation of women to continue. Women are deflected from their real struggle in the world for justice and engage in a marginal and essentially illusory search for a feminine essence. Safely analysing, talking, exchanging among themselves, patriarchal oppression goes on as before.

Critical as they are of Lacan, Kristeva and Irigaray still borrowed from him the theoretical bases on which their revisions operate. Their analytic thought was a reaction, structured by Lacan's previous statement. Given the symbolic as described by Lacan, given its necessary putting aside of the maternal or feminine as outside, given the exchange of women as symbolic foundation and therefore as the base of human society — *given* all that, the female subject still finds a way to assert herself. Kristeva's and Irigaray's strategies differed: Kristeva recommended a new kind of feminine theorising which calls attention to its own unstable foundations, while Irigaray proposed the rejection of theory and an exploration of the irrational feminine. In each case, Lacan's patriarchal symbolic remained, supplemented in order to give a precarious foothold to the feminine. Allowing Lacan's symbolic to stand as the correct analysis of patriarchy irrevocably commits feminism to what is marginal and socially harmless, as women accept, no matter with what gloss, the status of the Lacanian 'pas-tout'.

Analysing analysis

Orthodox Freudian analysis offered for feminist practice only the crippling effects of 'normal femininity', at best supplemented with Horney's legitimate protest. Psychoanalysts taught women that if they were to escape neurosis they would have to learn to accept some inhibition of their sex drive along with a reduced need for sublimation. They would have to realise that their achievements would be less than men's and be content with the second best gratifications of motherhood. Feminist revisionists offered more: Mitchell held out the visionary hope that the family might some day become obsolete; Chodorow advised a new kind of parenting that might eliminate some of the more destructive features of gender differences; Irigaray and Kristeva added a feminine element that could be encouraged or at least acknowledged. In each case, space is found for the feminine, either *after* Freudian Oedipal society, or *before* the Freudian Oedipal stage or *beneath* logical Oedipal thought, or *in addition* to male sexuality. However, nowhere is it clear that the feminine will be able to exist in any but a subordinate role. If, in all previous human societies, the individual has found his or her identity in family relations, if, in the Oedipal stage, individuals must still learn to be men and women, if maternal expressiveness must always be superseded by the symbolic law of the father, if feminine sexuality must co-exist with assertive male sexuality, then the feminine element will remain marginal and under the hegemony of male-dominated social forms. Mitchell, Chodorow, Kristeva and Irigaray circumvent the paternal authority of Freudian theory, but they do not challenge its basic terms — in the workings of an individual's unconscious mind can be found the universal structures of psychic and societal development where, like Oedipus, we are all guilty of an 'illegitimate' sexual love for the mother and a rebellion against the 'legitimate' authority of the father.

A feminine identity theorised in the shadow of paternal authority will necessarily be a negation of that authority. If male authority depends on an exclusive mothering role, then there should be no such role; if male authority is generated in the family, then there should be no family; if male authority is expressed in symbolic language, then the maternal language is non-symbolic; if masculine sexuality is unitary, the feminine will be plural. In each case, the opposing feminine must be asserted against masculinity and is identified by that opposition. The question is whether so much authority needs to be accorded the psychoanalytic theory. Who is this Oedipus, whose love for his mother and murder of his father are supposed to be the primary structure of the psyche? Does the feminine need to be theorised in terms of a prologue or supplement to this primal scene? Recent biographical work suggests that Freud's discovery of the Oedipus complex was in response to a very specific dilemma faced by Freud and other Victorian men. Radical feminists dismissed

Freud as describing only a historically specific Victorian family. The work of Marie Balmary and Jeffrey Masson suggests that far from *describing* Victorian family relations, Freud may have fantasised them as they threatened to fall apart due to some shattering revelations.

Freud's major interest, as he began early in his practice to see patients and try out his new talking cure, was the surprising and shocking fact that all of his female patients eventually confessed that as children they had been sexually abused, often by their own fathers. From these revelations Freud formed his first theory about neurosis — the 'seduction theory'. The cause of neurosis is childhood sexual trauma, a trauma that can remain hidden and unassimilated in the unconscious mind to erupt later in terrifying symptoms. Marie Balmary, in *Psychoanalyzing psychoanalysis*,[85] followed Freud painstakingly through the painful months of self-analysis during which he abandoned this early theory and discovered the Oedipus complex. Already he had been reviled by the medical community who refused to believe that so many good respectable fathers could be guilty of perversion. Freud's own father died with his character, Balmary convincingly documented, also under suspicion from an early hidden marriage, from Freud's falsified birth certificate, from the firing of an old family servant who knew too much. Elegantly analysing Freud's domestic peculiarities, his phobias and manias, his literary references, his taste in music and art, as well as his writings and letters, Balmary traced the course of an obsession to clear the name of the father and remove doubts as to his character and behaviour.

Finally, Freud announced that he had solved his problem. The 'seduction theory' is mistaken.[86] Fathers are not guilty of seducing their daughters. In fact, the daughters are the ones who wish to seduce their fathers. Daughters desire their fathers; so they fantasise that they have been seduced. In the same way boys desire their mothers, then in jealousy accuse their fathers. In this Oedipal 'interpretation', Balmary concluded, Freud finally managed the repression and displacement onto himself of the father's fault. Furthermore, the displacement is not only onto himself, but also onto his patients. His female patients are no longer victims attacked by evil fathers, but are themselves guilty of seduction and shameful fantasising. The real seducer, Freud hinted, is the mother or nurse who fondles a child.[87]

Jeffrey Masson in his *Assault on truth*[88] supplemented

Balmary's account of the discovery of the Oedipus complex. Freud, while he was working out the conflicting emotions caused by his father's death, faced yet another conflict. He had referred a patient, Emma Eckstein, also apparently seduced as a child, to his friend Fliess for a bizarre operation on her nose that was supposedly to correct the structural defects caused by masturbation.[89] Fliess botched the operation and Freud found himself in an embarrassing situation. Again, the Oedipus complex proved its explanatory value. Not only were fathers not to blame, neither were Freud and Fliess. Eckstein's near fatal haemmorhaging, constant pain, and permanent disfigurement were not the physical effect of Fliess's and Freud's malpractice,[90] but hysterical symptoms caused by Eckstein's unconscious desire for her father projected onto Freud. *We* are certainly not to blame, Freud was then able to reassure Fliess from the newly discovered perspective of the Oedipus complex; the source of hysterical symptoms is neither physical nor any actual traumatic event but a complex of emotions arising spontaneously in the individual's mind.

With this displacement from external event to spontaneously generated emotion, Freud was able to explain not only the painful consequences of his and Fliess's mistreatment of a patient, but also Freud's father's less than blameless character. Freud's suspicions could now be blamed on Oedipal jealousy. The troubling complaints of women patients could also be explained; they, like Oedipus, sexually desired the parent of the opposite sex. In one ingenious feat of intellectualisation, Freud was able to preserve his alliance with Fliess, dismiss his doubts about his father, and redeem himself in the eyes of the medical community by rejecting his controversial seduction theory.

Self-serving fantasy, however, does not often become a theory that shapes the way several generations think about personality and society unless the fantasy serves more than an individual's purpose. It is not necessary to posit a mysterious group mind to understand why the Oedipal complex would have had a general appeal. Freud's trouble, from the beginning, involved others, not only as an intrasubjective conflict between parts of Freud's self, but as an intersubjective conflict between men. How was a son to relate to a questionable father, or to the memory of that father? How was a male doctor to relate to the abusive male relatives of his female patients, or to an abusive male medical community protective of its reputation?[91] Freud's difficulty was a difficulty which he must have shared with other men, in fact, with any man willing to acknowledge his situation as a man in a male-dominated society. Any man might find himself to be the son of an aggressor, allied with aggressors, aspiring to enter a community of aggressors. Any man might have found this problem complicated, as it was for Freud, by the fact of an early attachment to and sympathy for women, for a mother, sister or nurse, or, as with Freud, for women patients who confessed to their doctor the wrongs done to them by other men.

The problem that Freud confronted was a problem of inheritance — specifically inheritance from generation to generation of male aggression. In the family histories studied by Freud in the period that pre-dates his discovery of the Oedipus complex, he was shocked to find a 'Genealogy of madness'.[92] Seducers were sons of seducers, perversion was handed down to nephews and younger brothers. Male victims of perversion became seducers themselves or psychotic, the assaulted daughters suffering inevitably from hysteria and neurosis. Typically the seducer himself had been previously seduced. Balmary reproduced a chart drawn by Freud to illustrate the sexual relations that took place between members of the family of one of his patients, a chart which makes clear the transmission of trauma across three generations.[93]

In his early analyses Freud was working towards a view of family relations increasingly inconsistent with traditional piety, which taught that fathers were to be respected and that sons should aspire to follow in the father's footsteps. In the testimony of his patients, and in his own memories, Freud was finding families where relations were based on an inheritance of brutality and perversion, thus posing a painful problem. What is a man to do? Is he to become the champion of hysterical women? Will he then forfeit the right to take his proper place as head of the family and member of the male community? The great achievement of the Oedipal theory was to make possible answers to these questions. Projecting the guilt back on to the son and eventually onto his female keepers, Freud makes reconciliation with the father and with the role of the father possible. The son, in assuming guilt as a resolvable childish complex, can re-ally himself with men. Freud's primal story of a pact between brothers covers another story:

Once there was a family headed by a brutal authoritarian father who in secret had a tendency to abuse his wife, his daughters and any women who came under his power. Sometimes he even abused his sons. His sons were uneasy about their father and about other men but they were men themselves. Therefore, they knew they were supposed to respect their father and learn to be like him. One son, however, listened to his mother, his nurse, and the talk of other women. He became very uneasy. The women told him of crimes that his father and other fathers had committed against women and about their suffering. But this son was also a man. He knew that he too had to become a father. Then he made his discovery. There was only one solution. The women were lying, they were in love with the father and wanted to be seduced. They had only fantasized the father's mistreatment. Now the son knew that he had been guilty also; he had suspected his father out of jealousy. And he repented. Now all the sons could come together, celebrating the father's memory and rejoicing that the father had committed no faults. Now they could follow in the father's footsteps and if accusations were made by the women or by any younger sons who happened to listen to women, the men would know what to say.

In particular they would know what to say to their female patients in psychoanalysis; and if the patient had been abused, as Freud's patients were, the result would be a further crippling destruction of self. The psychiatrist repeated the denial of the abusive family, and the skeleton of perversion remained in the closet to break out at intervals. The consequences for women patients were movingly described by Balmary and Masson. The memory of sexual trauma, still unacknowledged, does not go away. Women continue to be ill, suffering from the unconscionable[94] hidden knowledge of the traumatic event: 'Transmitted secretly, and by means of the secret itself, the fault nonetheless emerges in our lives. If perversion reproduces it, illness on the contrary, attempts both to disclose it and to prevent its transmission.'[95]

The original suppression of truth in the disturbed family is continued by the therapist, with disastrous results for the patient. Her inner life is again violated, she is again made to take the guilt onto herself. She is given only the alternatives of remaining crazy or accepting the Freudian account of her illness. Masson concluded that it would be better for women not to go to analysis:

> By shifting the emphasis from an actual world of sadness, misery, and cruelty to an informal stage on which actors perform invented dramas for an invisible audience of their own creation Freud began a trend away from the real world which it seems to me, is at the root of the present-day sterility of psychoanalysis and psychiatry throughout the world. If it is not possible for the therapeutic community to address this serious issue in an honest and open-minded manner, then it is time for patients to stop subjecting themselves to needless repetition of their earliest and deepest sorrow.[96]

It is not surprising that women would fare so badly in psychoanalytic practice. Freudian theory is a theory for men, a theory that attempts to solve a man's problem. Given the terms of that attempt, femininity must remain a mysterious phenomenon, poorly assimilated in psychoanalytic theory. As exchanged tokens, deprived of any right to property or to the means of an independent existence, women were in reality passed on from abusive father to abusive husband, from abusive psychiatrist to abusive surgeon. However, the veiled identities and object status of such tokens is not the price of civilisation; it is the price of a continuing refusal to acknowledge the concrete realities of women's situation. Once Freud decides that women are lying, they are condemned in theory to anonymity, speechless Lacanian 'femmes' who can never be known and can never know themselves.

Lacan as a third generation analyst had his own difficulties with male succession. Again the son listened to women.[97] Again the son was rejected by the community of mostly male analysts.[98] Lacan had to reinstate the pact between brothers in new terms and re-found his own male society. Lacan moved the initiation into male society back to the infant's first steps, making it the threshold of the human. In the mirror stage, the male infant conceives a stable self image, assumes it jubilantly, and begins to move away from the intersubjectivity of his relations with the mother in preparation for his introduction into the symbolic Oedipal universe of paternal law. For Lacan the pact between brothers that restores the father's memory, is a symbolic alliance to speak the same rational language, to follow the same logical law. Lacan, like Freud, names women as the seducers: as mothers they threaten to draw the male child back into animal intersubjectivity, in fusional psychosis they can be guilty of violent crime.[99] For Lacan, women are not victims; they are to be feared and at the same time revered — feared because they are a constant reminder of the precarious stability of the male self, revered because they represent a mysterious experience beyond the mirror images of symbolic thought.[100]

Lacan's charm for French feminists came from his appreciation of the fragility of symbolic structures. He commented on Freud's interpretation of a dream in which Freud sees his dead father. His father, Freud reported, talked to him but did not know he was dead. Freud, working toward his discovery of the Oedipus complex, interpreted the dream — like Oedipus he wished his father dead and so is guilty of murder. 'No', said Lacan: the son does not kill the father; he watches him die. Freud was only mastering a painful situation by becoming master of it and an aggressor himself; the Oedipus complex is a defence against something more terrifying — but against what? Lacan tells us that it is the son's fear of his own death. However, in the light of Balmary's and Masson's discoveries it is possible to be more precise. The fear is not of physical death but of death as a 'man' and as a 'father'. The Oedipus complex protects against revelations that would make life as a man and as a father impossible. The imaginary male self is threatened not by fusional maternal animality, but by the always-present possibility of renewed accusations from abused women; not by the nothingness of the intersubjective, but by an empathy that will make him vulnerable to others' experiences.

Freudian theory is not simply wrong. Just as Mitchell hoped, it explains the inheritance of male domination from generation to generation. Gone is a boy's *choice* to identify with a brutish father rather than with a powerless mother. Gone is any innate male viciousness, or anatomical tendency to oppression. Freud's man, terrorised by older males, is caught in a bewildering inheritance of aggression and violence; often himself abused as a child, constantly tempted by sympathy with his mother and other women, he must painfully try to come to terms with his inheritance as a man. There is no question of a simple choice. In the unconscious mind there is only conflict without any clear name. The myth of the Oedipus complex allows that conflict to settle into a coherent, if deceptive, imaginary schema.

However, it does so not as an accurate description of universal family or psychic structure. Both cross-cultural and contemporary intra-cultural studies show that the Oedipal triangle of a father, mother and child, is far from universal and may in some circumstances be a rarity.[101] The Oedipal family is a phantasm, an imaginative construct by which men have made sense of their life and conceptualised their relations to other men; Lacan only makes explicit the fragility of this phantasm. Although such imaginary constructs may be necessary in any form of human life, this does not mean that Freudian theory is the only alternative or that it is, in the last analysis, the best alternative. The Oedipal family is rooted in a lie; its conceptualisation is a process of covering up the truth. Victims whose experience is denied suffer more acutely, the truth they cannot speak continuing to make itself heard in symptoms and mental anguish. Those whose identity as men is based on the lie continue aggressively to maintain a fragile and paranoic alienation from others. Psychoanalysis complicates further its hermetic researches, weaving in ever more complex designs the tangled web of deception, practising arcane arts increasingly removed from human experience.[102]

Freudian theory begins from the fact of women's oppression. It is both a defence against the guilt that oppression occasions and a rationalisation of continued oppression. When feminist psycho-analytic theory accepts the Oedipal complex it must also accept women's oppression. From that point on, women must be different, and that difference can be defined in reaction to male culture. The myths on which that culture is based are allowed to stand, and women adapt their protest to mythic roles of female mystic, female hysteric. Inspired by Freud and Lacan, feminists turned to studies of madness and avant-garde poetry; a woman who speaks outside male culture has to be either mad or an artist who creates fictions. Feminists celebrated a mystic femininity without authority and without power, both of which are left to the Oedipal world of men, consoling themselves with Lacan's acknowledge-ment of the precarious, if not equally precarious, status of that authority and power.[103] Once the source of that precariousness is located in events in the actual lives of men, however, the necessity fades and Freudian theory need no longer set the perimeters for feminist theory, nor femininity bear the stigmata of a resurrected scapegoat.

Freud himself provided some tools for the dismantling of

psychoanalytic necessity. The discovery of the unconscious, of the unacknowledged images, dreams and thoughts which shape even rational thought, help women philosophers to understand better the gender distinctions inherent in Western thought. Freudian analysis allows Marie Balmary to uncover the unconscious motivation behind Freud's own theorising. However, Oedipal relations hardened into the universal law of the father cannot be a starting point for feminist theory. Even when psychoanalytic theory is revised, expanded and supplemented to include women, the masculine problematic remains. The maternal must exist in the shadow of the Oedipal dilemma, the feminine as an alternative to male legitimacy. Men's account of themselves is again accepted, their account of their psychological selves. Even when that account is projected back onto the primal history of the individual or of culture, it bears the mark of Freud's and other men's specific problem: how to conceptualise and rationalise the situation in which a man finds himself, the situation of oppressive father, husband, doctor. To accept men's account of their situation without an 'analysis' such as Balmary's means that women must again try to make a place for themselves in an already patriarchal world.

Notes

1. *Psychoanalysis and feminism* (Pantheon Books, New York, 1974), p. XVIII.

2. See Julia Kristeva's discussion of socialism and Freudianism in 'Women's time', trans. A. Jardin and H. Blake, *Signs*, vol. 7, no. 1 (Autumn 1981), p. 20, in which she described Freudianism as 'that lever inside this egalitarian and socializing field, which once again poses the question of sexual difference and of the difference between subjects who themselves are not reducible one to the other'.

3. See Sigmund Freud, 'Femininity', in *The standard edition of complete psychological works of Sigmund Freud*, vol. XXI (Hogarth Press, London, 1953), esp. pp. 132–4. See also, in the same volume, the earlier 'Female sexuality'.

4. This neglect of the theoretical basis of psychoanalytic findings on femininity is cited by Mitchell in some detail as the reason for a too hasty rejection of Freudianism. See *Psychoanalysis and feminism*, Part II, Section II, 'Feminism and Freud'.

5. Male analysts certainly did not neglect making connections between feminism and penis envy: see, for example, Karl Abraham, 'The female castration complex', in *Selected papers of Karl Abraham* (Hogarth Press, London, 1927).

6. See Freud, 'Femininity', where Freud considered, but also questioned, an analogy between the 'activity' of the sperm and the 'passivity' of the egg, and a masculinity characteristically active and a femininity charateristically passive.

7. *The second sex*, trans. H.M. Parshley (Vintage Books, New York, 1974), Book I, Part I, Chapter II, 'The psychoanalytic point of view'.

8. Ibid., p.53.

9. *The feminine mystique* (Norton, New York, 1963).

10. *Patriarchal attitudes*, (Virago Press, London, 1978), pp. 146–7.

11. The major texts here are 'Female sexuality' (1931) and its revision as 'Femininity' (1933).

12. 'Bisexuality' is Freud's term, though there has been considerable discussion as to whether this is a real bisexuality. Some analysts have argued that the libido which Freud claims is the same for each sex is masculine. See my discussion of Irigaray, p. 149–54 ff.: compare also Freud's 'Three essays on sexuality', pp. 219–20 and 'Femininity', p. 130.

13. 'Female sexuality', p. 239.

14. 'Femininity', p. 132. Freud lapses into anatomy again here, adding that frigidity may also have a contributing anatomical factor.

15. These were in essence the views restated by Ernest Jones, and argued against Freud in the so-called Jones-Freud controversy.

16. 'Female sexuality', p. 226. Freud speculated on the possibility of this 'blank's' connection with his masculine presence as analyst. A female analyst, he sometimes admitted, might have better luck, leaving it unclear whether the repression is his or his patient's.

17. 'Our insight into this early pre-Oedipus phase in girls comes to us as a surprise, like the discovery in another field, of the Minoan-Mycenean civilization behind the civilization of Greece.' — 'Female sexuality', *Complete Works XXI*, p. 226. See Jacquetta Hawkes, *Dawn of the gods* (Random House, New York, 1968), for an archaeological account of this prehistory of Western civilisation and the feminine qualities of the Minoan civilization, retained even after its 'marriage with', or conquering by, mainland Mycenae. Compare also Robert Graves, *The Greek myths* (Cassell, London, 1965) for a different kind of archaeology. Graves finds in myth the remnants of an older matrifocal order and traces of its violent overthrow by invading Acheaens imposing the 'Oedipal' relations of father and son.

18. Flax, 'Mother-daughter relationships: psychodynamics, politics, and philosophy' in Hester Einstein and Alice Jardin (eds), *The future of difference* (G.K. Hall, Boston, MA, 1980), p.22.

19. Ibid., p.37.

20. This split for Flax is the concrete correlate of the dualistic metaphysics which dominates Western Philosophy. See particularly her analyses of Descartes as rejecting the mother's world of the senses, and of social contract theories as fantasising a prehistoric without women.

21. Flax, 'Mother-daughter relationships', p. 37.

22. Denoel/Gouthier, Paris, 1980. See also arguments for shared parenting from American psychologists: Lilian Rubin, *Intimate strangers* (Harper and Row, New York, 1983); Louise Eichenbaum and Susie Orbach, *Understanding women* (Basic Books, New York, 1983).

23. 'One can already see designed there from infancy the differences which will mark the language of the man and that of the woman: one, "precoce", has for its function to establish a link, to deny the distance, resented as unsupportable, with the other. It's the feminine language which "enjambes" the void, which looks for similarities, which recovers consensus . . . The other, "tardive", manifests the distance to maintain with the other; it is a masculine language more often denuded of affectivity and anxiety. The man keeps to banalities of an order very general and little compromising.' — C. Oliver, *Les enfantes de Jocaste*, p. 87.

24. University of California Press, Berkeley, California, 1978.

25. *Reproduction of mothering*, pp. 187–8. Chodorow also cites critical theorists such as Horkheimer and Parsons.

26. D.W. Winnicott, 'Ego development in child development' in his *The maturational process and the facilitating environment* (Inter-Universities Press, New York, 1965), p. 62. See also Victoria Hamilton, *Narcissus and Oedipus: the children of psychoanalysis* (Routledge and Kegan Paul, New York, 1982) for a review of how the object relations theory of Winnicott and others rescues the infant from 'the solitary confinement' of primary narcissism.

27. D.W. Winnicott, 'Mother as mirror' in P. Lomas (ed.), *The predicament of the family*, (Hogarth Press, London, 1968).

28. See Monique Plaza, 'La même mère', *Questions Féministes*, no. 7 (Fev. 1980) for an interesting critique of this mother-blaming syndrome.

29. See also Jessica Benjamin's analysis of sado-masochism as a differentiating drive gone wrong, 'The bonds of love: rational violence and erotic domination' in Eisenstein and Jardin (eds), *The future of difference*, p. 60. The child does not, when it is aggressive, want the other to be destroyed but 'to place the other outside the sphere of mental control or omnipotence. Its aim, or at least its effect, is to collide with the other's resistance and so firmly to establish his/her solid independent presence.' A mother who only accedes to the child's wishes can set off such a repetitive 'rational' violence.

30. Chodorow, 'Gender, relation and difference in psychoanalytic perspective' in Eisenstein and Jardin (eds), *The future of difference*.

31. *Psychoanalysis and feminism*, p. 362.

32. *Totem and taboo: some points of agreement between the mental lives of savages and neurotics* (W.W. Norton, New York, 1950). 'The beginnings of religion, morals, society and art converge in the Oedipus conflict' — p. 156.

33. This story is told by Freud at ibid., pp. 141–3. Later, Claude Levi-Strauss re-told Freud's story as anthropology making the exchange of women the constitutive structure of society: *The elementary structures of kinship* (Eyre and Spottiswood, London, 1969). Some American feminists saw this account of the origins of society as a necessary supplement to Marx, arguing that the exchange of women operated across economic systems. See, for example, Gayle Rubin, 'The Traffic in women: notes on the "political economy" of sex' in R. Reiter (ed.), *Towards an anthropology of women* (Monthly Review Press, New York, 1975).

34. In *Moses and monotheism*, Freud found the same mythic murder of

the father in the Judaic/Christian tradition. In a virtuoso display of scholarship, he argued that Moses was an Egyptian (not Jewish) follower of Aten the Egyptian monotheistic god, who was murdered after he led the Jews out of Egypt. The crucifixion of Christ then further complicates the situation by offering a tempting mythic resolution of guilt — the sacrificial death of one of the sons.

35. *Totem and taboo*, pp. 157–8.

36. Ibid., p. 159.

37. Sherry Turkle's phrase. See her *Freud's French revolution* (Basic Books, New York, 1978), a fascinating 'ethnography' of psychoanalytic culture and an account of its very different theory and practice in America and in France.

38. 'Le stade de miroir comme formateur de la fonction du "Je"', *Écrits I*, (du Seuil, Paris, 1966), p. 89ff. *Écrits: a selection*, trans. Alan Sheridan (Tavistock, London, 1977). There are other less mythic accounts of this early narcissistic reflection. The English psychologist Winnicott, for example, sees the child as reflected in the face and expressions of the mother. Lacan prefers the inhuman mirror, perhaps because of his observation that with some animals a reflection is all that is needed for such supposedly interpersonal events as fertilisation.

39. 'Le stade du miroir', p. 96.

40. 'Signification du phallus', *Écrits II*, pp. 109–10. This and some other writings of Lacan ('Guiding remarks for a Congress on Feminine Sexuality' and some excerpts from *Encore*, Lacan's seminar on love) are collected and translated in Juliet Mitchell and Jacqueline Rose, (eds), *Feminine sexuality*, trans. Jacqueline Rose (Pitman Press, Beaconsfield, England, 1982).

41. For Lacan, intersubjectivity characterises animal rather than human life. The decoy, for example, draws the predator away from the flock and the mother limps to draw a hunter's attention from her young. All this is still on the animal level of 'need fulfilment'. 'Instance de la lettre dans l'inconscient', *Écrits I*, p. 285.

42. Again one can see the Lacanian shift in discussing the difference between conscious and unconscious. Freud had already rejected a naive conception of the unconscious as a basement location of physical drives that were to be removed to another level. Lacan, however, moved beyond Freud's 'reinvestment of energies'. It is not energies which are involved but significations. Unconscious thought is as much a language as conscious. The difference is that conscious thought is rational, i.e. it has a connection with the real (not to be taken as implying any connection with an independent reality). In mental dysfunction the subject suffers from the distance between the rational world of language and the unconscious. It is not a question, any more that it was for Freud, of sublating or eliminating either. Instead the goal is integration, for Lacan always a matter of language. The fragmentary, free-floating 'ça' of the unconscious will become the 'je' of language — that is to say, with help the subject will learn to express meanings in a public language. if the 'moi' must learn, so must the 'je' which must abandon the myth of a unitary essence and find its signifying source in its essential division from the unconscious.

43. It is questionable whether Lacan also must not fall back on anatomy to explain why the Phallus plays this central role. He was certainly not willing to admit this is either a contingent or historically determined choice. The Phallus is the master signifier because of its role in copulation 'both sexual and logical' and because of something that Lacan mysteriously called its 'vital flux'. 'Signification du Phallus', *Écrits II*, p. 110.

44. The Phallus as signifier has some results for men as well who, because they are constantly asked to give women what they have not got, always hold back a part of themselves and search for other partners. Ibid., pp. 114–15.

45. 'Instance de la lettre dans l'inconscient,' *Écrits I*, p. 252. Lacan cited Stalin in support, as realising that language is not just another part of the superstructure.

46. See Lacan's early connections with the surrealists, C. Clément, *Vies et legendes de Jacques Lacan* (B. Grasset, Paris, 1981), p. 70. Also in English, *Lives and legends of Jacques Lacan* (Columbia University Press, New York, 1983).

47. See footnote 2, above.

48. This split between generations of feminists, as Kristeva would have it or between national style, as some American commentators would have it, has been much discussed. See, for example, the introduction to Elaine Marks and Isabelle de Courtivron (eds), *New French feminisms* (University of Massachusetts Press, Amherst, 1980), a useful collection of excerpts from Kristeva's generation of feminists. Also, see Eisenstein and Jardin (eds), *The future of difference*, section on 'Language and revolution: the Franco-American dis-connection', with articles by Donna Stanton, Josette Feral, Christine Makward, Jane Gallop and Carolyn Burke.

49. Lacan's influence in French thought even after his death is phenomenal. See Sherry Turkle, *Freud's French revolution*, where she noted that even the hatred of Lacan's enemies formed a nexus around which anti-Lacanian thought turns. In the work of Kristeva and Irigaray, he is seldom mentioned directly but his presence is always felt in footnotes and, more importantly, in expressions borrowed from his seminars. Lacan was not just another text to be discussed but an internalised father always present, whether acknowledged or not, in one's thought. This dialogical/dialectical relation between Lacan and French feminists is explored by Jane Gallop in her *Feminism and psychoanalysis: the daughter's seduction* (Macmillan, London, 1982) (the clever reversal of Mitchell's title is itself a Lacanian tactic and an example of Lacanian wit, as is the sub-title. According to Freud, the hysteric believes herself to have been seduced, but the feminist reader of Lacan will seduce the father). See also Juliet Mitchell's review, 'The bisexual idyll', *Times Literary Supplement*, 14 Jan, 1983, p. 39.

50. Kristeva develops the idea of a pre-articulate economy of expressive meaning in her major text, *La révolution du language poétique* (du Seuil, Paris, 1974), trans. M. Waller, *Revolution in poetic language* (Columbia University Press, New York, 1984). Expressive semiotic meaning irrupts in avant-garde poetry and other non-rational texts to make 'budge' the rigid structures of rationally ordered symbolic meaning.

51. Reprinted in *Desire in language* (Basil Blackwell, Oxford, 1980), p. 237. See also on the maternal, 'Hérétique de l'amour', *Tel Quel*, no. 74 (Winter, 1977) where Kristeva explored the psychological function of the Virgin Mary for women.

52. Ibid., p. 239.

53. 'Jouissance' became almost a technical term in French feminism. Its literal meaning is enjoyment in general, but it is used colloquially for the enjoyment of orgasm. It was coined by Lacan and other post-structuralist theorists for a specifically feminine sexual pleasure which is supposed to transcend phallic release.

54. Here Kristeva made her own return to Freud, citing passages neglected by Lacan where Freud referred to such a primary identification. 'L'abject d'amour', *Tel Quel*, no. 91 (Spring, 1982).

55. See the opening passages of *Les pouvoirs de l'horreur* (du Seuil, Paris, 1980), *Powers of horror*, trans. Leon Roudiez (Columbia University Press, New York, 1985), for a definition of 'abjection', and its function in Kristevan thought. The 'abject' is neither subject or object, but the rejected 'debris' that makes possible the constitution of subject and object.

56. In *Les pouvoirs de l'horreur*, Kristeva, like Mitchell, draws on structural anthropology and especially the work of Levi-Strauss, to confirm Freud's view of society as constituted by an alliance between men. For Kristeva it is not so much the founding myth of patriarchy but a structural necessity that explains kinship. Patriarchal law is necessary to guarantee reproduction and at the same time to subordinate it to productive relations between men. See also *La révolution du langage poétique*, 'Le clivage entre rapport de production et rapport de reproduction', p. 455.

57. *Les pouvoirs de l'horreur*, p. 83.

58. Kristeva considers, among others, Mary Douglas's study of ritual uncleanliness, Greek drama, ancient Judaic prohibitions, as well as Christian teaching.

59. *Les pouvoirs de l'horreur*, p. 85.

60. Ibid., p. 87.

61. Ibid., p. 119.

62. Ibid., p. 131.

63. See *La révolution du langage poétique*, p. 455 ff. for the detailed argument.

64. Ibid., p. 458.

65. See Kristeva's remarks on women's writing in 'Women's time', p. 25. 'Nor am I speaking of the aesthetic quality of production by women, most of which — with a few exceptions (but has not this always been the case with both sexes?) — are a reiteration of a more or less euphoric or depressed romanticism and always an explosion of an ego lacking narcissistic gratification.'

66. *La révolution du langage poétique*, p. 614. Women all too easily move from their interest in emotional expression to making a fetish of their femininity, and end up again as the stability that supports patriarchal pleasure.

67. *Les pouvoirs de l'horreur*, p. 247.

68. See *Polylogue* (du Seuil, Paris, 1977), p. 519. This stance is also

recommended by other 'post-structuralist' feminists such as Larysa Mykyta, 'Lacan, literature and the look: women in the eye of psychoanalysis', *Sub-Stance*, no. 39 (1983). Women must, to assert themselves, Mykyta said, co-opt phallic power but every phallic gesture must be accompanied by 'a questioning of the conditions of power and the conditions of discourse' (p. 56).

69. *On Chinese women*, trans. Anita Barrows (Urizen Books, New York, 1977). 'And we know the role that the pervert — invincibly believing in the maternal phallus, obstinately refusing the existence of the other sex — has been able to play in antisemitism and the totalitarian movements that embrace it.' (p. 23).

70. The evidence cited by Kristeva for this fear is rather slim: only that there are women now involved in terrorist activities.

71. 'Women's time', p. 30.

72. See footnote 50, above.

73. Irigaray's own relations with the master show her daring in this regard. As a Lacanian analyst on the faculty of Lacan's department at Vincennes, her seminar was abruptly cancelled as unsuitable after the publication of her *Speculum de l'autre femme* (Minuit, Paris, 1974), *Speculum of the other woman*, trans. Gillian Gill (Cornell University Press, 1985). Lacan, for his part, reverted to silence on the matter, pleading that he must get back to his important topological representations of psychic structures. It was clear that Irigaray's questioning of the master/masters was not to be tolerated or even discussed.

74. This order, the order in which the articles are presented in *Speculum*, is itself significant. Irigaray worked back historically to the founding metaphors, models and motives of Western philosophy.

75. Irigaray also accused Lacan of resmuggling back anatomy by emphasising the 'organic' significance of the penis rather than the 'organic' significance of womb or ovaries.

76. 'Cosi Fan Tutti', Irigaray's critique of Lacan in *Ce sexe qui n'en est pas un* (Minuit, Paris, 1977), p. 86. *The sex which is not one*, trans. C. Porter with C. Burke (Cornell University Press, 1985).

77. *Speculum*, p. 63.

78. *Ce sexe*, pp. 24, 122.

79. See Irigaray's 'Quand nos levres se parlent', (When our lips talk to each other) in *Ce sexe* (reprinted and translated in Marks and Courtivron (eds.), *New French feminisms*), for Irigaray's attempt to evoke such a relation.

80. See Irigaray, 'And the one doesn't stir without the other', *Signs*, vol. 7, no. 1 (1981). In addition, in America there was renewed interest in the mother/daughter relation — for example, Adrienne Rich's *Of woman born* (W.W. Norton, New York, 1976).

81. See 'Les marchés des femmes' (The woman markets) and 'Les marchandises entre elles' (The merchanise gets together) in *Ce sexe*, in which Irigaray contrasted the two systems.

82. Irigaray made much of the dominance of vision to the exclusion of other senses in Western thought. She connected this emphasis on vision with the male visible sex.

83. *Ce sexe*, p. 126.

84. 'Pouvoir phallomorphic et psychologic de "la femme"', *Quéstions féministe*, no. 1 (1978), or in English, '"Phallomorphic power" and the psychology of "woman"', *Ideology and Consciousness*, no. 4 (Autumn, 1978), pp. 4–36.

85. Trans. Ned Lukaker (Johns Hopkins Press, Baltimore, 1982).

86. Freud's reasons can be directly related to his stalled self-analysis: he cannot seem to bring analysis to a conclusion (he cannot bring his own to conclusion); it is hardly credible that perversion is so general (he cannot accept it); the unconscious cannot distinguish fact from fiction (he cannot); unconscious memories (his own?) do not break through. Ibid., p. 145.

87. See Balmary's chapter on the 'Nannie', pp. 134–8, for a discussion of the nurse's role in Freud's biography.

88. *The assault on truth: Freud's suppression of the seduction theory* (Farrar Strauss and Giroux, New York, 1984).

89. Fliess diagnosed Eckstein's symptoms — stomach ailments, menstrual difficulties — as due to masturbation which he believed caused menstrual problems and in turn structural abnormalities in the nose. These abnormalities, he decided, could only be cured by an operation: *The assault on truth*, pp. 58–9. The fact alone that Freud credited such a fanciful theory and allowed Fliess to operate on his patient would seem enough to cast doubt on Freud's lucidity at this period in his life.

90. In what must be one of the more horrible of medical horror stories, Masson described Eckstein's ordeal. After the operation she suffered from persistent infection and haemorrhage, expelling from the nose sometimes 'two bowlfuls of pus' (*The assault on truth*, p. 61). Finally, Freud called in another doctor. Eventually, along with the pus and blood, a large piece of gauze was expelled, a piece of gauze that Fliess had left in the wound. The damage, however, was done. Eckstein continued to suffer and was, according to one witness, permanently disfigured.

91. On medical treatments such as cauterisation of the uterus, clitorectomy, and rest cure, see Ann Douglas Wood, 'The fashionable disease: women's complaints and their treatment in nineteenth century America' in Mary Hartman and Lois Banner (eds), *Clio's consciousness raised* (Harper and Row, New York, 1974), pp. 1–22.

92. Balmary, *Psychoanalyzing psychoanalysis*, p. 111.

93. Ibid., p. 112.

94. See Balmary's fascinating conflation of consciousness and conscience in her account of unconscious trauma, where the orthodox separation between the psychoanalytic unconscious and moral consciousness become increasingly 'entangled'. Ibid., pp. 159–62.

95. Ibid., p. 171.

96. Jeffrey Masson, 'The seduction theory', *The Atlantic Monthly* (Feb. 1984), p. 50.

97. For Lacan's early fascination with sensational crimes committed by women, especially the Papin sisters, two maids who hacked to pieces their demanding employers with kitchen knives, see Clément's chapter 'Le chemin des dames' in *Vies et légendes*.

98. See Catherine Clément's *Vies et légendes* for a lively account of Lacan's expulsion from the Psychoanalytic Institute for unorthodox

practice such as the variable length session.

99. Lacan's analysis of female psychotics, including the Papin sisters, was that they did not keep a 'good distance'. They were too close to some other woman, forming an unhealthy 'identity for two'. Clément, *Vies et legendes*, p. 92.

100. For example, this passage from Lacan's Seminar *Encore*: 'Naturally vou are going to all be convinced that I believe in God. I believe in the "jouissance" of the woman in so much as she is more of it . . . this "jouissance" that one experiences and of which one knows nothing, isn't it what puts us on the road to ex-sistence? And why not interpret a face of the Other, the face of God, as supported by feminine "jouissance".' *Encore, le séminar de Jacques Lacan, Livre XX* (du Seuil, Paris, 1975), p. 71.

101. See, for example, studies cited by Elise Boulding in 'Familial constraints on women's work roles' in M.W. Zak and P.A. Moots (eds), *Women and the politics of culture* (Longman, New York, 1983), pp. 204–5.

102. Balmary points out that some therapists, such as Laing, Bettelheim and Mannon have been able to ignore official doctrine and create humane therapeutic institutions. *Psychoanalyzing psychoanalysis*, p. 154.

103. For example, Jane Gallop, *Reading Lacan* (Cornell University Press, Ithaca, New York, 1985), p. 20. Gallop argues that the realisation that everyone is castrated is the cure for patriarchy.

6

A Woman's Language

Lexical discrimination

With the Lacanian equation of 'the nature of things' and the
'nature of words', sexism is located in language itself. This, Lacan
declared, in his famous reference to feminism, was only what
women had been claiming all along:

> There is only woman as excluded by the nature of things
> which is the nature of words, and it is necessary to say that
> if there is something of which they themselves complain at
> the moment it's very much that — simply they don't know
> what they say, that is all the difference between them and
> me.[1]

It is not 'nature' or any physical reality that determines women's
inferior position but a 'thought' difference, a 'signified difference'.
The only real difference, Lacan asserted, was that women do not
know what they are saying.[2] This is not surprising according to
Lacanian teaching. There is only one language and in it women
are at a significant disadvantage. They will always speak with a
borrowed authority and always have trouble with the analytic-
rational knowledge of 'what one says'. When asked about their
sexuality women cannot answer. When asked about their mystical
experiences they are inarticulate. Moreover, although Lacan's
hardly empirical enquiry into women's speech might be rejected
as unfounded in fact, other investigators were also noting differences
in women's language and giving scientific credence to Lacan's
ministerial pronouncements. In the 1970s a growing number of
empirical studies related sexual difference to language use.

Women speak less and less often than men.[3] Women are more careful than men to use correct grammar,[4] are more conservative when it comes to stylistic innovation[5] use adjectives of emotion rather than pace,[6] form conflicting, ambivalent, rather than stereotypic, metaphors.[7] Women also show a preference for modal structures such as 'might have been', indicating uncertainty and indecision.[8] Other, empirically less well established but observed, differences are women's use of 'empty' adjectives such as 'charming' or 'lovely', or of tag questions to dull assertive force, in addition to women's tendency to be more polite and more responsive.[9] In some cultures the 'abnormality' of female speech is institutionalised,[10] or built into phonological structure.[11] Women may use different dialects than men, or write in a vernacular while men write a more formal language.[12]

There is, however, from the sociolinguistic point of view, a more obvious explanation for women's silence and different speech than Lacan's 'lack' of the symbolic phallus. That women are silent is not surprising considering women's lack of power. Certainly the right to speak at all had been hard won. Even when the right of women to speak in public is not contested overtly, few women do. In their intimate conversations with members of the opposite sex, women speak less, and less often and are interrupted more. Sociologists located this 'disability' not in a woman's symbolic identity but in her situation as powerless.[13] If the topics that women introduce fail, it is not because their symbolic ability is impaired, but because men do not bother to work reciprocally to respond to what they say. On the other hand, when men speak, women do listen, make comments, further develop men's ideas. Men control conversations not only by veto but also by lack of interest. This control is not a peculiarity of male/female relations, but of any power relation.[14] Whenever one conversant is more powerful, then similar restraints on the powerless will result. To speak is to take power, and women, as Beauvoir noted, fail to assert themselves here as in other areas. The prescription was obvious. Women must assert themselves. Women must refuse to be interrupted, insist on their right to speak, and suppress linguistic devices like tag questions which blunt assertive force.

There was also, however, the realisation by some researchers that a restitution of speaking privileges, a receptive audience, and linguistic assertiveness, might not be enough. 'Language', Robin Lakoff observed, 'uses us as much as we use language,'[15] suggesting that even a woman determined to speak might not find an instrument adequate to her purposes. If women had been coerced into using a neutral language discretely, had been taught to be 'seen and not heard', then they could be taught to be linguistically assertive; but if in language itself, just as Lacan claimed, there is systematically instituted the inequalities of gender[16] difference, this would indicate that no aggressive ascension to the podium, no 'talking of the word' could finally solve the problem of the woman speaker. If the language available for her to use is itself sexist, then she will always either replicate sexist attitudes or fumble inarticulately and impotently. Some linguists studying the vocabulary of English and other languages thought they found such asystematic encoding of feminine inferiority. Gender differences, they argued, were written into lexicons, inherent in the very discriminations that make linguistic meaning possible.

Common in language are pairs of words, similar in meaning but denoting a difference in gender, such as master/mistress, man/woman, bachelor/spinster. Logically it would be expected that the semantic content of such words would remain the same and only the gender would change. This, however, is not the case. 'master' implies dominance and control, but 'mistress', instead of dominance and control, suggests a kept woman or sexual object. The marriage relation as well as the extra-marital relation is asymmetrical. Women cannot be gracefully substituted in locutions such as 'man and wife', the peculiarity of 'woman and husband' indicates that a man may have a female helpmate but a woman may not have a male helpmate. Unmarried and unattached, the asymmetry persists. 'Spinster' has none of the sophisticated, satisfied air of 'bachelor', but indicates unattractiveness and failure. It would seem that there are no neutral words in which one could even attempt to indicate a male/female relation in which the woman was dominant, or even equal. Power and femininity being contradictory, the semantic component of dominance is masculinised and women's inferiority coded into the language in such a way so as to make equality inconsistent with femininity. Supporting this analysis are findings that there are many more sexual derogatory words in vocabularies for women than there are for men,[17] and that female marked words in the vocabulary systematically carry a negative connotation.[18]

Similar in the linking of femininity and powerlessness is the semantic force of feminine endings. There are poets and poetesses, stewards and stewardesses, majors and majorettes, authors and authoresses. Here where there is no obvious connotation of power in the root word, the sexual shift is still indicated in the diminuitive force of the added endings. The proper poet, steward, author, is male, but room must be made in the lexicon for the feminine exception marked as such. Furthermore, that exception, as shown by the diminuitive ending, will be a lesser, more frivolous, even fraudulent, version of the real thing.[19]

In *Language and woman's place*, Lakoff noted the frequent use of euphemisms for women. This, she argued, is typical of powerless and oppressed groups. Given that 'women' or 'black' carries the connotation of inferiority or even sub-humanity, then it is necessary in polite conversation not to refer explicitly to women or blacks. Instead of being black, one is 'coloured'; instead of being a woman, one is a 'lady', or a 'girl', the latter combining politeness with an implication of immaturity and inferior status. Given the stigma attached to the feminine, even honorific female words can quickly become perjorative. 'Lady' is an example, originally indicating high status, now when used in 'Hey lady', indicating contempt. In *Gyn/Ecology* Mary Daly gave other examples of words which originally referred to female power, but which are now derogatory. The term 'hag' meaning ugly old women originally meant 'untamed' as applied to a hawk; other obsolete meanings of 'hag' include 'intractable', 'wilful', 'wanton', and 'wild-eyed'. Here female sexuality as conjoined with power must be expunged, and a hag becomes the least thinkable of sexual objects. Power a hag may have, but it is power only to repulse, or to disgust. Feminine sexuality is reciprocally transformed into a woman's status as sexual object for men. 'Glamour', the trap of the man-identified woman and 'spinster', the punishment of the man-refusing woman, Daly noted, originally indicated female power and female skill respectively: 'glamour' was the charm of a witch, a 'spinster' was someone who spins.[20] The incompatibility of feminine sexuality and power is further shown in qualifying adjectives such as the masculine 'potent'; a woman's sexuality, on the other hand, is expressed by the passive 'frigid' or 'hot'. Investigators like Muriel Schultz argued that 'virtually every originally neutral word for women has at some point in its existence acquired debased connotations or obscene references or both'.[21]

Titles are another way in which male/female difference is coded into language. Each individual must be formally addressed as either masculine (Mr), or feminine (Mrs/Miss). Again, the difference is asymmetrical: the woman's marital status is coded but not the man's, reflecting the expectation that a woman's identity depends on her husband's. Interesting in this regard is the sometimes unpredictable result of consciously instituted linguistic change. 'Ms' has been proposed as a title neutral as to a woman's marital status and so symmetrical with the masculine 'Mr'. However, the usage of 'Ms' itself quickly became asymmetrical: either it carries the same old connotation of unmarried or, more often, an even more contemptuous imputation of feminist pretension open to ridicule. Therefore, the proscribed change only manufactures another abusive term for women who insist on being unfeminine.[22]

Even adjectives are sexually coded. 'Beautiful', 'fragrant', 'neutral', 'soft' — all apply to women and not to men, suggesting an underlying semantic scheme that assigns different adjectives to different sexes. This, Gunther Kress and Robert Hodge argued,[23] constitutes an ideology, a prescriptive schema for femininity in which women are not active but weak, obedient, pleasing and caring. Such an underlying schema is more efficient than direct statements for perpetuating sexism as it covers contradictions (e.g. between 'caring' and 'inactive') and operates at a conscious level below critical awareness.

The most frequently criticised example of linguistic sexism is the generic use of 'man'. Here it is not so much that language encodes the inferiority of women as that it valorises what is male. 'Mankind', the 'rights of man', 'the ascent of man' — all indicate that to be properly human is to be male. The objection that 'man' is generic misses the point. Terms like 'man' and 'mankind' function as they do because they are both masculine and generic. Then the identification may be made between what is general and male, while at the same time, when necessary or politic, an illusive solidarity can be asserted.[24] The generic use of male pronouns completes this strategy, by extending the implication of generic masculinity, even in cases in which the term 'man' is not explicitly used.

These and other examples caused feminist linguists to conclude that sexual difference is built into available vocabulary, making it unlikely that in its present state language could be a vehicle for women's expression. This was the argument, for example, of Shirley and Edwin Ardener.[25] The dominant group, i.e. the males, also dominates communication. Women have different perceptions and experiences but their experience must be filtered through the male-constructed language. Determination to speak is not enough. Even to name female subjugation is difficult when 'female = powerlessness' is written into the language.

Nevertheless, vocabulary is one of the most mutable features of language as new words are added to the lexicon and old words become archaic. There therefore seemed to be available a variety of strategies for instituting linguistic change. Projects such as the American Heritage School Dictionary (1972) indicated a conscious effort to break down sex-role stereotypes.[26] Publishers circulated to their readers and editors non-sexist manuals of style. In educational and governmental institutions, 'chairman' was replaced with 'chairperson' or more simply, 'chair'. Ms was to be used on official correspondence. Masculine pronouns were replaced with 'his or her', or, where that was stylistically inelegant, rewritten in either a neutral plural or using the ungendered 'one'. 'Man' was replaced with 'humanity'.[27]

Such efforts, however, all too often seemed to constitute only another euphemism deceptively covering the fact of feminine inferiority. The distance between official, polite language and ordinary language remained. Most continued to think and speak as before; only now for public consumption some editing was required. Even feminists caught themselves using the old generic masculine pronouns or referring to themselves as 'chairmen'. It was not so easy to decide to speak in a new way. Other, more radical strategies were proposed.

Mary Daly, for example, argued that masking anti-women sentiment with politeness was not enough. Deceptive euphemisms as well as directly anti-feminist vocabulary must be exposed. Women should not accept a polite neutral alternative that leaves the powerful semantically charged anti-woman expressions still in the field and dominant over any revision, but literally crack sexist language apart. They should 're-cover' old meanings, add novel prefixes, make up creative etymologies, split words to show their real semantic significance. Women-made words, like 'chairperson', are for Daly more dangerous than overt sexism because they mask the reality of feminine oppression, patching it over with deferential linguistic wall-paper which must soon crack again in even more insidious ways along the faults of misogynism.[28]

However, it was not clear that Daly's linguistic terrorism was any more able to change general usage than official deference to feminist sensitivities. Women, instead of accepting a token inclusion, were to form a secret society whose membership is identified by catch-words detached from the body of language and so incapable of engaging the lives of masses of women. The only reality touched by such a language is its point of separation with 'normal language', and consequently with the masses of non-radical, 'fem-bot' women. In Daly's chants and incantations reappeared Lacan's inarticulate female saint lost in inexpressible experience:

> Sounds of joy echo through the chamber, and reverberate through other and deeper chambers of the labyrinth. The voyagers glimpse our Paradise that is beyond the boundaries of patriarchal Paradise . . . Those who have been called bitches bark; pussies purr; cows moo; old bats squeal; squirrels chatter; nags whinney; chicks chirp; cats growl; old crows screech.[29]

The alternative to patriarchal language, just as Lacan warned, is no language at all, a regressive return to the inarticulate animal. The unsatisfactory choice remains between a superficial erasure of offensive words for women, and on the other hand a refusal to participate in any publicly constituted meaning. It is Daly's awareness of the depth of sexism's involvement in language that drives her to the latter, self-defeating, style of feminist protest.

The inequities in semantic structure cannot be so easily remedied. One term in an opposition that should be symmetrical is marked as superior. Linguistic reform was to restore equality; if the male term denoted power then so should the female. Either women must be 'poets', or 'poetess' must be revalorised. Such a restitution of symmetry is consistent with liberal feminism's focus on equality as the common ground and goal of feminist effort. The tendency of the language to unbalance itself after any such reform seemed to indicate, however, that inequality might be present not only in laws, economic relations, or the social practice of language, but in the very constitution of meaning. It might be changeable historical accident that some word, or worse, the masculine word, to use a sexist image, must always 'wear the trousers'.

Faced with this impasse, the feminist critique of sexist language required a more adequate theoretical base, one that did not take words as simple stand-ins for objects that can be rearranged at will, or naively assume that there is a natural meaning substitutable for patriarchal distortion. The problem is not only with individual words which, as simple offensive epithets, may be expunged, replaced, or edited out, but with the relationship between words. If the very structure of meaning depends on sexual difference, then a simple expulsion or reinstatement of meanings may not have the desired effect. If the structure of the language demands hierarchialised gender, then no matter what new words are invented or rediscovered, the same asymmetrical relations will eventually reconstitute themselves, as other words shift in meaning to accommodate the addition or deletion.

The inequalities of semantic structure

That language is not a list of disconnected items is the founding insight of structural linguistics. Words and the sentences made up of words are related to one another in systematic ways. A 'woman' is 'not a man'. A 'father' is 'not a wife', a 'mother' is always 'female'. An account of language must explain and describe these relations — hence the 'science' of semantics. Because these are relations of necessity and are not optional, semantics will take the form of exhibiting a necessary structure to meaning. Although the inventory of vocabulary of any language may be one of its mutable features, the deep structure of the lexicon is not. The founder of structural linguistics, Ferdinand de Saussure, explained the theoretical basis for this insight.[30] Linguistic signs do not represent things because that would assume that ideas come ready-made and that naming is a simple labelling process. What is, in fact, combined in a sign, whether audible or visible, is a concept and a 'sound image', which should be referred to respectively not as object and word but as signified and signifier. Although it might seem that a speaker chooses what word might best represent her idea, signifiers are instead 'fixed' in place. The 'masses have no voice in the matter' but are 'bound to the existing language': 'Language furnishes the best proof that a law accepted by the community is a thing that is tolerated and not a rule to which all freely consent.'[31]

Given this view, it was clear that feminist attempts to legislate linguistic change would encounter difficulties. Even if mass support could be rallied for such a cause, language is, Saussure argued, engrained at such an early age and linguistic competence is so unconscious that conscious instituted change is impossible. More importantly, there is no alternative natural meaning that can replace established connections between words: any meaning outside of these relationships is no meaning at all. The sign is arbitrary: that is, there can be no connection between a sign and any natural fact. Instead the sign constitutes the facts it is to represent. For this reason, language 'blends with the life of society, and the latter, inert by nature, is a prime conservative force'.[32] This is not to say that language does not change, because it obviously does. It does not, however, change in the same way that law, fashion, or customs might change, all of which are in some sense based 'on the natural relations of things' and so can be altered to accommodate women's legal equality or more active feminine lifestyles. Instead, the arbitrary nature of the sign removes it from conscious human control. Even an artificial language, once in circulation, escapes the control of its designer.

Saussure used the example of a game of chess to illustrate the relation of speakers to language.[33] The chessmen have no value in themselves; their choice as pieces is arbitrary. Their value depends instead on their position on the board — that is to say, on their relation to other pieces. Furthermore, these relative values are immutably fixed. To question the rules of the game is to destroy the possibility of play. It is true that when one piece is removed the entire configuration is changed, but at this point — the point at which feminists might hope that small changes in the lexicon might bring about larger conceptual change — two facts must be observed. Firstly, any change that occurs in the feminine position is still governed by the rules of the game. Secondly, it is at this point that the analogy with chess, according to Saussure, breaks down. The chess player as a part of her strategy may intend to shift the balance of power, but 'the pieces of language are shifted — or rather modified — spontaneously and fortuitously'. For the linguist it is not any such random and uncontrollable mutations in time which are to be studied, but instead the permanent rules that constitute the only linguistic 'reality'.

Thought, in the psychological sense, Saussure claimed, is only a 'shapeless and indistinct mass'.[34] Without language there is no distinguishing one thing from another; there are no given concepts or ideas that we then find words to represent. The divisions of language operate between the two shapeless masses of thought and of sound.[35] If there is no idea for which a sound can be deputised, and no distinguishable sound for which an idea can be formed, the value of the sign that combines sound and idea must depend only on its relation with other signs.[36] It is the same with any system of exchange. All value, Saussure argued, is so constituted; a dissimilar object is exchanged for something else (money for a loaf of bread) and similar things are compared (four quarters with a dollar). Money has value because it can be exchanged for fixed quantities of goods, but it can be exchanged only because it can be compared with equivalent items in the money system. The 'value' of language must be determined in the same way. Neither words nor money are intrinsically useful; both are arbitrary. Their value depends on the fact that they are ordered systems of differences and equivalences whose particular material manifestation is irrelevant to their value. This Saussurian view of language as neither created nor controlled was further developed by Lacan. To be someone is to find one's place within a system of signs; it is 'to have a value', and possible identities are only constituted within a network of relationships that are linguistically defined.

Although the first successes for structuralist linguistics were in grammatical models,[37] soon the meaningful elements of language were also submitted to structuralist analysis. Again the naive idea that words referred to things was rejected; the meaning of linguistic units was a function of relationships between words; the logical relations such as synonymy and antonymy.[38] These are the stable objects which a semanticist must study, or, to put it in Lacanian terms, the Law of the Father, that any speaker must obey. One cannot contradict oneself if one is to be understood; so understanding depends not on any relation between words and things but on the relations between words.

> We have already seen that the vocabulary of a language will contain a number of lexical systems the semantic structure of which can be described in terms of paradigmatic and symtagmatic sense-relations, and we have stressed that these relations are to be defined as holding between independently determined senses.[39]

The implications for linguistic reform are obvious. If linguistic meaning is constituted by systematic differences, the possibilities for feminist revision of language are limited. Linguists saw themselves as describing the essential structure of meaning. Feminists would also have to speak within these sense-relations, and if the sexism they deplore is inscribed in semantic structure, no escape would seem to be possible.

An explanation for the resistance of language to feminist

revision can be found in the component analysis frequently used to exhibit semantic relations between words. In order to describe and explain the relations of synonymy, autonomy and hyponomy, semanticists could not simply list permissible relations: 'A father cannot be female', 'a brother is a male sibling', etc. The list of such relations would be intolerably long. Instead, semanticists take each word as a divisible unit made up of component meanings. The meaning of a word can then be 'factorised' to take account of the fact that words are related and provide economical descriptions of those relations. The components, for some[40] universals that form the semantic base of any language, are oppositional: male/female, living/non-living, animal/human. By reference to an oppositional grid the meaning of an individual word can be mapped.[41] 'Woman', for example, = (female, human). To make the mapping even more economical, the opposition can be turned into (+) and (–), making (woman = – male, + human, + living).[42] The oppositions are hierarchical — that is to say, one term is positive and therefore governs the opposition. To confuse this hierarchy, or to combine opposite components, is always to lapse unintelligibly into nonsense.[43]

To 'be' something and to 'not be' something, then, frame our thinking — in fact make thinking possible. To think or say anything is to think or say that it 'is' or 'is not'. It is necessary that the positive feature be defined or understood with reference to its opposite or lack. Only by way of such a contrast can any meaning be established. 'Woman' cannot have any meaning in isolation: it can only have meaning in relation to 'man'. Although 'man' also can only have meaning in relation to its opposite, or lack, 'woman', the positive male presence governs the contrast. Nor are sex-linked terms such as 'mother', 'wife' and 'father' an isolated, eccentric, part of the vocabulary. In fact, in almost all cases, these sex-marked oppositions are the examples used by semanticists to explain the oppositional structure of language in general.[44] Component analysis is almost always illustrated with reference to kinship words or their animal analogies (cow, bull, calf). Words like 'mother', 'father' and 'child', are taken as the model for the relation between componential and word meaning.

Although semanticists in their careful, if not tedious, attempts to formalise rules which can generate well-formed meaningful sentences have not been much interested in the implications of such examples, their paradigmatic function could be used to explain the resistance of the lexicon to feminist revision. If the oppositional character of meaning is modelled on family relations where the father is a positive authoritarian presence and the mother is the lack of that authority, then it is no accident that in all representations masculine is taken as the positive presence and feminine as deficient. The coupling of activity and presence with masculinity in pairs of words would be the very generating principle of meaning. Lacan's assertion of the male phallus as a master symboliser is confirmed. Masculinity is the positive presence around which the meaning of words like 'father', 'mother', and 'child' is structured, and around which, by extension, all meaning must be structured.

So systematic is this structuring of meaning around masculine presence that gender is often a part of the very grammar of language. English does not have grammatical gender. The universe of discourse, in English, is not separated without remainder into inclusive sets, as it is in the root languages of Latin and Greek which divide all nouns and adjectives into masculine, feminine and neuter and require that all modifiers agree. Often, however, the effect of grammatical gender and 'natural', semantic gender is the same. In either case, the choice of pronouns is governed by the gender of the noun replaced, whether grammatical or natural. It is this agreement that determines the use of the generic 'he' criticised by feminists. A pronoun replaces a noun. Furthermore, nouns, if unmarked, are always masculine. As the linguist Chafe puts it:

> I shall here assume that a human noun, if not otherwise specified, is understood to be what we would normally term *masculine*. In other words, I shall take masculine to be the unmarked state of a human noun and feminine marked state.[45]

For this reason; Julia Stanley argued that there is in fact grammatical gender in English:[46] one large generic masculine encompassing all words marked as active, powerful and positive, and a small group of specifically feminine words. Any crossing of gender categories must consequently be marked as in 'lady lawyer', or 'male nurse'. The fact that grammatical gender is not simply linked to any physical organic difference allows a marking out of gender categories which both identifies and prescribes gender differences as masculine-active-present versus feminine passive-lack.

183

A similar point was made by Kress and Hodge.[47] Sexual difference is a 'principle internal to language, part of the structure of its "science"'. English may not have the overt gender of Latin and Greek, but it does have 'covert gender'.[48] This can be seen in the fact that even in English masculine pronouns are considered appropriate for some nouns (doctor, lawyer, etc.) and feminine for others (ship, car, etc.). This is not arbitrary. The choice of pronouns is governed by perceived analogies: women, like cars or ships, are possessed and controlled. By examining adjectives appropriate for women and those appropriate for men, one can, Kress and Hodge argued, set up an 'abstract scheme' for femininity with the defining characteristics: -active, + weak, + obedient, + pleasing, + caring. Such a system of covert gender may be even more coercive than a system of overt gender. Because it operates unconsciously and is not subject to critical awareness, inconsistencies, such as between an active caring and passivity, can be ignored. In systems of overt gender, inconsistencies result in surface irrationalities that demand attention. Given a gendered language, women have two choices: they may refuse standard usage and insist on an inhuman, inarticulate femininity; or they may as speakers accept an always defective feminine humanity. These choices are the only ones available.

The conclusion drawn by feminists such as Kramarae was that masculinist ideology is embedded in language. The lexicon is a 'structure organised to glorify maleness and ignore, trivialize, or derogate, femaleness'.[49] Not only is the master-slave conflict institutionalised in the oppositional structure of linguistic meaning, but again the male element is the master-presence against which a female lack is defined. Any female victory then must amount to a taking of phallic power, a victory which can never, by definition, be feminist, but only constitute a masked assertion of essentially masculine power. The more seemingly radical alternative that the feminine becomes the presence against the masculine lack, is equally illusory. Although such a reversal, pace Lacan, might be logically possible,[50] it could do no more than again put femininity in the masculine position, and so perpetuate sexist society.

It is not surprising that a woman would have trouble finding her voice in such a language. No coining of new words or editing out of old can give her eloquence. The language described by Lacan is not a transparent medium available to any determined speaker; the position of speaker is itself sexed. Although linguists, in their discovery of formal grammatical and semantic models, ignore the subject who speaks in favour of synchronic structural relations within languages, feminists called attention to the kind of speaker linguistics presupposed. To speak is to be able to use 'I' even when the 'I' or speaker is not made explicit. Although linguistics cannot deal with such a subject or subject place, it remains as the ideal speaker whose grammatical intuitions are encoded in semantic and grammatical theory. The position of this speaking subject, the centre around which semantic distinctions revolve, is already fixed in language. There can be no illusion, then, that sexist use of language can be avoided by a non-sexist speaker. There is no pre-existing speaker who *uses* language; instead, a place is already determined in language for the entry of the speaking subject, a place that, according to Lacan and, apparently, according to semantic theory, is masculine.

Masculine bias goes further than even vocabulary or grammar, elements of which can be seen as eliminable archaic features of language. If the function of speaking is male, then so is the constitution of our identity as speaking subjects: 'It is in and through language that man constitutes himself as a *subject*, because language alone establishes the concept of "ego" in reality . . .'[51] If this observation of the linguistic Benveniste is correct, and subjectivity is shaped in language, then it is not surprising that a woman would find it difficult to become such a speaking subject. Language is not just a functional ordering of sounds; it is by way of that ordering that one comes to have an identity. If that identity is masculine, then a woman's identity will always be problematic. More is at stake than the linguist's attempt to formalise gender in rules of agreement. To obey such rules is to be a subject, and that subject, that 'I', is male.

In order to understand how such an identity is constituted, Benveniste examined the linguistic feature of 'person', ignored by structural linguists. The ability to pose oneself as subject cannot depend on any pre-linguistic 'feeling' of self. Consciousness of self is only possible in contrast, by way of an opposition between an 'I' and a 'you'. The 'I' or ego always stands in a special relationship to a 'you'. There is no equality or symmetry, the 'I' is 'transcendent' and allows a speaker 'to appropriate to himself an entire language'.[52] According to Benveniste, there can be no more equality between an 'I' and a 'you' than there can be between 'man' and 'woman'; and 'I' always has a position of superiority with regard to the 'you'. The function of 'I' is to order all language around one centre; all demonstratives and personal pronouns relate to the 'I' that speaks. To become a speaker it is necessary to become this subject formed in the confrontation between 'I' and 'you'. The woman's otherness, her status of the 'you' or 'other', or the 'it', has been prepared in the very function of speech. She is the other, the one addressed, ordered, constrained; or she is the 'it', the woman-object-nature on which language makes its ordering marks. She is not, the appropriating, masterful 'I', with his compliment of masculine pronouns, hierarchicalised meaning, overt or covert gender.

The psychogenesis of this masculine 'I' was described by Lacan. In the mirror stage, the child for the first time experiences himself as a unity, and as a unity that he can control. This sense of mastery is further confirmed in the playing of the Fort/Da game as the child learns to control the frustrating appearances and disappearances of the mother by playing a symbolic game with himself. The 'I' who is the 'I' whom I see in the glass becomes the 'I' detached from his bodily dependence on his mother and his feeling self. This is a process from which the woman, identified with the feminine maternal, is excluded. She can only mimic a man; as speaker she is always a sham, an interloper, someone who cannot know what she is saying.

Derrida: the purveyor of hope

According to Lacan, a woman must either submit to phallic order or lapse into feminine inarticulateness. However, an alternative was soon suggested by another French philosopher, Jacques Derrida, who also laid claim to be the theoretician for French feminism. Lacan, Derrida argued, was no 'ladies' man', but represented the patriarchal authority that feminism must seek to subvert. In 'The purveyor of truth',[53] Derrida exposed Lacan's version of analysis as prescriptive rather than descriptive.

Derrida agreed with Lacan's claim that the unconscious is a language, but unconscious language, he argued, is not structured around the self-present symbol of the phallus: language is instead a kind of writing, a series of graphic differences or traces. Freud realised this himself, in his 'analogue of the magic writing pad', the child's device where one may write on a surface with a pointed instrument and then erase that surface by pulling off an upper sheet of plastic. Psychic content or memory is like such a writing pad. The marks of experience remain on the underlying surface of the unconscious even when the conscious is erased. The trace of the unconscious imprint left on the writing pad of the mind is non-hierarchical, composed of repetitions, differences, deferrals in time. Language, conscious or unconscious, is only 'a topography of traces', 'a map of frayings'.[54]

The hierarchical oppositions that supposedly order meaning around presence and absence are for Derrida metaphysical. The idea of a privileged presence of phallic identity is linked to the supposed authority of the spoken voice. Speech can then be related to a conceptual order or system of meaning, which is supposed to exist independently of language and provide the basis for linguistic truth. The authority of the self-present voice, Derrida argued, must be ultimately theological, an appeal to a God, or Logos, who embodies absolute presence and absolute truth. Once such a God is rejected, speaking is not revelatory of any transcendent truth but is only a kind of phonemic graphism not prior to or essentially different from writing. It is not that an authoritarian ordering of language cannot or does not exist. Psychoanalysts, linguists and grammarians play a major role in maintaining conceptual order.[55] Hierarchical oppositions do form the semantic matrix of thought and cannot be simply removed or refuted. If the premises of a supposed truth are criticised by way of logical argument and an alternate 'truth' asserted which is more consistent with the facts, in both cases the metaphysical 'presence' of truth is reaffirmed.

Instead of traditional philosophical criticism, Derrida proposed a more sophisticated 'deconstruction'. The conceptual order supposedly discovered by semanticists, by philosophers, or by Lacan, must be disordered, rearranged, unbalanced. Derrida suggested a variety of 'strategies'. The hierarchical opposition can be turned on its head and the supposedly present term exposed as really a lack against which the other term is defined. This is not to establish a new hierarchy but to unbalance and subvert the old, showing that what is in question is not dominance, but a two-way relation between terms. The deconstructor may read between the lines of a text and discover ways in which the author subverts his or her position in asides or in 'supplements'.[56] Again this must be distinguished from the philosophical technique of finding inconsistencies in an opponent's arguments. The deconstructor may also take an apparent opposition and show that the supposedly opposed terms both represent the lack of presence and

the desire for something lacking which are the basis of signification. For Derrida, there is no question of finding the meaning,
the truth, or even any author's intended meaning in a text.
Released from any such project, the reader/thinker can proceed
to explore an infinite chain of textual differences and associations
in which there is no canonical order. In this process new meanings emerge and different logics not based on 'is' and 'is not' but
subject to ambiguity and paradox.

For Derrida, there is no unified subject from which any
authoritative semantic ordering can issue. Lacan had shown the
subject's origin in the splitting of the self between an imaginary
'I' and a feeling 'me'. The self, Lacan argued, was neither, but
was instead the tenuous middle ground between the two. Nevertheless, with the Law of the Father, Lacan restored a unity to the
self, a unity supposedly necessary for rational communicable
thought and based on the self-presence of phallic authority. This
unity, Derrida claimed, is the imposition of a theological self-
presence. Lacan's split subject remains split. Once rational self-
presence is unmasked, the deceptive unity disappears and with it
the imposition of patriarchal authority.

Derrida identified the unmasking of that authority with
femininity. In the 'Double session',[57] he used feminine
'hymenal' imagery to describe language without Lacan's 'phallo-
gocentricism'. Language, like the hymen, is both a veil and a
closeness, both sacred and vicious, both desire and fulfilment.
Language, as hymen, is a kind of ideal orgasm, the 'supreme
spasm'. In language it can seem as though desire is fulfilled, that
the difference between the object and expression has been
eliminated. The hymen is the dream of this fusion, but the
hymen is also a barrier or difference. There is no phallic self-
presence, no oppositional logic; instead the hymen is both a
difference and a celebrated union, a marriage and the barrier to
marriage. Instead of a simple (+) or (–), the hymen illustrates
a 'lexical richness', a 'sedimentation' that produces layers of
often contradictory meaning. The hymen is literally a lack of
communication, but that lack of communication allows a meta-
phorical fusion or marriage. The hymen is both virginity and
sexual intercourse. The hymen is a kind of 'hymn' in which
differences are 'unfolded' without oppositions and without hierarchy as the hymen puts contraries into confusion and at the
same time holds itself as the barrier between them. The hymen
is 'between', emblematic of the dual relationship between the

male and female 'of murder and of love'.

Hymenal language requires a new feminine 'style'. In *Spurs: Nietzsche's style*,[58] Derrida explored Nietzsche's misogyny,[59] and surprisingly uncovered an affirmation of the feminine. The women that Nietzsche seems to insult constantly are, according to Derrida's eccentric reading, the key to Nietzsche's rejection of rationalism.[60] If Nietzsche had simply launched a critique of Western philosophy and Christianity, he would have ended with only a 'clamourous declaration of the antithesis'.[61] Instead, what is important is Nietzsche's style which constitutes a kind of parody, or miming. Around Nietzsche's 'heterogeneous', often contradictory comments on women always plays the question of truth. Women reject 'phallogocentristic' truth and so are false. Women assert a different revealed truth to be glimpsed at a distance. Women represent the position beyond this opposition from which there is no truth. The latter position, feminine though it may be and acknowledged as such by Nietzsche, Derrida claimed as the true Nietzschean position. 'This knowledge is part of my Dionysian patrimony. Who knows: Maybe I am the first psychologist of the eternally feminine,'[62] Derrida quoted Nietzsche as affirming.

By adopting a 'feminine style' himself, Derrida claimed to be able, unlike philosophers such as Heidegger, to approach Nietzsche 'without prejudice'. Once there is no truth, he can read, 'freed from the horizon of the meaning or truth of being'.[63] For the deconstructing reader, assertive content is dissolved into style — a multilayered, self-referring, proliferation of images. Truth/falsity, veiled/unveiled, hidden/revealed — all become part of a play of meaning in which the priority of any term can be uncentred to reveal the mastery of its opposite. Although possession and mastery, always sexual according to Derrida,[64] still provide the structure of language as symbolic exchange and 'the history (of) truth (is) a process of appropriation',[65] that 'propriety' can be interpreted and subverted. This can be done from the standpoint of femininity. The woman as the gift, as what is exchanged, is outside appropriation. For her there is no 'the truth' and no 'the woman' either: instead there is a multiplicity of meanings, a withdrawal, an ambiguous distance. A woman seduces from a distance. In feminine fashion, Nietzsche's style also kept its distance from any asserted truth by the use of breaks, hyphens and quotation marks. Nietzsche did not, argued Derrida with approval, make the mistake of the dogmatic philosopher who would take the truth or the woman by storm, showing that he understands neither.[66]

Derrida's 'feminine' is not any essential female nature or feminine sexuality. This would only constitute another 'essentialising fetish'. Instead it is a certain kind of 'operation' which, he asserted, 'we ourselves' [i.e. men] — who we? — might learn from her'.[67] Derrida's feminine is not feminist. To be feminine is to realise that any 'feminist' reversal of power only deprives a woman of her 'dissimulating' power and reinstates phallocentrism only now with the 'rowdy student as master'. Derrida's feminine operator avoids these feminist mistakes. Instead of claiming maternal power, she/he plays with symbolic structures. She amuses herself, and 'as she plays she is gleefully anticipating her laughter, her mockery of man'.[68] She does not reverse or reject oppositions, but finds an anchor in their conflatibility. These techniques are opposed to the 'feminism' derided by Nietzsche, in which the woman becomes the man and lays claim to truth and objectivity. 'Feminism has no style', any more than Nietzsche's sterile, pompous scientist has style.

Derrida agreed with Lacan that femininity and masculinity are embedded in the meaning of words; however, not only is there a way for the woman cleverly to subvert the hierarchical order of the symbolic, but she may also amuse herself in the process. He agreed with Lacan that there is no escape from the signifying chain, but showed how a feminine operator could interrupt the order of that chain to create new 'folds' of meaning and new relations. This operation was not confined to women; certainly Derrida and Nietzsche were to be its practitioners. However, women could take heart. Derrida seemed to offer an alternative to feminine inarticulateness and Lacan's phallocentric language in a new kind of feminist textual practice. Not attempting the impossible task of speaking outside established meanings or remaining restricted within the conceptual perimeters of patriarchal thought, a woman writer could 'displace' patriarchal thought. Derrida offered strategies for use within the 'text of patriarchy', mining the gaps and inconsistencies in phallocentric thought and emulating deconstruction's dazzling feints and reversals to decentre the stability of the Father.[69] In the silence that resulted, women could begin to speak with their ally Derrida, to 'make our voices resonate throughout the corridors in order to make up for the breakup of presence'.[70]

Derrida's approach to language avoided any naive feminist

expectation either that the token inclusion of women could bring about significant conceptual change, or that legislated language reform could ensure social reform. The feminine writer would not phallically campaign for the deletion of offensive surface constructions but would attempt to derange the syntactical and semantic structures which generated those constructions. This new feminist 'textual practice' is best exemplified in the work of two French writers, Luce Irigaray and Hélène Cixous. In the work of both it is possible to see Derrida's influence.

Firstly, both saw writing, as opposed to speech, as the privileged place for feminist confrontation and discovery. Speech, according to Derrida, was the supposed bearer of phallic truth; writing's claim to truth had always been secondary, based on the claim to represent a self-present voice. When the philosophy of presence was deconstructed, speech was revealed as itself only writing — a series of graphic phonemic traces, of differences, repetitions and deferals which only have meaning inter-textually.[71] Irigaray and Cixous joined with Derrida in rejecting logocentrism. In her 'The laugh of the Medusa',[72] Cixous called for an '*écriture feminine*', a feminine writing that would free women from masculine language governed by the phallus. Alone, faced with only a blank sheet of paper, the woman writer would escape constraints of logic and 'propriety'. Freed from the pressure and self-consciousness inevitable in any actual speech situation, her words would flow. 'To write is always to break the value of exchange that maintains speech on its rail, to have super-abundance and uselessness play their savage role.'[73] In writing a woman can defy the role assigned to her in the symbolic and think 'between' the words not bound by the plus' and minus' of oppositional categories.

Luce Irigaray also called for an 'écriture de la femme'[74] (woman's writing) that would be an 'excess' or 'derangement' of the male logic in which women are always a lack or an inverted reproduction of a masculine subject. Specifically in writing, masculine logic, based on visible form, can be questioned. A woman's 'style' will expose established categories to go beyond critique and beyond the analysis of patriarchy to 'destroy its discursive functioning'.[75] This can only be accomplished in a certain 'travail du language' (work of language). If feminists attempt to analyse femininity in the old theoretical language, they remain bound by patriarchal thought where the woman is the subject/object of research. Instead, 'a feminine operation'[76] is necessary to 'jam theoretical machinery itself, to suspend its pretension to the production of truth, and to a univocal sense'.[77]

Reflecting on her re-reading of Freud and the philosophers of the Western tradition in *Speculum*, Irigaray described her method: what is necessary is to institute a kind of purposeful mimiticism.[78] There is, she agreed with Derrida, no quick way out of patriarchal symbolic systems. However, in a conscious re-telling and re-reading of the core texts of patriarchy, a woman can turn submission to affirmation. She can play with the text, and in this playing, in this 'ludic effect', maintain a kind of independence from masculine categories. Irigaray's questioning of Freud in *Speculum* is an example of such a feminine operation. She did not criticise Freudian theory from a superior theoretical position, but rather, traced the course of Freudian thought in all its heterogeneity, complexity and diversity. She did not reduce Freud's argument to a simplistic logic of presence in order to refute it, but exposed the tangles, reading between the lines, listening to tone, nuance, to what is not said. She questioned the *functioning of the 'grammar'* of each figure of discourse, its syntactical laws or necessities, its imaginary constructs, its metaphoric networks, and also its silences.[79] The writing 'de la femme', Irigaray believed, would be able to 'put to the fire' the fetish words of patriarchy in a style always fluid, never allowing itself to be defined and restricted, never consisting in taking a fixed position.

Cixous also agreed with Derrida that masculine authority is constituted in hierarchical oppositions. Symbolic meaning, structured around the primary opposition male/female, and therefore around the phallus, ensures that what is male is always positive and what is female is negative. Thus, logocentrism, or the philosophical assertion of self-present, self-evident truth is a mask for male domination. Cixous gave as illustration in *La jeune née* the following set of oppositions:

> Activity/Passivity
> Sun/Moon
> Culture/Nature
> Day/Night
> Father/Mother
> Head/Heart
> Intelligible/Sensible
> Logos/Pathos[80]

The masculine/feminine contrast supplies the underlying symbolism for the whole set. It is no accident that linguistics chooses to illustrate semantic structure with the example of father/mother. Ordering means law, Cixous maintained, and the law 'organises the thinkable' into 'couples'. Then all relations, whether religious, familial, political or linguistic, can be 'thought' in the same way. Cixous's way with such oppositions was, like Irigaray's, no simple reversal: instead, she probed deeply into oppositional thought, deconstructing its apparent purity and simplicity. If there is to be paternal authority versus female submission, then there will be conflict between different fathers, different authorities; father will turn against son, master against slave, to create hierarchies among men. In this ensuing war, woman will be forgotten. She will drop out, although something of her must always remain, as the necessary maternal backdrop for male exploits.[81]

Irigaray identified the oppositional contrast between masculine presence and feminine absence with the subject/object opposition foundational in Western philosophy. The objectification of the feminine, Irigaray agreed with Lacan, is the 'hypothetical guarantee of all irreducible constitution of the object',[82] and therefore of discourse itself. The linguistic categories of masculine subject and feminine object are reflected in philosophy, the masculine subject becoming the Sun around which the feminine Earth revolves.[83] Probing this metaphor further, Irigaray asked what would happen if the Earth moved itself, turned on its own axis. That would mean that the feminine may have a kind of 'self-knowledge' which does not depend on the other for a foothold. The object Earth would then no longer be so inert, or so dumbly resistant and the hierarchy of subject and object collapses. The feminine was to be an opposing object perfectly reflecting masculine knowledge, but even a mirror has its own characteristics. Seen as dependent on an object, the supposed dominance of the masculine subject falters. If its supposedly stable, inert object should begin to speak or move, its very identity is undermined.

Following Derrida, Irigaray did not criticise the opposition of subject/object as unfounded or even as sexist; she deconstructed it, teasing out implications to show how the surface logic conceals hidden complications. Like Derrida in his study of Nietzsche, she concentrated not on the apparently important foreground elements in philosophical theory, but on the assumed emptiness, or silence, which is the backdrop for theory.

To insist also and deliberately on the 'whites' of discourse which recall the places of (the woman's) expulsion, spacings which assure in their silent plasticity the cohesion, articulation, the coherent expansion of established forms. To reinscribe them in gaps, otherwise and elsewhere than there where they are expected, in ellipses and eclipses which deconstruct the logical grids of the reader/writer, derails his reason, troubles his view until there results, at least, an incurable double vision.[84]

The goal was not an unsatisfactory reversal of male/female positions, but a radical decentring of established meaning.

Like Derrida, Irigaray proposed alternate feminine symbolism for language. Again the choice was sexual — instead of Derrida's hymen, the female genitals. Phallic language is based on a semantic economy of 'has' and 'has not', an endless repetition of the same, the priority of a repeatable visible form. A vaginal symbolism, Irigaray argued, would produce a different economy of meaning, a different syntax. 'Women's desire most likely does not speak the same language as men's desire, and it probably has been covered by the logic that has dominated the West since the Greeks.'[85] From the phallic point of view, the vagina is a 'hole', a flaw. Seen, however, as a founding symbol, a new configuration of meaning appears. The 'one' of the male subject becomes the two of the vaginal lips, constantly in touch with each other in an interaction in which the two are not separated by negation but interact and merge. The vagina is neither one or two, but two in one, unlike the unitary phallus that can only repeat itself. The pleasure or the meaning represented is not unitary, but diffuse, diversified, multiple, decentred. Although from a phallic perspective 'temperamental, incomprehensible, perturbed, capricious', a vaginal language would in fact require a different kind of listening to be understood:

> One must listen to her differently in order to hear an 'other meaning' which is constantly in the process of weaving itself, at the same time ceaselessly embracing words and yet casting them off to avoid becoming fixed, immobilized.[86]

Instead of the relation of identity, vaginal symbolism suggests contiguity. The law of non-contradiction does not rule because the point is not a repetition of the same. Asked for clarification, a woman cannot answer; she has already moved on, or turned her back on her own thought, in a kind of vaginal 'fold' within herself.

In this feminine operation, this play with signs, is produced a textual *jouissance*, a sensuous pleasure forbidden by patriarchal language.[87] Feminists took delight in discomforting, decentring, deconstructing masculinist dogma. *Jouissance* came as the pent up energy repressed was released in a rejection of patriarchal law. A restoration of this 'feminine pleasure', unspeakable within phallic language, was promised by Derrida as a result of the feminine operation of *Spurs*. Both writer and reader would experience a kind of delicious *frisson* as oppositional purity was interrupted and grammatical rules broken. *Jouissance* would bring the liberating realisation that conceptual order is not sacred but that a plurality of meanings can be spun out from the signifying chain. Pleasure is identical with the linguistic function itself, described by Derrida as a play which brings about 'nominal effects' — the relatively unitary or atomic structures we call names, plus chains of substitutions for names. This play can then be 'affirmed with a certain laughter and a certain dance'. Derrida's 'grammatology' becomes Nietzsche's 'joyful science', always anathema to logocentrism which maintains itself by rigid adherence to canonical truth.

At the same time there were differences between Derrida's feminine operation and feminist textual practice. The starting point of feminist play with the text was not a theoretical interest in the nature of language, but the painful and interested recognition of women's oppression; a feminist deconstruction of discursive functioning had a practical and not a theoretical aim. In her strategy of mimeticism, Irigaray's goal was not, as it sometimes seemed to be for Derrida, the liberating naughtiness of play itself. Instead, she probed for the role that women play in language as the object 'mother-matter-nature' which must 'nourish' male theorising, but which, at the same time, must be put down or rejected. The realisation of this function put the woman 'elsewhere',[88] able to deconstruct but also experience what is inexpressible in phallic language. Deconstruction was only a preliminary to the main task of the woman writer/thinker — the forbidden expression of her femininity. This would require what Derrida's metalinguistics could not allow — a language in which a feminine presence can make itself known.

The woman-text

In the foundational text of deconstruction, *Of grammatology*, Derrida rejected as metaphysical the idea that a lost presence could be restored to language. His principle target was Rousseau's attack on alienated language which Derrida took as reflective of the dodges, ambiguities and ambivalence inevitable in thought about language. French feminists revived Rousseau's distinction between rational language and expressive language. Rousseau's languages of the North and South became the languages of the sexes — patriarchal language dominated by the masculine element and a woman's language expressing the material maternal presence that patriarchal language suppressed. The purpose of feminist deconstruction was not to affirm a kind of imaginary sexual play at of the heart of language, but to rediscover what both rational ordering and the play of differences must presuppose — a material base or footing that makes imaginary play or ordering possible. If rejection of the natural or feminine is constitutive of the symbolic, *écriture féminine* would reappropriate the deleted feminine presence. The mirroring, the redoubling, the refolding of Derridean representation were as much to be broken through as the Lacanian symbolic, as a feminist Alice proceeded behind/through the looking glass of language.[89]

The discovery of a feminine presence, always necessary but always repressed, will allow the woman thinker/speaker to recover her own 'auto-affection',[90] and with it a new way of relating to herself and others. This different way of being and speaking is not dependent on any redoubling of images, no matter how complex or devious. Nor must femininity remain in place as the lack of presence that affirms a derivative masculine presence and as the 'support, more or less complacent, for the acting out of the fantasies of men'.[91] What is in question is not a seamless web of graphic textual relations, but exploitation and victimisation. As exploited, rather than as a motif in the various designs of textuality, femininity becomes a liberatable presence beyond the oppositions of patriarchal language. The oppositions allow an exchange between men, but there must be something to exchange. If language is oppressive action in the world, the opposition between masculine and feminine is no longer only the dominant strand in a conceptual network that can be rearranged but not escaped. These 'objects' of exchange are real, exist in a feminine 'elsewhere' beyond the 'text' of patriarchy; this 'elsewhere' is not the necessary redoubling contrast of an equally dependent opposite, but a place from which women can begin to speak in a new way. 'And if the "merchandise" refuses to go to the "market"?'[92] Irigaray asks. The result is not a trickster's change of tactic, but an undermining change in the speech situation. Irigaray thus proposed what Derrida proscribes, an escape from the matrix of established meanings.

Cixous also attempted to restore an expressible feminine presence. In *Angst*,[93] she described the agony of the male-identified woman whose existence is defined by men. Her feminine subject is possessed by the desire to be saved by a deified male lover, dependent on scraps of his attention in letters and phone calls, incapable of being alone, terrified of abandonment. Writing provides the entry to a new life, an escape from this masculine-defined woman

> already written, caught in the old book where it is said to each woman: You will not live. You will give life and you will pour out love, and they will be given back to you a hundredfold in hate and in folly. You will give body and it will be given back to you as absence.[94]

This, however, is an 'old' book. It is not necessary to continue to live by it. The mere fact of the survival of the woman in *Angst* through all her hate and hysteria is proof to Cixous that there is another kind of woman to be discovered. This woman had to have existed before; a woman

> committed to the affirmation of life, decisive, a thought without model, without peers, without master, without response, capable of thwarting the work of death, of returning the negative to its impasse, . . . not a fantasy, not a '*lettre*', but a real, always present in the present, always at the same time three lives in advance.[95]

It is this real woman, no 'letter' or sign, whose search Cixous documents in *Illa*.[96] At first there are no traces of her; she has disappeared 'through a fissure of time' as utterly as Persephone was swallowed up, abducted by Hades to the Underworld. The searching woman is in the position of the despairing, grieving mother Demeter searching for her disappeared daughter; but even mythology can give no substantial clues, only faint echoes and visions of the lost feminine.

The woman/writer must venture beyond the categories male/female that structure language, beyond the stability of a subject who has found herself with reference to these categories. The woman in *Illa* hesitates before the door marked 'Men' and 'Women'.[97] She opens the first door, the men's, she passes to the next, opens it. 'Same game, same place.' There is no substantial difference marked in sexual difference; one sex is the reverse, the lack, of the other, but beyond such empty oppositions Cixous searches for a 'language that speaks before speech',[98] 'an index of truth on the other side of words',[99] a meaning which is not expressible in articulated speech but is heard as a faint 'bubbling' or 'stammering'.

Once such a rhythm is heard, the way is still by no means easy. The more the woman searches, the more she may find herself wandering, at a distance. She may only 'augment the thickness of distances, the luxuriance of labryinths'.[100] She may find herself lost in a Derridean chain of signification, lost in a wilderness of signs far from any real presence, 'journeying along language, lost in its mirages. Each sentence seems the last curtain, but never is, as curtains rise on curtains, veils on veils.'[101] Nevertheless some flavour, some faint melody leads the woman on past this 'cortege of thoughts'. She will 'bite that tongue with her very own teeth to invent for herself a language she can get inside of'.[102] This 'inside' must be outside the text of patriarchy.[103]

The exit for Cixous is not to be found in tricks of representation[104] or in a jubilatory play with categories, but in a different kind of experience, of the body and of other bodies. The discovery of the feminine is a discovery of the female body, and a discovery of the body's relation to other bodies. One must 'write the body', Cixous urged, echoing Rousseau's yearning for a sensuous language. In the 'Laugh of the Medusa', Cixous described such a rediscovery of body:

> By writing her self, the woman will return to the body which has been more than confiscated from her, which has been turned into the uncanny stranger on display — the acting or dead figure, which so often turns out to be the nasty companion, the cause and locus of inhibitions.[105]

With the female body is discovered female sexuality, the female drives, the female organs which we have been taught to denegrate and ignore. In order to discover this real female body, codes must be broken, including in a defiant reference to Derrida, 'the one that laughs at the very idea of pronouncing the word "silence", the one that, aiming for the impossible, stops short before the word "impossible" and writes it as the end'.[106] Women are, Cixous claimed, bodies in a sense that men are not. It is women who allow drives to surface in hysteria, who allow their feelings to colour or distort thought. Men, on the other hand, sublimate and control their impulses. Women have never lost touch with their bodies and so constitute the dangerous presence that men need but must always master. The woman-text will take on the shape of a woman's body. Like an egg, it is not closed but endless. There is no beginning and no end; instead, the text at some point leaves off, while the thought in the reader is to go on. Just as the female body gives birth, so the female text 'sends off' the reader. The text does not master material, it is a 'body that overflows, disgorges, vomiting as opposed to a masculine incorporation'.[107]

For Cixous the discovery is not just of one's own body but also of other bodies. Language with its matrix of categories can be a barrier to understanding of the external world, of what is there before our physical eyes. In a series of mystical passages in *Illa*, Cixous described this experience of things, an experience which does not attempt to master or to classify, but listens, looks, feels, hears. To speak a rational language is to kill the things, to refuse to hear them or look at them. Another way of seeing can be recovered through the eyes of the child, an innocent seeing-speech before language imposes its categories.

> But I have a childhood who knew. She lived in the Jardin d'Essais. She knows still that which alone I don't know anymore . . . Language recounts to us the walk we are to take before we take it in fact, and we walk in language following its indications.

In contrast to this guided tour, Cixous suggests:

> To enjoy a walk from the high trails to the earth of the Jardin d'Essais, to make one's way with fidelity, according to life and the body, we must leave gently, give the slip to all recommendations, and now live, beginning as it begins,

letting come things which arrive according to their fashion, let the rose make itself felt in the order rose, descend to the garden, drawn, led by the appeal of its freshness, to go down, before knowing the names of streets, but the senses know the way, before proper names and common names, through the perfumes, walking with sandaled feet, in the heavy odors, in the movement of the market.[108]

So Cixous described the experience of the pure child, who has not yet learned the categories of male thought, but who takes in colours, tastes and smells in an ecstatic communion between physical thing and physical body.

In these prescriptions for a new kind of woman-text, Cixous and Irigaray called into question not only particular words or expressions but language in its deepest functioning: the grammatical requirement that sentences be constructed according to rule, semantic well-formedness, and predication itself as an act of alienated mastery and appropriation. They saw rationally ordered language not as an instrument for communication whose neutrality could be restored with proper revisions, but as the embodiment of sexist theory. With this realisation, the distinctions between a critique of patriarchy, a critique of patriarchal thought, and a critique of patriarchal language were dissolved. Any critique of patriarchy or patriarchal thought must also be a critique of language. Furthermore, any critique of language that does not reach the ideological roots of grammatical and semantic functioning must be superficial and in the end impotent to correct the sexism inevitably generated in language. The roots of language are also the roots of science and logic; a critique of language must therefore also be a critique of thought and of knowledge — that is, of philosophy and science. No longer is the goal of feminist theory the right for women to participate politically and economically. If that participation is conducted in and regulated by science and logic, any such achievement must once again signal the downfall of the female race.

Instead Irigaray proposed a speaking of the female-objects among themselves. 'What if the objects began to speak?' These objects would speak not as masculine subjects but from their feminine position as objects, as 'merchandises'. In her 'Mechanique de fluids',[109] Irigaray tried to explain the syntax of such a speaking. It would be a language that flowed, with no rigid concepts or fixed senses to interrupt that flow. Two would not necessarily mean two ones, but categories and boundaries would be shifting and flexible. Because there would be no simple identity, so there would be no contradiction. Just as woman's sexuality cannot be contained in a single organ, so a woman's speech would encompass all plurality. A logic based on atomic bits, whether ideas, semantic components, or mathematical entities, could never represent this flow that is characteristic of nature and of bodily experience. A woman's language would not seek to project on nature an alien rigidity that could only, in the end, represent itself, but would expressively flow without closure or boundary.

Such a language, Irigaray acknowledged, has affinities with the language of dreams. She identified a woman's language with the unconscious, the excess whose repression is necessary so that the conscious can be defined. There is, she argued, a 'double syntaxe', of conscious rational thought and the unconscious feminine repressed.[110] A woman's language has something in common with the breakthrough of the unconscious in the deviant language of psychotics or hysterics. Although such language is symptomatic of the woman's enforced silence, it has the same 'gestuality' and expressiveness that would characterise the language of a woman speaking in her own tongue.[111] Dream language also belongs on the feminine side of the 'double syntax' as in dreams, figures and images are not ordered by logic. Later the dreamer may be 'seduced' into imposing a rational explanation, a theory of dreams that will represent the dream content in the other, masculine syntax.[112]

A feminine language would offer no 'discourse', adopt no coherent strategy of argumentation. It would offer no theories, no new methods of research. It could not constitute a 'practique' or a 'politique'; any political praxis would be 'masculine through and through'. The woman speaker would not propose a political theory or any canonical agenda for feminist revolution. This would be impossible without theorising and establishing conceptual objects. No feminist 'theory' can be articulated in a woman's language: to think so would be to risk the danger of an unconscious importation of the masculine into feminine thought.

This 'position' [of not developing a politique] is explained by the difficulties that women encounter in making themselves understood in situations already determined in and by a society which at one time uses them and excludes them, and which continues especially to ignore the specificity of their 'revendications' while at the same time adopting certain of their themes, indeed their slogans.[113]

Liberalism might espouse women's rights, Marxism might include women in the labour force, psychoanalysis might show how femininity is not biological, but the theorising male subject is still always present, constructing the logic of his politics. Now women will speak with their own syntax, with their own voice, and outside any politics.

If Irigaray was the theoretician of such a woman's language, then Cixous was its practitioner. Her search for the disappeared feminine was not pursued by way of any theory or academic scholarship. She produced no treatise on femininity: femininity would always escape any attempt at definition. Instead she pursued a female voice, a female speaking, singing, chanting, that has been silenced by male language and that makes no sense according to male reason. It is a voice that will be able to express the anguish of the captured female body in *Angst*, as well as the desperation of the woman freed but surrounded by male thought and institutions in *Illa*. Cixous's texts do not provide a theory or a sequential argument, they do not disprove male theses on women: instead, they struggle to speak a certain way.

Like Irigaray, Cixous rejected the hierarchical oppositions upon which semantic order is based in favour of a plurality of meaning. The style of *Illa* is exemplary. Sentences are not structured grammatically, but are more often fragmentary, spaced by the passing of the breath, and therefore by feeling rather than by grammatical law. Words and thoughts are expressed as they come to mind, not according to any logic. No unitary voice holds the argument together but a variety of voices intermingle, transform, and shift without warning. No thought is complete; instead, thinking goes on until, by often tortuous associations, it takes another turning. There are no logical divisions, no 'coupures' of the text.

Cixous carries on a never-ending interrogation, of herself, of the text, of other texts, of friends, of historical and mythological figures. Nor does this questioning proceed from any stable position as would a critique. The questioner himself is questioned in a complicated weaving of transformations, voices, and associations. Although Cixous admitted that a man could write in this feminine style,[114] in fact few men, she maintained, would be brave enough. Men always have something to gain by sustaining the established order and hierarchy of meaning. Women, on the other hand, not only have nothing to lose, but their desire is in fact endless and plural. Although she may learn to function rationally, a woman will not like it and where she succeeds in expressing herself will always produce a free-flowing writing without rational contours.

This writing is a writing close to the voice.[115] It is paradoxically in 'l'écriture féminine' that a woman will find her voice, Cixous argued, in reversal of the Derridean discovery of writing or graphic formalism in spoken language. In a woman's writing will be heard the rhythm of the felt expression and the rush of breath which will make the text 'pant', shaken with cries.[116] The voice will be heard that cries out the body's pains and joys, a kind of singing flesh that existed before patriarchal law, before the 'breath was cut by the symbolic'. In each woman sings the first love without name',[117] says Cixous in a Rousseauean celebration of a language of the South, born of love and song, passionate, warm, not yet solidified in the logic of the practical masculine North.

There can be no logic in such a language. Senses of words that are the most opposite will be united, linkages will be made and unmade, a thing can be thought along with its contrary, without one being excluded.[118] It is not any conceptual order that gives substance to such a language, but the words themselves. Cixous dwells on the flavour, on the sounds of words, on the way they feel on the tongue and strike the ear. This writing is not visual but tactile, as the writer/reader savours the substance of the living words. Cixous's childhood garden is a way to approach such a writing. To attempt to fit the garden into any classificatory scheme, to be a botanist, would be to fail to grasp it at all, would be to kill it. The garden must be allowed to express itself. The word 'frui' comes to Cixous, the result not of study but, in her words, 'hatched' on her lips and in the feel of this word is the speech of the garden: '"Frui" is the noise which a buttercup exhales towards the light. "Frui" is one of those prim-words, especially yellow or white, which arrives sooner than any thought, and dazzles our mouth.'[119]

This tactile appreciation of the colours, shapes and sounds of words returns the writer to the things themselves. In names there is revelation. In the sound of 'panther', for example, Cixous was able to hear how the animal walks, to hear the 'music of her paws', to taste the 'chantory vibration of her allure'.[120] Even in the names of friends, Cixous discovered a tactile access to the person herself, beyond rational assessment. An example is the Brazilian writer, Clarice Lispector, whom Cixous very much admires and whose name, like the panther's, enters, leaves, enters. 'Lispector', Cixous maintained, has a colour — orange — which expresses Lispector's voice of clarity and light. The sounds of the name are taken apart by Cixous like a cipher into separate kernels, 'lis, spec, rice, rire, respect, etc.'.[121] In this poetic play with words, in a writing that sensuously lingers on the surface of words, Cixous tried to evoke another, feminine, world.

Certainly the subject who would write such a language is not the unitary, appropriating subject of logical thought. The point of such a writing is not to gain control of material, but to lose control, to allow the words to speak, to allow one's body to speak, to allow things to speak. There is no unitary 'I'; instead, the writer is constantly shaken, traversed by, vulnerable to other voices, other ideas, other writings. Cixous's texts illustrate the result. They are not structured in any sense, there is no ordered centred design, but instead a weaving in which the weaver[122] is guided as much by strands which randomly come to hand as by her own suspect design, whose letting go may in fact be the requirement for her success. Then with no plan, no design, no ending in mind, she writes and as she does the strand of a thought appears, disappears, reappears. The important thing is to keep the writing going, not to stop the loom or the weaving, not to censor, tidy, or edit the thought. When blocks are encountered she does not stop, but somehow moves through, around, not insisting on a truth but moving through the tangle, working it free. Such a procedure is necessary if the truly new feminist thought is to appear, and not the always tempting masculine thought in feminine dress.

There is a price to pay for a definitive break with patriarchal language, a price which was acknowledged by both Irigaray and Cixous. The result of such a separation must be marginality and/or political impotence. A 'parler-entre elles' or 'l'écriture féminine' requires withdrawal from a conceptual universe dominated by men. Cixous's woman writer would shun the academic world where her insights would always be compromised.[123] Nor would she attempt to penetrate commercial publishing where she would be subject to standards set by culture at large. The practitioner of an 'écriture féminine' would write for herself and her friends without the restraints of department review or consumer preference.[124]

For Irigaray participation in the existing political process would require a masculine politique inconsistent with a woman's language. Women must, if they are not to compromise, intervene marginally. The communication between women must take place apart from male-dominated power relations. Until women break their silence and can speak their experience, a politique can too easily turn against them. The speaking of women/objects among themselves is the revolutionary step because their object status is what sustains male hegemony. Therefore, the fact of their exclusion, or their exteriority, should not be ignored or denied. It may in fact constitute the only real possibility for critique as women learn from their position of exteriority to speak a language outside of traditional political theorising and also outside of its 'metaphysical presuppositions'.[125]

This denial of traditional forms of political intervention in favour of a dialogue between women away from seats of power or an 'écriture féminine' practised in a community of women has seemed to other feminists a dangerous rejection of feminist power that threatens to reduce feminism to a position of marginal impotence. *La jeune née* ends with a dialogue between co-authors Clément and Cixous in which Clément expressed some Marxist doubts about the implications of Cixous's style of feminism.[126] She begins by comparing Cixous's half-fictional literary manner to Clément's own discursive demonstration and references to the historical treatment of women. Clément adopted the tone of a teacher, of an authority who transmits ideas, who writes to persuade. Cixous, she suggested, rejects such a taking of linguistic power as masculine mastery of a subject.[127] However, it is not that a woman might 'steal' masculine power; there is no outside position from which such a theft could be conducted. Men and women are in and think within the same cultural system, phallocentric or not: there is no other. To think so is to be 'utopian', to think that one could dream up another world.

Cixous claimed to go behind Lacan's mirror to see that the Law of the Father does not exist. For Clément, however, mastery of the symbolic is the fundamental and necessary presupposition of any knowledge. Knowledge is a 'body of coherent statements whose coherence is not neurotic, does not hold by virtue of a singular fantasy point of view (une partie fantasmatique singulière) of she who transmits it'.[128] When discourse, argumentation and theory are given up, so at the same time is any feminine knowledge. Women are returned to their mythic status as hysterics or sorceresses. In fact such an exclusion is not only a mythic, but also an historical fact with its explanation in economic and social conditions, facts which can be known.[129] Just as Marxists have managed to conceive an economic knowledge uncontaminated by ideology, so could feminists produce a theory of sexism which is not sexist.[130]

The historian Christine Fauré even more specifically criticised 'l'écriture féminine' as historical. The very concrete problems of the 1980s threaten, she maintained, to push the individual 'back into a position of isolated refusal outside the context of his work and his habits of life and thought'. The ominous popularity of conservative policies on women and the family cannot be countered, however, in 'a retreat into aesthetics' where the old stereotypes revived by conservatives are repeated, 'draped in the trappings of a supposedly "feminine" lyricism'.[131] Fauré criticised Irigaray, especially for devaluing the historical, economic and political presence of women in favour of their sexuality and the inner world of their passionate experience. From this perspective there can be no critique of women's past or present condition and no proposal for social change.

This abdication of a position of mastery and retreat from the symbolic order was also criticised by Julia Kristeva. For Kristeva the problem was not a concentration on language instead of historical fact, but a failure to understand how language functions. Giving up the paternal world of stable concepts, women will fail to engage the system at all and will be reduced to self-indulgent confession or a psychotic outpouring of emotion. Neither, she argued, is likely to advance the cause of revolution. The most revolutionary tactics are, she agreed, textual, but should not regressively deny the necessarily alienated function of representation. Nor is a textual revolution to be carried out exclusively or even primarily by women. A 'woman's language' would be a retreat into privatism that leaves linguistic power, whether academic, literary, scholarly, or scientific, as it stands. Feminists who think that they can discard the symbolic must make one of two mistakes: either they uncritically accept some unacknowledged rational order, or they slip into incomprehensible and impotent babbling. At best, the result is a self-indulgent 'expression' that does nothing to challenge the conceptual structures that hold sexism in place, but instead returns women to the banishment of the 'sacrificial contract'. For Kristeva, women's relation to the maternal disadvantages them as textual revolutionaries: either they psychotically reject the symbolic in a regressive attempt to return to the mother, or they desperately assume an always defective identity as women and cling to the traditional roles allotted to them by men. Even as they listen, fascinated, to women's poetry, they either return to a defence of home and family, 'the most solid support of the social order',[132] or they lock themselves up in their feminine identities, becoming: 'militant romantics of the final "cause" to be thus revived, theologians of an inverted humanism rather than its iconoclasts'.[133]

This is a condemnation that, although no names are mentioned, one must assume was aimed at defenders of feminine specificity such as Irigaray and Cixous who, Kristeva charged, wished to create a sacred and secret society of women with its own private language. In contrast Kristeva proposed her perilous, simultaneous, participation in and subversion of symbolic structures. Women must acknowledge the paternal function while at the same time facilitating its breakdown in the maternal semiotic. Patriarchal language must be spoken by the feminist but spoken to be exposed, reconstituted only to be shattered again. 'Jouissance' is not the joy of a communion in which there are no boundaries but the perverse laugh of someone who knows the clay feet of any male idol.

The difference is an important one. If Kristeva is right, rejection of form, whether logical, poetic or social, constitutes self-delusion, if not self-destruction. Although women have a role as the perennial negative outside that will always threaten authoritarian male order, there can never be a feminine victory. Language and culture mean, for men and for women, repression of, but not extinction of, maternal intersubjectivity. Rather than regressively seek to recapture such a communion in uncontrolled outpourings of emotion, women, like men, must escape the maternal and master the symbolic. They must match male theory in all fields; at the same time, they must call attention to theory's unstable beginnings in a symbolic contract sacrificial of the feminine. The political goal of Kristeva's textual practice is not a total escape from paternal authority, but a less repressive variety of symbolic structures in whose authority women as well as men could share.[134]

The history of the signifier

Feminist textual practice provided a rejuvenating antidote to the frustration of feminist projects in the late 1970s. Blocked by an order both conceptual and institutional that always, no matter what job was obtained or law suit won, returned women to traditional roles, conscious of a void in feminist thinking that appeared whenever positive goals rather than negative criticisms were needed, plagued by the paradox of political action that one had to 'beat them at their own game',[135] and frustrated by a resurgence of conservative political and economic policies, women saw in women's writing both freedom from the compromises necessary in any confrontation with male power and also a space in which a feminist future could be imagined outside the distortions of male theorising. Women scholars, with elegance and wit, disrupted the smooth functioning of academic discourse with puns and anagrams. In experimental fiction that transgressed rules of syntax and genre, women writers evoked ecstatic women's communities on mythical Mediterranean islands, and in surreal landscapes of deserted prairies and infernal machines led women warriors to victory.[136] Women poets explored in incantatory verse non-alienated lesbian relations, new images for a woman's body, mythic Amazons and African queens.[137] With this joyful and defiant escape into a world of sensation, imagination, and myth, disappointing struggles for employment rights, marital parity, equal pay, social services, and control of sexuality could seem insignificant attempts to negotiate hopelessly with men in a world that holds it as axiomatic that a woman can have no power.[138] Textual practice produced a garden of the mind, a 'jardin de textes'[139] that would bloom whether there was seed to plant, drought, war, or men in control of the means of production who cared more about their own power than about meeting human needs.

The hope of 'écriture féminine' was that feminism could finally move *beyond* masculine political, economic and psychoanalytic thought. However, once post-structuralist theory identified masculine thought itself with symbolic meaning, the feminine 'beyond' became a vacuum which could only be filled with fragments of poetry and fantasy. What was to have been outside masculinist thought became what rational thought was not — a definition that prescribed a specific place and function for the 'feminine'. Again, femininity was placed within men's accounts of their own conflictual relations.

Lacan's alienated symbolic was a way to escape from the confusions of interdependence. In a doubling of self, the male subject creates the possibility of representing an object and an imaginary universe of symbols. In language he can live another kind of existence regulated by desire that has nothing to do with physical need. Out of this redoubling, a syntax and a semantics can be articulated and an existence created in which women are no longer the needed, but not always available, warmth of a maternal presence, but a sign, in fact *the* sign, that provides the contrast necessary for meaning. Learning to 'signify' is learning a linguistic functioning independent of any actual physical presence or physical need. Now the other can be the 'moi' as opposed to the 'je', an experienced loss in opposition to a stable self image.

Derrida's discussion of the 'dangerous supplements' of writing and masturbation illustrates a similar avoidance of the physical and the maternal. Derrida quoted Rousseau describing masturbation:

> This vice which shame and timidity find so convenient, possesses, besides a great attraction for lively imaginations — that of being able to dispose of the whole sex as they desire, and to make the beauty which tempts them minister to their pleasures, without being obliged to obtain its consent.[140]

Masturbation, the dangerous supplement, reveals the essence of sexuality and of language. What is in question for Rousseau commented Derrida, is the absence of a certain kind of mother, an absence which allows the representation of an imaginary presence. Rousseau, Derrida rightly points out, delights in this sort of flirting sexual presence/absence in which the conflict between his rigid sexual ethics and the perversity of his desires is projected onto an imaginary duality between the woman as unattainable pure virgin and as degraded seductress. In masturbation, this contradictory duality can be realised in fantasy. Writing, Derrida suggested is a similar 'supplement'. If the Lacanian mother is an avoided presence, Derrida's, like Rousseau's, has already disappeared and the poor orphan attempts to conjure up an imaginary substitute. Thereafter, even when Rousseau/Derrida takes a real living woman into his arms, his pleasure must be governed by that imaginary economy.

Derrida's discussion of Pierrot's murder of his wife in *Dissémination* explored similar themes. The 'hymen' is attractive as a metaphor for language because as screen protecting the lover from entering the loved one and, at the same time, as the imaginary marriage, it symbolised for Derrida the complexity of the linguistic function as well as the sexual: 'It is the hymen that desire dreams of piercing, of bursting in an act of violence that is (at the same time or somewhere between) love and murder.'[141] Hence the interesting violence of Pierrot against his wife whom he kills not by any physical violence but by tickling her to death so she dies laughing in a kind of spasm which Derrida related to the spasm of writing. Language and the hymen allow what is impossible in fact: one can love and kill at the same time; one can make of death or of absence the affirmation of presence. In a kind of textual masturbation one can manufacture out of nothing a universe of desire to replace an unattainable or unreliable physical reality. Although Derrida no longer allowed himself the illusion of any self-present Law of the Father, the problematic with which he began was no less masculine.

Kristeva in her account of language, also remained within this problematic. The poet-son must separate from the semiotic-maternal and learn to enter the masculine world of concepts. He must, as son and father, both challenge the father's authority and yet not destroy it; because he is a man himself, paternal authority is his heritage also. 'Father names that which prevents writing and that which gives pleasure in permitting writing.'[142] The questions which Kristeva's semiotics answered were male questions, generated in the conflict between father and son, in which the mother stands apart as the nutritive base without which neither can survive. The 'feminine' has become a female impersonator, the son who in his attachment to his mother and rejection of his father acts out the role of a woman, the son who in his 'homosexuality' expresses both his love for his father and the flaunting of paternal authority.

Neither Lacan, Derrida, nor Kristeva presented their discussions as descriptions of particular kinds of masculine speech or speech strategies. It is not the fragile male ego's fear of or avoidance of women that makes necessary the rejection of physical need, but the founding moment of any linguistic expression. It is not the rebellious son's refusal to become a 'bon père de famille' that intrudes into the symbolic, but the semiotic. At the same time, it is difficult to see how a woman can find a point of reference in Lacan's mirror or Derrida's masturbation. Admirable as such accounts might be as an *exposé* of the necessary solipsism of a certain not unfamiliar male logic, they are not directly related to any problematic with which a woman can easily

210

identify. Daughters do not have to deal *in the same way* as a son with an authoritarian, perhaps violent, father with whom they are supposed to identify. Daughters do not have to resist, as a son does, the feminising 'fusional' influence of the mother. Women do not, in order to preserve their masculinity, have to maintain a distance from their emotions that turns human 'need' into alienated 'demand'.

Nevertheless, French feminists began their thinking about language from the supposedly general truths of post-structuralist analysis. Language has grammatical rules, therefore these must be broken in a feminine writing. Language has a phallic logic, therefore feminine thought will be illogical. Language is based on an exchange of women so these exchanged women must also begin to speak. Representation involves a self-delusive doubling that objectifies the flesh, so a woman must permit her objectified flesh to speak. In each case feminist thought about language, beginning with theory, reacted to theory, attempted to valorise within theory a place from which a woman might speak, a place all too graciously indicated by the 'purveyors' of theory themselves. Rules are made to be broken, logic requires a contrasting illogic, exchange requires objects of exchange, representation requires objectification.

A woman's language, whether an independent woman's language or a maternal semiotics, became the rediscovered under-side of male logic and all that rationality imagines it must cover, reject, or fear. As such, it continued to be a language of the oppressed, a language without authority, a language which makes no assertions, a language which cries and communicates but cannot establish or prescribe. Such a language, however, need not be theorised as a necessary effect of femininity. Derrida's feminine operators, Lacan's female saints, and Kristeva's maternal semiotics are images of women projected by masculine anxieties and shaped by a masculine problematic; they do not define the feminine or restrict how a woman may speak or what she may say. Those 'structures' against which French feminists claimed to resurrect the rejected debris of femininity were not universals, but particular responses to specific anxieties and contradictions, responses that conveniently removed the theorist from the concrete realities of his situation. Not only are other responses possible but the situations which occasion such removals are historically specific.

Lacan's positing of patriarchal symbolic order against the

'nothingness' of animality, intersubjectivity, and physical need projected onto both past and future an ahistorical synchronity. Lacan, however, in his very early work on 'The family',[143] before he read the structural anthropologist Levi-Strauss,[144] recognised that the Law of the Father had an historical beginning. In his 1938 essay he criticised Freud for making the Oedipus complex the specific form of the human family and proposed to situate it in history in the 'paternalist' family. Freud, Lacan argued, was mistaken in making the 'leap' from the families of his Victorian patients to a hypothetical primitive family with a patriarch at the head. This is not consistent, Lacan pointed out, with either anthropology or primate studies. Noting repeatedly that the Oedipus complex applies very poorly to girls, Lacan proceeded to explore those Oedipal relations between father and son which eventually give rise to 'an immense patrimony of cultural norms, statutes, creative institutions'.[145] If the light of historical traditions only strikes fully the annals of patriarchs, and only as marginal the matriarchy everywhere underlying ancient culture, Lacan continued, this is a matter of 'structure'.[146] Although Lacan went on to argue for the moral superiority of that structure as perpetuated in the paternalist family, and to mourn the contemporary decline of the paternal image in favour of 'collectivities' and 'economic concentration',[147] in 1938 he left open an historical space surrounding patriarchal structures that he later refused to acknowledge.

The structural linguistics and anthropology which would soon change Lacan's mind about the historicity of paternalist structures was, from its very first conception by Saussure, ahistorical. Linguistics never proposed to describe actual speech events. The theory of linguistic value as exchange value that inspired both Levi-Strauss and Lacan to place women as the exchanged objects, is explained by Saussure as an attempt to provide an object of study *beyond* the arbitrarily imposed rules of historically situated grammarians and logicians. However, where could such a linguistic reality be found?[148] The *facts* of language are, Saussure acknowledged, that each time a word is used it is used with a different expression and intonation and also with a different meaning, depending on the situation and the speaker's history and intentions: when we speak we make a word our own. In what, then, could a transpersonal linguistic identity consist? Saussure concluded that it could only consist in exchange value, in the fact, outside of ordinary linguistic communication, that some words or sets of words could be *exchanged* for others.[149] The language linguists study, he concluded, must be a multi-layered system of such systems, of phonemic identities and differences, of graphic identities and differences, of conceptual identities and differences,[150] in which something 'positive' occurs only when one layer is superimposed onto another, generating the oppositions that are the substance of linguistic meaning.

The subject, then, of structuralist linguistic enquiry is not speech or the way people actually communicate in language. Speech, Saussure agreed, exhibits no 'identity' of meaning but only a 'flow' of nuances, colour, transformation — a 'freedom of combination' that cannot be the universal, timeless object of scientific knowledge. On the other hand, in linguistic 'value', removed from meaning and also from physical sound, Saussure found a stable unchanging object for scientific enquiry. The reality that linguistics can reveal is not reality in the sense of any independently substantive linguistic existence, but reality only because it is universal and unchanging. So linguistics rescues language from its 'irrationality' and 'natural chaos'.[151] That 'rescue', carried out in the theory of the signifier, was in fact a retreat from the intentional sources of language use, and the complex, variable experiences out of which we speak and have spoken.

Neither 'a maternal semiotics', nor a 'feminine operation', nor 'écriture féminine' returned speech to its concrete human situation. These strategies of French feminism either disrupted conceptual order, or supplemented the ahistoricity of structures with an ahistoricity of pure bodily and emotional expression. In neither case are meanings seen as a function of historically grounded intentions. Both the social order which must be maintained and the rebellion which must be permitted to loosen the rigidity of social order became barriers in the way of a coherent social or political practice: Irigaray supported the dictatorial takeover of the French feminist movement by one militant faction; Kristeva endorsed rightist candidates against the socialists; Derrida defended the hierarchical, elitist French education system against leftist reforms. By the very terms of post-structuralist theory of language, there are no other possibilities except to exist on a narrow edge between necessary social order and anarchic rebellion.

Once, however, the intentional sources of language use are taken into account, a different linguistics is possible. Julia Stanley, instead of emphasising the structural/universal quality of grammar's sexism, placed grammatical studies in historical context and so was able to criticise the gender system of English as historical imposition and not as immutable structure. Grammar is not the sexist barrier beyond which feminist thought cannot go without a 'work of language'. Grammar is not language, but a theory about language. In fact, Stanley pointed out, the generic use of 'man' has a history that can be correlated with the historical fact of the increasing domination by men of public and printed discourse. The Law of the Father is dictated not by the signifier but by male grammarians who did not neglect giving the reason why 'man' *should* now be used as the generic. The man, they argued, is the more 'noble' and the more like God.[152]

In another paper Stanley traced the history of the marked feminine pronoun 'she' in Middle English, relating this linguistic innovation, borrowed from Swedish to supplement the deficient egalitarian English, to the patristic teachings of the Medieval church.[153] Grammar is not a universal structure *discovered* by grammarians and linguists, but an interested imposition on language of a certain kind of speaking. To say that change is grammatical is not to say that there has been observed some spontaneous change in the economy of the signifier, but that certain systematic rules are imposed on speech, rules which may or may not be followed.

This is not to say that the order so imposed has no substantial reality: but that reality is not an insubstantial network of textual differences. There is instead a relation between the meanings expressed in a language or family of languages and particular institutions. This was brought out clearly by the linguist Benveniste in his study of Indo-European language and society.[154] Benveniste described a 'common culture', a 'material culture', that stretches from Russia, to India, to Europe, to America, and is reflected in the vocabularies of different modern languages, all stemming from a common Indo-European source. Benveniste related the formation and organisation of the vocabulary of those institutions not only to systems of justice, government, or religion, but more importantly to ways of life, social relations, ways of thinking and acting. After a first section describing an economy of livestock breeding, exchange of commodities, and prices and wages, Benveniste turned to the vocabulary of kinship: 'Father and mother, brother and sister, do not constitute symmetrical couples in Indo-European. Unlike

mater, "mother", pater does not denote the physical parent
. . .'[155] In Indo-European, 'mother' and 'father' are not equals,
nor is father a biological concept. The concept of patriarchy is the
foundation of Indo-European society; the father is not a male or
physical sire but a function. The mother, on the other hand, is the
physical parent. There can be no 'matria' to complement the
'patria' or 'world of the father' conceptualised in Indo-European
vocabularies, because in Indo-European the mother has no legal
status. There are corresponding asymmetries in the vocabulary for
the marriage relation. In Indo-European, a man 'leads a woman
into marriage', a woman that another man has given to him; the
woman, on the other hand, enters into a 'state' of being married,
she does not *do* anything but is the passive recipient of a function.
The vocabulary of Indo-European marriage leaves no room for
equality. It is not surprising that semanticists, confounding
English, or other Indo-European languages, with all languages,
claimed that hierarchical opposition is built into symbolic
functioning.

These facts about a language family, however, are not just facts
about texts; they are facts about a way of life. A familiar description of such a way of life can be found in Aristotle's *Politics*. There,
Aristotle described an ordered world of relationships and mutually
supporting hierarchies. A good society is one that retains these
relationships and it is only further evidence of their rightness that
one can be defended in terms of the other:

Greek/barbarian
master/slave
man/woman
husband/wife
mind/body
reason/emotion
human/animal[156]

For Aristotle, these hierarchies represented an order which is both
institutional and symbolic, both practical and theoretical, both
familial and political. Nor are these hierarchies foreign to the
subsequent history of Western society. As they continued to be
articulated, Greek/barbarian became Euro-American/Third World;
master/slave became civilised/primitive; mind/body became
materialism/idealism; and reason/emotion became conscious/
unconscious. In structuralist theories of language, this nexus between
particular ways of life and ways of speaking is dehistoricised

in a 'symbolic', from which there is no final escape, only the terrorism from within of a textual practice. A new dimension is added to men's account of themselves and their situation. The laws that mediate between competitive acquisitive men, the economics by which the production of male workers is organised, the psychoanalysis in which conflicts between fathers and sons are reconciled, all share a common language. Furthermore, that language is the only language anyone can understand.

It is not hard to see why feminists would want to escape a language structured around masculine presence and feminist absence, but it is not necessary, for that refusal, to find a new language other than the English, French, Spanish, etc. that we already speak. Nor is it necessary to revert to the powerless speech of dreamers and hysterics. If theories of language, whether as grammar, linguistics, or philosophy of language, have power over our talk and practice, that power is not a metaphysical given: it comes from the power over our lives of teachers, experts, publishers, academicians, grammarians, a power asserted at various historical times and in various ways. Even if Benveniste is right and Indo-European languages share a common semantic structure, the conquest of Europe by Indo-European invaders was a concrete historical event, and one not written unambiguously into Indo-European semantics. Benveniste also noted the retention of non-Indo-European concepts, such as *adelphos/adelphi* (brother/sister in Greek) which indicates a parity between children of the same mother.[157]

To see a particular semantic structure as an absolute social beginning is, as the early Lacan realised, a question of 'structure' — that is, of projecting back onto human history the reality of a particular human situation: Saussure, craving for timeless scientific certainty in the face of the diversity of spoken language; Levi-Strauss, worrying in *Tristes tropiques*[158] about the subjectivity of his response to the 'primitive' objects of his research; Lacan, deploring the father's lack of power and the son's inability to find in the disintegrating family a paternal figure against which to rebel. In each case a transcendent object is posited beyond the unsatisfactory reality of linguistic and cultural diversity and change: 'La langue', 'the elementary structures of parenting', the 'Law of the Father'. If, later, room is made for a rebellious son, this is a matter of hygiene, of providing a convenient conduit for the inevitable and unconceptualisable anxieties, urges and pulsions that must always surge up under a repressive social order. However, this is already an order within which women have been assigned their roles, as unintelligible expression, as exchanged objects, as the maternal body which even a rebellious son must eventually reject.

Structuralist and post-structuralist theories of symbolic meaning complete the philosophy of man, not only because they give to man a language, but also because they show us something about the philosophies which revealed his nature. Divorced from practice, symbolic structure becomes a substitute world; the theorist makes a definitive break with the ambiguity, violence and death of physical existence. Language provides a textual arena where ambivalent relations can be acted out, while at the same time real life continues with its murders and cruelties. The removal from practical life which makes such a language possible is itself a practice. It is not, as Sartre argued, the metaphysically necessary 'ekstasis' of the conscious subject, but a way to deal with the painfulness and ambiguity of men's situations. The projection of an alienated symbolic back to the dawn of man's history covered over the fact of that choice. When French feminists urged a textual practice, they collaborated in this deception. Lacan left a space for the mysterious 'beyond' of the female; Derrida gave permission for a masturbatory play with the text. However, drawn into the Law of the Father whether to obey or subvert, women lost the perspective that would have allowed them to see a certain way of speaking for what it is — an attempt to escape painful intersubjectivity in alienated textual relations.

Feminist critique of a masculine symbolic showed that attention must always be paid to the terms in which we think about what we are doing. It also revealed something about theory itself. Liberalism, Marxism, existentialism and psychoanalysis, tried to make sense of the concrete historical situation of men by searching for origins — of society, consciousness, personality. Some universal constant would rule the variety of cultural and political practice. Lacan's Law of the Father was instantiated in natural law, economic law, Oedipal structures. The phallus, centre of meaning, became man's identity with himself. 'Man is competitive', 'man is productive', 'man is a subject', 'man is Oedipus' — each in turn became the self-evident starting point from which social, economic and psychological theory was derived.

The exposure of the symbolic form of the philosophy of man suggests a new direction for feminist thought. Not only may yet another theory devised by men to rationalise men's activities be rejected as inadequate, but theory itself, as a search for self-present origins and deductive laws, is called into question. Feminist theorists have also searched for origins; they have found the source of sexism in the superior strength of men, in male viciousness, in biology, in a sexual division of labour, and in the family. All of these explanations illuminated parts of women's experience, but as universal law they also obscured the various practices, contemporary and historical, Western and non-Western, that might yield new feminist concepts, values and knowledge. Although a deconstruction of the text of patriarchy may be needed to clear the way for these new ideas, a feminine counter-text can only offer a mirror image of masculinist thought. At that point, however, at which post-structuralist theories have made explicit the conflictual and alienated sources of the philosophy of man, it may finally be possible to turn away, to women's history, women's literature, women's lives, with no Law of the Father to dictate what we might find there.

Notes

1. *Encore, le séminaire de Jacques Lacan, Livre XX* (Editions du Seuil, Paris, 1975), p. 68.

2. In the year of *Encore*, 1973, Lacan was accepted by many French feminists as having made a significant contribution to the understanding of femininity. Even now there are still many in France who believe that his was the last word on women.

3. Pamela Fishman, 'What do couples talk about when they are alone' in D. Butteroff and E.L. Epstein (eds), *Women's language and style* (University of Akron English Department, Akron, Ohio, 1978); or Donald Zimmerman and Candace West, 'Sex roles, interruptions and silences in conversation' in B. Thorne and N. Henley (eds), *Language and sex: difference and dominance* (Newbury House Publishers, Rowley, Massachusetts, 1975), pp. 64–75. See in the latter volume a useful annotated bibliography of studies on sex differences in language, p. 204. See also a second volume of papers on gender difference in language, *Language, gender and society*, also edited by Barrie Thorne and Nancy Henley as well as by Cheris Kramarae, with further annotated bibliography (Newbury House, Rowley, Massachusetts, 1983).

4. Francine Wattman Frank, 'Women's language in America: myth and reality' in *Women's language and style*, citing surveys of the literature by Roger Shuy (1969) and Cheris Kramarae (1974). See also Peter Trudgill, 'Sex, covert prestige and linguistic change in the urban British English of Norwich', *Language in Society*, no. 1 (1972), pp. 179–95.

5. Mary Hiatt, *The way women write* (Teacher's College Press, New York, 1977), chapter 3.

6. Ibid., chapter 4.

7. Ibid., chapter 3.

8. Mary Ritchie Key, *Male/female language* (Scarecrow Press, Metuchen, New Jersey, 1975), p. 75.

9. Robin Lakoff, *Language and women's place* (Harper and Row, New York, 1975). Lakoff has often been criticised for the unscientific nature of her introspective findings.

10. Edward Sapir, 'Abnormal types of speech in Nootka', reprinted in David G. Mandlebaum, (ed.), *Selected writings of Edward Sapir in language, culture and personality* (University of California Press, Berkeley, California, 1968), p. 179. See also Ann Bodine, 'Sex differentiation in language' in Thorne and Henley (eds), *Language and sex: difference and dominance*, p. 130, for a summary of difference in male and female language in other cultures.

11. Key, *Male/female language*, pp. 68-9.

12. Ibid., p. 119. Key cites tenth-century Japan when males wrote theology, science and law in a formal court language while women wrote novels such as Lady Murasake's *Tale of Genji* in the vernacular.

13. See Pamela Fisher, 'What do couples talk about . . .' and Key, *Male/female language*, pp. 35-6, and also Cheris Kramarae, *Women and men speaking* (Newbury House Publishers, Rowley, Massachusetts, 1981), chapters VII-X, for a review of the literature relating differences in women's and men's speech to different power strategies. This linking of sex difference in language and male dominance is cited by Kramarae as a socio-linguistics that does not treat language as isolated from society but as a social act itself. For a general description of this approach, Thorne and Henley, 'Difference and dominance: an overview of language, gender and society' in *Language and sex*, pp. 5-42, is useful.

14. See, for example, Basil Bernstein 'Social class, linguistic codes, and grammatical element', *Language and Speech*, no. 5 (1967), pp. 221-50, for evidence that other power differences such as class differences also can be related to language differences. See also Trudgill (1972), footnote 4.

15. Key, *Language and women's place*, p. 3.

16. This change from sexual difference to gender difference reflects both a linguistic turn and the Freudian insight that sexuality is not *a priori* gender but must be engendered.

17. See, for example, Julia Stanley, 'Paradigmatic women: the prostitute' in D.L. Shores and C.P. Hines (eds), *Papers in language variation* (University of Alabama Press, 1977), in which Stanley lists 210 derogatory sexual words applied to women.

18. Julia Stanley, 'Gender-marking in American English: usage and reference' in A.P. Nilsen *et al.* (eds) *Sexism and language* (National Council of Teachers of English, Urbana, Illinois, 1977), pp. 46-50.

19. The situation in French is if anything worse. There, even the possibility of a neutral word for certain professionals — for example, 'professeur' — is grammatically precluded. Every French word is gendered and must exhibit its gender in articles and agreeing adjectives. Consequently, 'le professeur' does not admit the possibility of a female form. See Jacques Céllard in 'Madame le Président', *Le Monde*, 27 Mars 1983, describing some of the series of 'grammatical heresies' needed to accommodate a growing number of female professionals.

20. *Gyn/Ecology: the meta-ethics of radical feminism* (Beacon Press, Boston, 1978), pp. 3, 24.

21. 'The semantic derogation of women' in Thorne and Henley (eds), *Language and sex*, p. 64.

22. For example, the following, quoted from the 1972 Nation's Schools Survey by Kramarae, *Women and men speaking*, p. 46: 'Sexism in textbooks may be a hot topic with ladies who like Ms in front of their names but not with school administrators.'

23. This is the argument of G. Kress and R. Hodge in *Language and ideology* (Routledge and Kegan Paul, London, 1979), p. 80.

24. See in this regard the interesting study by Wendy Martyna, 'What does "he" mean?: use of the generic masculine', *Journal of Communication*, vol. 28, no. 1 (Winter 1978), pp. 131–8, where she shows that whereas men tend to associate masculine imagery with 'man', women associate abstract imagery.

25. S. Ardener and E. Ardener (eds), *Perceiving women* (Malaby Press, London, 1975).

26. For an account of this ground-breaking project, see Alma Graham, 'The making of a non-sexist Dictionary', *Ms*, Dec. 1973, reprinted in Thorne and Henley, (eds), *Language and sex*, p. 57.

27. For a resource list of publishing and professional guidelines, see Casey Miller and Kate Swift, *Words and women* (Doubleday, New York, 1975), p. 164–5.

28. *Gyn/Ecology*, p. 24.

29. Ibid., p. 423.

30. *Course in general linguistics*, trans. Wade Baskin (McGraw-Hill, New York, 1966), pp. 65–70.

31. Ibid., p. 71.

32. Ibid., p. 74.

33. Ibid., p. 88.

34. Ibid., p. 111.

35. Ibid., p. 112. Saussure's somewhat surprising image is of a body of water (sound) and a body of air (thought). When the atmospheric pressure changes (it is not indicated what might precipitate such a disturbance), then the water will be divided into waves and, at the same time, the air with currents, creating the reciprocal divisions in sound and thought that constitute linguistic meaning.

36. To think otherwise is to confuse value with signification (ibid., p. 115). With this move away from the duality of the signifier and signified to exchange value, the arbitrariness of the relation between signifier and concept, no longer functional, begins to resemble an empty conceptual identity.

37. Chomsky's generative grammar is the front runner with a model of linguistic competence in which an underlying propositional 'kernel' is transformed by way of transformational rules into grammatical 'surface structures', a process which Chomsky believes to be innate to the human mind.

38. These are the standard relations that semantics is to describe and/or explain. See, for example, John Lyons, *Introduction to theoretical linguistics* (Cambridge University Press, Cambridge, 1968), p. 443. Although views

on the sort of representation appropriate to such relations and on the relation between semantics and grammar differ, there is no disagreement that the 'sense of a lexical item may be defined to be not only dependent upon, but identical with, the set of relations which hold between the item in question and other items in the same lexical system'. Ibid.

39. Ibid., p. 443.

40. For example, Jerrold Katz has consistently so argued, in the midst of a lively discussion. See Charles Ferguson and Edith Moravisk (eds), *Universals of human language* (Stanford University Press, Stanford, 1978). Emmon Bach and Robert Harms (eds), *Universals of linguistic theory* (Holt, Rinehart and Winston, New York, 1968). Certainly individual words from different languages seldom exactly coincide in meaning. Once word meaning, however, is reduced to component parts, the common conceptual atoms of meaning are supposedly revealed.

41. The model is phonetics in which the sound substance of language is similarly described with reference to a grid of 'distinctive features' whose presence or absence defines each phoneme.

42. Although (male) and (female) are sometimes preserved, as in Katz, 'The structure of a semantic theory' in J.A. Fodor and J.J. Katz (eds), *Structure of language* (Prentice Hall, Englewood Cliffs, New Jersey, 1968), p. 496; or the gender numbered (gender 1, gender 2, gender 3) as in Chomsky, *Aspects of a theory of syntax* (MIT Press, Cambridge, 1965), chapter 4, section 2.

43. Even when the form of predicate logic is adopted so that relations and arguments (the individuals of whom predicates are true) can be semantically represented, predicates are still represented as positive or negative.

44. A few examples among many: Ruth Kempson, *Semantic theory* (Cambridge University Press, Cambridge, 1977), p. 83; F.R. Palmer, *Semantics* (Cambridge University Press, Cambridge, 1981), p. 109; Joseph Greenberg, 'Language Universals' in T.A. Seboek (ed.) *Current trends in linguistics III*, (Mouton, The Hague, 1966); George Dillon, *Introduction to linguistic semantics* (Prentice Hall, Englewood Cliffs, NJ, 1977), p. 11, as well as Lyons, *Introduction to theoretical linguistics*, p. 470, and also Saussure, *Course in general linguistics*, p. 121.

45. Walter Chafe, *Meaning and the structure of language* (Chicago University Press, Chicago, 1970), p. 111. A Lacanian ambivalence might also be noted in Chafe who later surprisingly 'treats' generic terms as unmarked (p. 261) and then must posit post-semantic rules to get from the unmarked to the masculine pronoun.

46. Julia Stanley, 'Gender marking in American English' in Nilsen *et al.* (eds) *Sexism and language*, p. 66. Further proof might be found in the difficulties a component analysis encounters with words like 'baby' as the contradictory (male) and (female) must be accommodated in the semantic analysis in order to explain the permissability of both the feminine and masculine pronouns. See Katz, *Semantic theory* (Harper and Row, New York, 1972), p. 369.

47. *Language as ideology* (Routledge and Kegan Paul, London, 1979), pp. 78-82.

48. Kress and Hodge attribute this insight also to Whorf in J.B.

Carroll (ed.), *Language, thought and reality* (Wiley, New York, 1956).

49. Kramarae, *Women and men speaking*, p. 42.

50. Even Levi-Strauss, for example, admits that logically, women could exchange men, only, he insists, that has *never* happened in any human society.

51. Emile Benveniste, *Problems in general linguistics* (University of Miami Press, Coral Gables, Florida, 1971), p. 224.

52. Ibid., p. 225.

53. 'The purveyor of truth', trans. W. Domingo, J. Hulbert, M. Ron, *Yale French Studies*, no. 52, (undated), pp. 31–113.

54. 'Freud and the scene of writing', trans. Jeffrey Mehlman, *Yale French Studies*, no. 48, (undated), p. 84.

55. See also the sociologist Pierre Bourdieu in *Ce que parler veut dire* (literally, *That which to speak means*) (Fayard, Paris, 1982), who, in his investigation of the social production and utilisation of meaning, cited the power of grammarians, teachers and ideologies to legislate what can be said.

56. See 'The dangerous supplement' in *Of grammatology*, trans. G. C. Spivak (The Johns Hopkins University Press, Baltimore, 1976), in which Derrida showed in a classic deconstructing move how what is presented as an insignificant addendum by Rousseau provides the key to his whole project.

57. In *Dissémination*, trans. Barbara Johnson (Chicago University Press, Chicago, 1981), pp. 174–286. The occasion is his juxtaposition of two texts, one from Plato on true and false ideas or images, and a meditation by Mallarmé, the symbolist poet, on a mime of the story of Pierrot's murder of his wife, Columbine. Derrida compared Mallarmé's approach to language with Plato's. Mallarmé's appreciation of the miming of the story of Pierrot and Columbine involved no privileged truth, or platonic logocentrism. In Mallarmé's account there was a kind of interplay of metaphor and association, a chain of relations with other texts, an 'interminable network' of images and cross references, or 'grafts' as Derrida called them. The mime does not imitate anything the way Plato's artist imperfectly imitates the real forms. The mime does not seek any kind of truth, nor does he create a truth. He copies, but he copies a copy for which there is no Platonic original. Derrida takes this miming as revealing of the text itself, and therefore of language.

58. Jacques Derrida, *Spurs: Nietzsche's styles*, trans. Barbara Harlow (University of Chicago Press, Chicago, 1978).

59. When Nietzsche's various pronouncements on women are examined, Derrida finds that there is not one but several attitudes towards women revealed. Firstly, the woman is condemned by Nietzsche as a 'figure or potentate of falsehood'. In the second place, the woman is also 'censured, debased and despised' as the figure of truth. However, in a third kind of statement, beyond this double negation, the woman is affirmed as having moved beyond the opposition of truth and falsehood — ibid., p. 97. Derrida finds that Nietzsche's anti-feminism applies only to the women who play the roles of the first or second figures, either rejecting male truth or affirming a female truth.

60. It is this 'key' to the text that Derrida accused Heidegger — whose

interpretation of Nietzsche is Derrida's real target — of ignoring, specifically in Heidegger's reading of *The twilight of the idols*, in which Nietzsche describes the change from Platonism to Christianity as the idea becoming 'female'. In such a way', Derrida charges, 'does one permit oneself to see without reading to read without seeing' — *Spurs*, p. 85. Heidegger can then mistake Nietzsche's thought as 'metaphysical' — ibid., p. 79.

61. Ibid., p. 95.

62. *Ecce homo*, quoted by Derrida, *Spurs*, pp. 105–7.

63. *Spurs*, p. 107.

64. See, for example, ibid., pp. 109–11, where Derrida discusses Nietzsche's two ways of describing the possessor-possessed relation between man and woman. The man is the master because he takes, but the woman is the master because she gives.

65. Ibid., p. 111. Derrida 'plays' with a pun between 'propriéte' and 'propre'. In standards of the 'propre' or correct, a kind of 'property' in language is implied. See also p. 119.

66. Ibid., p. 55.

67. Ibid., p. 61.

68. Ibid.

69. See Derrida's description of these strategies of deconstruction in 'The ends of man', *Philosophy and Phenomenological Research*, vol. XXX (1969–70), p. 31.

70. Derrida, *Speech and phenomena*, trans. David B. Allison and Newton Grover (Northwestern University Press, Evanston, Illinois, 1973), p. 104.

71. It is the study of those relationships which constitutes Derrida's 'Grammatology'. *Of grammatology* clears the way for such an approach to a language, freed from authoritarian presence and so reduced to a kind of 'graphic spasm' or writing.

72. 'Laugh of the Medusa', trans. K. Cohen and P. Cohen, *Signs*, vol. 1, no. 4 (1979), which also appears in revised form in Elaine Marks and Isabelle de Courtivron (eds), *New French feminisms* (University of Massachusetts Press, Amherst, Massachusetts, 1980), p. 245.

73. C. Clément and H. Cixous, *La jeune née* (Inedit, Paris, 1975), p. 171.

74. *Ce sexe qui n'en est pa un* (*That sex which is not one*) (Les Editions de Minuit, Paris, 1977), p. 76.

75. Ibid., p. 73.

76. Ibid., p. 74.

77. Ibid., p. 75.

78. Ibid., p. 72ff, cf. Derrida, *Of grammatology*, p. 24. 'The movements of deconstruction do not destroy structures from the outside. They are not possible and effective, nor can they take accurate aim, except by inhabiting those structures.'

79. Ibid., p. 63.

80. *La jeune née*, p. 115 excerpts reprinted in Marks and Courtivron (eds), *New French feminisms*, p. 90.

81. This is the argument of ibid., p. 115ff (Marks, p. 91ff).

82. *Speculum de l'autre femme* (Les Editions de Minuit, Paris, 1974), p. 165.

83. Specifically the reference is to Plato whose journey to the Sun represents such a distancing. Irigaray brilliantly deconstructs the Platonic metaphors of sun and cave in *Speculum*, p. 300ff.

84. Ibid., pp. 176–7.

85. *Ce sexe*, p. 25. This passage is translated in Marks and Courtivron, (eds), *New French feminisms*, p. 101.

86. *Ce sexe*, p. 28 (Marks, p. 103).

87. Roland Barthe's *The pleasure of the text*, trans. Richard Miller (Hill and Wang, New York, 1975) is the classic description of this textual jouissance.

88. 'Ailleurs', *Ce sexe*, p. 74–5.

89. *Ce sexe*, p. 75; also see in the same volume 'Le miroir de l'autre côté' (The mirror from the other side), pp. 9–20.

90. See Derrida's discussion of auto-affection in *Of grammatology*, pp. 97–8, as the source of the self-present certainty of the Platonic forms and of the Cartesian cogito. God must be the example of perfect auto-affection. Irigaray is careful to distinguish masturbatory feminine 'auto-affection' from 'the auto-sufficing infinity of God' — *Ce sexe*, p. 75.

91. *Ce sexe*, p. 25.

92. 'Des marchandises entre elles', *Ce sexe*, p. 193, trans. in Marks and Courtivron, (eds), *New French feminisms*, p. 107 as 'When the goods get together'.

93. *Angst* (Editions des Femmes, Paris, 1977).

94. Ibid., p. 281.

95. Ibid., p. 283.

96. *Illa* (Editions des Femmes, Paris, 1980).

97. Cixous referred to Lacan's famous two doors, Hommes/Dames, which 'submit public life to urinary segregation' and illustrate 'how signifier enters in fact in the signified'. 'L'instance de la lettre dans l'inconscient', *Ecrits I* (Editions du Seuil, Paris, 1966), p. 257. *Illa*, p. 66.

98. *Illa*, p. 67.

99. Ibid., p. 176.

100. Ibid., p. 177.

101. Ibid.

102. 'The laugh of the Medusa', Marks and Courtivron (eds), *New French feminisms*, p. 257.

103. *Of grammatology*, p. 158. There is, Derrida argued, no 'outside the text'. If one seeks to escape from textuality into 'the real life of these existences of "flesh and bone"' or into any historical or psychological fact, not only is one still in a textual matrix of meanings but one blinds oneself to the assumptions made. 'Real' itself only has meaning within the signifying chain, which can be subverted but not escaped.

104. Notwithstanding such overquoted puns as Cixous's 'Let the priests tremble, we're going to show them our sext' — 'Laugh of the Medusa', p. 885.

105. 'The Laugh of the Medusa', *New French feminisms*, p. 250.

106. Ibid., p. 256.

107. Cixous, 'Castration or decapitation', *Signs*, vol. 7, no. 1 (1981), p. 54. Although *Illa* and *Angst* both exhibit this uncensored outpouring there is at the same time a problematic and a working through of that

problematic that gives an organic kind of form.

108. *Illa*, p. 137.

109. These points are made in all Irigaray's texts, but see especially 'La méchanique des fluides', *Ce sexe*, pp. 103–16, and 'L'incontournable volume', *Speculum*, pp. 298–300.

110. *Ce sexe*, p. 130.

111. Irigaray is not quite ready to equate the two. Asked whether to speak-woman was the same as to speak hysterically, without denying the affinity, Irigaray attempts to distinguish the two. The hysteric does not speak, 'It' ('Ça') (or in the English translation of Freud the 'id') speaks in her, while she still speaks a rational language. *Ce sexe*, p. 134.

112. *Speculum*, pp. 170–71.

113. *Ce sexe*, p. 125.

114. See *La jeune née*, p. 160, on the question whether the writing Cixous urges is 'specifically feminine'.

115. Ibid., p. 162. See also 'Castration or decapitation', 'All the feminine texts I've read are very close to the voice, very close to the flesh of language.'

116. Ibid., p. 170.

117. Ibid., p. 172.

118. For example, *Illa*, p. 40. 'There is in this extraordinary woman, moreover, the tendencies which unite in her the senses the most opposite, a tendency to link-unlink, a tendency to precede-suspend, in this extraordinary language, an aptitude for thinking a thing and its opposite.'

119. *Illa*, pp. 140–41.

120. Ibid., p. 143.

121. Ibid., p. 145.

122. Ibid., pp. 66–71, where Cixous spins out this complex metaphor.

123. This is especially true in France where the educational system, hierarchical and elitist, has not proved fertile ground for feminine scholarship. In French universities, with some exceptions, such as Vincennes where Cixous holds her seminar, there were no Women's Studies departments or Women's Studies programmes.

124. With respect to publishing, French feminists may be in a somewhat better position than their American counterparts, given the more decentralised and non-commercial style of Paris publishing. *Éditions des Femmes*, for example, founded and supported by the radical feminist group *Psychoanalyze et Politique*, provides both publishing and a bookstore for feminist works, including those of Cixous.

125. *Ce sexe*, p. 81. The grass-roots movement of consciousness-raising groups, somewhat surprisingly stronger in America than in France, is an example of an attempt to create such an exterior place. In France, the 'talking-among-themselves' tended to go on among educated avant-garde women rather than among the masses of women.

126. *La jeune née*, 'Une maitresse femme', pp. 152–75.

127. Cixous admits (p. 252) that she does not totally give up such a 'parler'. She, in fact, she maintained, exercises it in class with her students. Given her theorising of a free writing, 'traversed by the other', visitors, especially those who are used to the American Women's Studies anti-authoritarian classroom praxis, have been surprised at her

magisterial manner in seminar. Either the prevailing master-to-initiate tone in French education is too pervasive for Cixous to avoid, or too threatening to face unarmed. Whether or not Cixous is able to practise a more egalitarian approach to teacher/student relations, she did seem to describe something similar later in her dialogue with Clément: 'that one *gives* to the other all the "gaps" in knowledge and then lets it appear. That one is "in the notch of" occupying a position which one has not the right to occupy and that one shows just how one occupies it and why' (original emphasis). The nuances of the last sentence are revealing. The 'notch', the 'position' cannot be done away with but must be 'occupied'. Still a consciousness of the unfoundedness of any such position can still be communicated. 'In the master, love (must) struggle against the will to power' — *La jeune née*, p. 258.

128. Ibid., p. 265.

129. Clément's contribution to *La jeune née* consisted of a comparison of two figures, the witch (or sorceress) and the hysteric. These figures are related to socio-economic conditions as well as explored 'symbolically'.

130. Clément's critique of feminist separatism could be extended along Marxist lines. For Marx, ideas must reflect real experience and so any attempt idealistically to dream up a new world could only re-duplicate, perhaps in reverse form, the old. Given the materialist base of ideology, the equation of knowledge and ideology is a sensitive issue in Marxism. Clément's argument illustrates some of the difficulties. At the same time as Cixous's separatism is declared as utopian, Clément must defend a knowledge above ideology that will be the basis for 'la maitresse femme', duplicating the Marxist problem of defending an authoritarian Marxist knowledge when ideational-ideological structures are supposed to be determined by material conditions.

Cixous, on the other hand, as a textualist and not as a materialist, posits ideology as an 'immense membrane which envelopes everything. A skin which, even if one is enveloped in it like a net, or as behind closed eyelids, one must know exists.' *La jeune née*, pp. 266–7. Her practice then consists in attempting to tear, to penetrate this text. One may never succeed in destroying it, but one must continue to break it up so it will not grow over.

131. 'The twilight of the goddesses or the intellectual crisis of French feminisms', *Signs*, vol. 7, no. 1 (1981), p. 81.

132. *La révolution du langage poétique* (du Seuil, Paris, 1974), p. 615, trans. M. Waller, *Revolution in poetic language* (Columbia University Press, New York, 1984).

133. *About Chinese women*, trans. Anita Barrows (Urizen Books, New York, 1977), p. 15.

134. See A. Nye, 'The woman clothed in the sun: Julia Kristeva and the escape to/from language', *Signs*, vol. 13, no. 4 (1987) for a critique of the theory of language that forces this choice between irrational expression and alienated logic.

135. The struggles within the American NOW (National Organisation for Women) are a painful example. The political efficacy of a hierarchicalised organisation with charismatic leaders was challenged by the more idealistic, pluralistic, grass-roots approach of feminists like

Ti-Grace Atkinson. See *Amazon odyssey*, esp. 'Resignation from now', (Links Books, New York, 1974), for Atkinson's criticisms.

136. For example, Monique Wittig, *Lesbian body*, trans. David LeVay (Owen, London, 1975) and *Les Guérillères* (Editions de Minuit, Paris, 1969), trans. David LeVay (Avon Books, New York, 1973).

137. See the poetry of Adrienne Rich, Audre Lorde, Olga Broumas.

138. The more theoretical French feminism made little attempt to engage sexism at a practical level. Irigaray's comments on pornography are characteristic. She noted, as did other feminists, pornography's violence against women. However, this does not mean, she argued, that women should militate against pornography. One might even say that pornography serves a useful purpose and should be encouraged, because it makes clear the relation between men and women that underlies our society and so provides a kind of unveiling of women's oppression. The important thing for women to do is not, she argued, to ban pornography, but to free their sexuality from male imagery and 'do what comes to you, what pleases you'. *Ce sexe*, pp. 197–202, with which might be compared recent attempts in the United States to declare that pornography violates a woman's civil rights.

139. Cixous, *Illa*, p. 186.

140. Derrida, quoting from Rousseau's *Confessions* in *Of grammatology*, p. 151.

141. *Dissémination*, p. 213.

142. Kristeva, *La révolution du langage poétique*, p. 465.

143. *Les complexes familiaux* (Navarin, Paris, 1984). This is a reprint of Lacan's entry on the family for the Encyclopedia Française, vol. VIII, 'La vie mentale', 1938.

144. The articles which cured Lacan of any remaining historicism were Claude Levi-Strauss's 'L'efficacité symbolique', *Revenue de l'Histoire des Religions*, vol. CXXXV, no. 1; 'Language and the analysis of social laws', *American Anthropologist*, vol. LIII, no. 2.

145. *Les complexes familiaux*, p. 67.

146. Ibid.

147. Ibid., p. 72.

148. Saussure, *Course in general linguistics*, pp. 107–11. 'What supports the classing of words as substances, adjectives, etc. Is it done in the name of a purely logical, extra-linguistic principle that is applied to grammar from without like the degrees of longitude and latitude on the globe? Or does it correspond to something that has its place in the system of language and is conditioned by it?' (p. 109). The former is possible, Saussure admits, but it is the discovery of the latter, linguistic 'reality', at which linguistics aims.

149. Saussure here rejected the idea that there are any conceptual universals. Instead, each language has its own system of exchange: ibid., pp. 116–17.

150. Saussure seemed to admit here that the conceptual chain of differences is derivative and has no substance of its own (ibid., p. 117). The disturbances in the undifferentiated sound mass are registered in/on the undifferentiated thought mass. It is not hard to see how Derrida is his logical successor.

151. Ibid., p. 133. The relation of the invention of money (Saussure's analogy for linguistic value) to mathematical thought and to the quantification of reality characteristic of modern society, as well as its relation to the alienation of capitalist exchange of commodities, is analysed by Alfred Sohn-Rethel in *Intellectual and manual labour* (Macmillan, London, 1978).

152. Julia Stanley, 'Sexist grammar', *College English*, vol. 39, no. 1, (1978), pp. 800-11.

153. Julia Stanley and Susan Robbins, 'Going through the changes: the pronoun She in Middle English', *Papers on Linguistics*, vol. II, no. 1–2 (1978), pp. 71–88. In a fascinating exploration of the generation of the generic masculine, Stanley and Robbins show how the feminine came to be separated from the originally generic pronoun forms in English by way of an astonishing borrowing of the distinguishing (s) from Swedish.

154. Emile Benveniste, *Indo-European language and society*, trans. Elizabeth Palmer (Faber and Faber, London, 1973). Languages in the Indo-European family include: Russian, Polish, Czech, Swedish, Danish, Dutch, English, French, Spanish, Greek, Persian, and most modern Indian languages.

155. Ibid., p. 193.

156. Aristotle, *Politics, complete works of Aristotle*, ed. Richard McKeon (Random House, New York, 1941). See Chapters 3–13, 'Household economy. The slave. Property. Children and wives'.

157. Benveniste, *Indo-European language and society*, p. 172ff.

158. Claude Levi-Strauss, *Tristes tropiques* (Plan, Paris, 1955). *Tristes tropiques*, trans. J. Weightman and D. Weightman (Cape, London, 1973).

7

The Theory of Feminist Practice

Feminist theorists expertly unravelled tangles of theory and practice, only to find resistance to feminist projects more securely knotted. This resistance was not in any biological nature or necessary conceptual structure. Theory has its origins in neither nature nor logic, but in the struggle to make sense of human action. The philosophies of men are theories of men's activities, activities which from the beginning exclude women; the goal of male theorising is to rationalise the inconsistencies and destructiveness of these activities. Marked indelibly with this project, the philosophies of man cannot serve feminist purposes without compromise. Although liberalism, Marxism, psychoanalysis, and structuralism may be temporarily useful in helping a woman to negotiate in a man's world, in the end they allow her only Kristeva's precarious dance on the volcano of male politics, economics, thought, and language.

But what is a feminist theorist to do? Without Athena's thread, is there only an abyss of nothingness into which she must fall, swallowed up as utterly as Cixous's Persephone into the great chasm of the Underworld? Some support is necessary for theory, some beginning from which coherent practice can begin to take form, some vantage point which will allow an understanding of the past, a situating in the present, and a vision for the future. There must be some design for a feminist history, feminist analysis, feminist projects; and where can this design come from if it is not borrowed from male thought, if it does not take the form of rights, privileges and immunities agreed between men to mitigate and perpetuate the effects of men's possessiveness, if it does not take the form of a centralisation of the means of production that will finally imprint on all natural things the image of

229

man, if it does not take the form of psychological complexes that rationalise male aggression, or linguistic structures in which men escape their physicality and their emotional needs? Moreover, how can these designs be denied when they are maintained and supported by the military power of West or East, by a dogmatic psychoanalytic establishment, by the seductive power of Parisian intellectual fashion?

Is there any way a woman can still turn Athena's thread to her own advantage, weave a pattern in which she will not be trapped herself? Is there another way to tell the story that neither futilely rehearses male crimes, nor argues for women's token inclusion on male terms? Who were those rebellious women who were punished and whose images adorned the corners of Athena's tapestry? Can they be made to move, to speak, to tell the story, not of their defeat, but of the life they lived, or hoped to live? Can a new kind of rendering give them voice? — release them from the fixed immobility of their punishment? That punishment was reworked in the very theories that feminists embraced. In democratic theory, women's life in the family became the natural, 'private sphere', subject to patriarchal will. In Marxism, women's work became regressive non-productive activity. In psychoanalysis, the mother became an inexpressible mystery hidden behind a wall of repression. In structuralism, the feminine became a residue of animality cast out of society. Can some future Arachne make these icons speak? Can she retrieve from the privacy of the family a new vision of non-alienated relations in which each understands his or her well-being as related to that of others? Can she take from women's domestic labour a model for work whose goal is not 'production' or the image of man but a liveable human space? Can she restore the intimacy of mother-daughter relations buried under Oedipal relations between father and son? And how, once she has restored voice to the mountain, stork, stone, is she to get the missile-makers, the pedants, and the fashion mongers to listen?

The practical feminist goes back to her confrontations. Was it all in vain? — all the weary intellectual labour, all the volumes of Marx, the mysteries of Lacan, the untranslatable puns of French feminism? It did not tell her what to do, did not point to the magic lever that would lift the weight of oppression. If anything, she learned how finely worked and deeply knotted is the fabric of sexist culture, and how cleverly interwoven are its political, economic, psychic, and linguistic designs: equal rights that are of no use to poor women, economic success nuanced by psycho-logical disability, egalitarian family relations that might correct the disability unthinkable and unsayable, every time sexism located more deeply in life and thought.

At the same time, however, as feminist theory successively uncovered the designs of sexist thinking, that thinking began to take on a particular tone of voice. Women began to hear not the voiceless reading of a universal natural law, economic law, law of the father, law of the signifier, but men's voices in response to conflicts between and within men; and this realisation alone might have been worth all the trouble. Because now the feminist knows how to probe for that raw nerve so cleverly hidden in the theoris-ing: the abject dependence of men on women's domestic labour, the shameful obscenity of male violence against women, the insecurity of the male ego based on alienation from others. Feminist theorists wove a revealing portrait of men's activities; of those men industrialisation turns into competing individuals, of those men socialism joins in a production machine, of those men for whom power over others is a way to avoid vulnerability, of those men who must reconcile with abusive fathers, of those men who retreat to the alienated language of rationality. Just as Arachne's portrayal corrected Athena's pious portrait of male gods, so liberal feminism, Marxist feminism and post-structuralist feminism corrected the distortion in the philosophies of man. Gone is the illusion of freedom that condones the brutality of capitalism, the ideal of brotherhood that justifies totalitarianism, the revered figure of the father that covers over the abusive reality of family life, the logic that condemns women to silence. In each feminist reworking of theory, the conflictual nature of men's prac-tices was exposed. Nowhere is this more evident than in post-structuralist theory. There, the son's inability, or refusal, to embrace wholeheartedly his paternal role and his painful sense of the fragility of a masculinist order is the acknowledged starting point of theoretical construction. This faltering of masculine resolve, this deep questioning of the stability of male culture, articulated in different ways by Derrida and Lacan, begins to bracket a conceptual universe.

That universe is not the only universe. The material/symbolic order on which Western culture is based had its beginning roughly with the Greeks. The supposed inpenetrable barriers of time and space which separate us from 20,000 years of pre-Hellenic human life have turned out to be often only the limited perspectives of male anthropologists and archaeologists. As more women enter these fields, evaluating old studies and undertaking new ones, different perspectives on 'pre-history' emerge, and woman-focused kinship systems, religions, values and philosophies are reconstructed. No longer is the world the narrowly circumscribed symbolic world of Western culture, with its defining complement of alien barbarism. Instead, in a kind of Copernican revolution, Western culture begins to seem not the sun, grand centre of all thought, but only one of Irigaray's earths travelling at its own speed and in its own particular orbit.

Nor at this point in history is Western culture the only culture or the only perspective possible. Although there may be no existing society in which women are not, to some degree, oppressed, there may be cultures in which women's worlds and women's values remain relatively intact. In an evolving Third World practice, philosophy, symbolism, the hegemony of Western culture are challenged — a challenge which is particularly timely, given the threat of nuclear extinction, the destruction of the environment, and the alienation of modern life. These are increasingly understood, not as transitory, correctible accidents but as necessary implications of a particular man-made social order that emphasises the sovereignty of man over nature, the subjection of the body to the mind, the logical impossibility of intersubjectivity. Even within Western countries, enclaves and outposts of women-oriented social orders exist and have existed: in convents, girl's schools, settlement houses, lesbian communities. Although they are always vulnerable to retaliation or reassertion of masculine control, their subversive power can be measured by the anger they often provoke in men and man-identified women. Even when repressed, they reappear, as the cutting radical edge of the feminist movement.

If patriarchy had an historical beginning, it can also have an historical end. This is not to say that feminist action based on the philosophies of liberalism, Marxism, existentialism, psycho-analysis and linguistic theory was or is useless: one cannot simply step painlessly and effortlessly outside the web of one's world and begin spinning a new one; such an escape can only be won. Each time, the centre, the nerve of power, is gained only with a meticulous separation of strand after strand until the mechanisms of oppression are finally understood. There is no other way to such an understanding, except by trying on the theory and the actions of men, and then judging the feminist results. Not only does the history of feminism illustrate this process, but each of us also — women and men — as we work through the layers of understanding, separating out the threads that constitute identity in a masculine world.

However, it is no longer enough to continue to assuage the unhappiness of that world or to learn from men strategies of survival. Turning away from the captive Arachne, struggling to survive on Athena's terms, a new kind of feminist thought is conceivable based on feminist action, not feminist action already theorised as male, but feminist action in a feminine world. Women living together, struggling together, identified with each other, acting together, would constitute in their thoughtful decisions, the ethics, the economy and the symbolic structure that order an alternate social reality. Feminist theorising would attempt to make coherent a feminist practice that knows no necessities beyond the necessities of feminist action. This is, in fact, the direction of a new wave of feminist activity and theory. Women scholars create enclaves in academia from which new approaches to knowledge are pioneered. Women historians research the diaries, letters and archives in which women tell about their lives. Lesbian women practice a sexuality outside heterosexuality, explore and begin to theorise new ways of intimately relating to others. Black women, Islamic women, Asian women, already situated outside the mainstream of Western culture, develop their very different social networks. Women travellers and scholars begin to experience non-Western cultures as other than backward repositories of primitivism. Most important of all, everywhere Arachnes turn back down the tangled thread of their thought to face once again the awesome Athena, to wait out her hysterical fury, her blustering, her shame at her admittedly inferior craftswomanship, and take Athena's hand firmly but gently. 'Leave them,' Arachne says, 'come with us. We will rebuild another world, in the memory of Crete, of the goddesses, of the Pygmy queen, of disobedient Antigone, of Aphrodite. Listen how the trees, the mountains, the birds, and the stones are speaking.'

233

Epilogue

Athena was originally a pre-Hellenic goddess ('na' is a non-Greek suffix) of Cretan-Mycenaean origin (her name appears on linear B tablets from Knossos as 'a-ta-na- po-ti-na-ja'). Although she was parthnogenetically born from the Mother goddess Metis (Hesiod Theog. 886ff), in later Greek myth she was reborn, motherless, a faithful father's daughter, from the forehead of Hellenic Zeus.

Arachne's Lydia, like the rest of Anatolia and many of the Aegean Islands, was never completely Hellenised. The Lydians maintained their local customs in the face of Greek colonisation. The rivalry between Athena and Arachne was not only personal but also economic. The Lydians and the Milesians operated a profitable textile industry which dominated Black Sea trade and blocked Athenian hegemony in the Aegean. Seals with the device of the spider appear in many places in the ancient world and identify goods of Lydian origin. Pliny, for example, reports that Arachne invented linen cloth, although, he adds, Athens claimed the discovery. The conflict between Athens and non-Hellenic Aegean peoples was also ideological. Indo-European Greeks, in successive waves of migration, forced the older Cretan-Mycenaean civilisation from mainland Greece and most parts of Crete to outlying Mediterranean settlements. The Greeks, worshipping the supreme sky-and-thunder god Zeus and bringing with them male-dominated social structures, confronted, often with violence, sophisticated cultures in which a feminine generative principle of all life was worshipped and in which women were accorded a high degree of independence and pre-eminence. In the Dark Ages, following the destruction of the last Mycenaean palace, traditions of excellence in art and music were preserved only in settlements far from Hellenic Attica. Not only was the fine art of weaving kept alive by the rebellious Lydian, Arachne, but Lydian music was an important source for the revival of lyric and epic poetry in Ionia, and Lydian coinage made possible the economic prosperity of Ionia and the eastern Aegean islands.

Greek myth, as compiled by Hesiod and others, constituted a textual reworking of these historical conflicts. The Greek's neutralisation of the sacradotal power of Minoan-Mycenaean goddess worship was co-optive, unlike the biblical Israelites' total destruction of the shrines of the goddess Ashera (related iconographically with the Cretan goddess), in which the followers of Yakweh ground idols to dust, murdered priestesses and priests, and desecrated graves and holy places. Zeus became the father-head of a family of gods and goddesses, sovereign over various aspects of the Cretan goddess who was reduced to individual, multiple, and inferior female deities:

Epilogue

Artemis, Aphrodite, Hera, and Athena herself.

The rapes which occur so regularly in Greek myth were the textual reflection of incidents which must have occurred as Greeks — whether Achaeans, Hellenes, or Dorians — imposed their warrior culture on Pelasgians, Cretans, and Cretanised mainlanders and islanders. Attacks on shrines would have included the rape and subjugation of priestesses. Abduction and forced marriage of local women allowed Greek men to intermarry with local aristocracy, and therefore exercise, as husbands, the prerogatives of their wives.

'The Pygmy Queen' was an African Queen, worshipped as a goddess, who reputedly despised the degraded Olympian female deities subject to Zeus. In punishment for her disobedience, she was turned into a crane.

Antigone was daughter of Laomedon, King of Troy. Troy, as described in the Iliad, retained matrilineal customs that were not Hellenic. Antigone claimed to rival Zeus' shrewish, but subject, wife, Hera. In punishment she was turned into a stork.

Cinyras was king of Cyprus, ancestor of the Cinyrodes, priests of Aphodite, of Phoenicion origin and founders of the cult of Aphrodite on Cyprus. Cinyras's beautiful daughters were resented by Hera who changed them into the steps of the temple and turned their father, as he lay prostrate with grief, into a stone.

Select Bibliography

Althusser, Louis (1971) 'Ideology and ideological state apparatuses' in his *Lenin and philosophy*, Monthly Review Press, New York

Ardener, S. and Ardener, A. (eds) (1975) *Perceiving women*, Malaby Press, London

Atkinson, Ti'Grace (1974) *Amazon odyssey*, Links Books, New York

Auclert, Hubertine (1908) *Le vote des femmes*, V. Giard and E. Brière, Paris

Balmary, Marie (1982) *Psychoanalyzing psychoanalysis*, Johns Hopkins University Press, Baltimore, MD

Barnes, Judy (undated) *The case for women's rights*, Society for Libertarian Life

Barrett, Michele (1980) *Women's oppression today: problems in Marxist feminist analysis*, Villiers Publications, London

────── and MacIntosh, Mary (1981) *The anti-social family*, Verso, London

Beauvoir, Simone de (1948) *The ethics of ambiguity*, trans. B. Frechtman, Philosophical Library, New York

────── (1972) 'La femme revoltée', *Nouvel Observateur*, no. 379 (14 au 20 Fev.)

────── (1974) *The second sex*, trans. H.M. Parshley, Vintage Books, New York

Bebel, Auguste (1904) *Women under socialism*, Labor News Press, New York

────── (1979) *La femme dans le passé, le présent, et l'avenir*, Ressources, Paris

Bentham, Jeremy (1876) *An introduction to the principles of morals and legislation*, Clarendon Press, Oxford

Benveniste, Emile (1971) *Problems in general linguistics*, University of Miami Press, Coral Gables, FL

────── (1973) *Indo-European language and society*, trans. E. Palmer, Faber and Faber, London

Bois, Carol du (1978) *Feminism and suffrage*, Cornell University Press, Ithaca, NY

Briffault, Robert (1977) *The mothers*, abridged by G.R. Taylor, Atheneum, New York

Brownmiller, Susan (1975) *Against our will: men, women, and rape*, Simon and Schuster, New York

Buhle, Mari Jo (1981) *Women and American socialism*, University of Illinois Press, Urbana

Burke, Edmund (1969) *Reflections and the revolution in France*, Penguin, Harmondsworth

Butteroff, D. and Epstein, E.L. (1978) *Women's language and style*, University of Akron Eng. Dept, Akron, OH

Chodorow, Nancy (1978) *The reproduction of mothering*, University of California Press, Berkeley

Select Bibliography

Cixous, Hélène and Clément, Catherine (1975) *La jeune née*, Inedit, Paris
—— *Angst* (1977) Éditions des Femmes, Paris
—— *Illa* (1980) Éditions des Femmes, Paris
Clark, Alice (1968) *Working life of women in the seventeenth century*, Augustus Kelly, New York (first published in 1919)
—— (1981) *Vies et légendes de Jacques Lacan*, B. Grasset, Paris
—— (1983) *The lives and legends of Jacques Lacan*, Columbia University Press, New York
Courtivron, Isabelle de and Marks, E. (eds) (1980) *New French feminisms*, University of Massachusetts Press, Amherst
Coward, Rosemary (1985) *Female desires*, Grove Press, New York
Dalla Costa, M. and James, S. (1975) *The power of women and the subordination of the community*, Falling Wall Press, Bristol
Daly, Mary (1978) *Gyn/Ecology: the metaethics of radical feminism*, Beacon Press, Boston, MA
Delp. .y, Christine (1984) *Close to home: a materialist analysis of women's oppression*, trans. D. Leonard, Hutchinson, London
Derrida, Jacques (1976) *Of grammatology*, trans. G.C. Spivak, Johns Hopkins University Press, Baltimore, MD
—— (1978) *Spurs: Nietzsche's styles*, trans. B. Harlow, University of Chicago Press, Chicago, IL
—— (1981) *Dissémination*, trans. B. Johnson, University of Chicago Press, Chicago
—— (undated) 'Freud and the scene of writing', trans. J. Mahlman, *Yale French Studies*, no. 48
—— (undated) 'The purveyor of truth', trans. W. Domingo, J. Hulbert, and M. Ron, *Yale French Studies*, no. 52
Dunayevskaya, Raya (1982) *Rosa Luxemburg: women's liberation and Marx's philosophy of revolution*, Humanities Press, New Jersey
Dworkin, Andrea (1981) *Pornography: men possessing women*, Perigee Books, New York
Easton, L.D. and Guddat, K.H. (eds) (1966) *Writings of the young Marx on philosophy and society*, Anchor Books, New York
Eisenstein, Z. (1979) *Capitalist patriarchy and the case for a socialist feminism*, Monthly Review Press, New York
—— (1981) *The radical future of liberal feminism*, Longman, New York
Engels, Frederick (1972) *The origin of the family, private property and the state*, Lawrence and Wishart, London
Farnsworth, Beatrice (1980) *Aleksandra Kollontai, socialism, feminism and the Bolshevik revolution*, Stanford University Press, Stanford
Figes, Eva (1970) *Patriarchal attitudes*, Faber and Faber, London
Firestone, Schulamith (1971) *The dialectic of sex*, Bantam Books, New York
Flax, Jane (1980) 'Mother-daughter relationships; psychodynamics, politics, and philosophy' in H. Eisenstein and A. Jorden (eds), *The future of difference*, G.K. Hall, Boston, MA
Foreman, Ann (1977) *Femininity and alienation: women and the family in Marxism and psychoanalysis*, Pluto Press, London
Fourier, Charles (1841) *Théorie des quatre mouvements*, Bureau de la Plalange, Paris

Freud, Sigmund (1950) *Totem and taboo: some points of agreement between the mental lives of savages and neurotics*, W.W. Norton, New York
——— (1953) 'Female sexuality' (1931) and 'Femininity' (1933) in *The standard edition of complete psychological works*, vol. XXI, Hogarth Press, London
Gallop, Jane (1982) *Feminism and psychoanalysis: the daughter's seduction*, Macmillan, London
——— (1985) *Reading Lacan*, Cornell University Press, Ithaca, NY
Gilligan, Carol (1982) *In a different voice: psychological theory and women's development*, Harvard University Press, Cambridge, MA
Goldman, Emma (1931) *Living my life*, A. Knopf, New York
——— (no date) *La tragedie de l'emancipation féminine*, Syros, Paris
——— (1970) *The traffic in Women and other essays on feminism*, ed. Alix Shulman, Times Change Press, Washington, NC
Gouges, Olympe de, *Declaration des droits de la femme et de la citoyenne*, reprinted in Auclert, Hubertine (1908) *Le vote des femmes*, V. Girard and E. Brière, Paris
Graves, Robert (1965) *The Greek myths*, Cassell, London
Greer, Germain (1971) *The female eunuch*, Boston Books, New York
Griffin, Susan (1980) *Women and nature*, Harper Calaphone Books, New York
——— (1981) *Pornography and silence: culture's revenge against nature*, Harper and Row, New York
Harding, S. and Hintikka, M. (eds) (1983) *Discovering reality: feminist perspectives on epistemology, methodology and philosophy of science*, D. Reidel, Boston, MA
Hartsock, Nancy (1983) *Money, sex and power*, Longman, New York
Hawkes, Jacquetta (1968) *The dawn of the Gods*, Random House, New York
Hawthorne, Nathaniel (1964) *The Blithdale romance*, (Ohio State University Press, Cent. Ed. vol. III)
Hayden, Dolores (1982) *The grand domestic revolution: a history of feminist designs for American homes, neighborhoods, and cities*, MIT Press, Cambridge, MA
Henley, N. and Thorne, B. (eds) (1975) *Language and sex: difference and dominance*, Newbury house, Rowley, MA
Hiatt, Mary (1977) *The way women write*, Teachers' College Press, New York
Higginson, Thomas Wentworth (1882) *Common sense about women*, Lee and Shepard, Boston, MA
Hodge, R. and Kress, G. (1979) *Language and ideology*, Routledge and Kegan Paul, London
Huguenin, Elisabeth (1949) *La femme à la récherche de son âme*, Editions de la Baconnière, Neuchatel
Hume, David (1965) *Treatise on human nature*, ed. Selby-Bigge, Clarendon Press, Oxford
Irigaray, Luce (1974) *Speculum de l'autre femme*, Minuit, Paris
——— (1977) *Ce sexe qui n'en est pas un*, Minuit, Paris
——— (1981) *This sex which is not one*, trans. C. Porter, with C. Burke, Cornell University Press, Ithaca, NY

Select Bibliography

——— (1985) *Speculum of the other woman*, trans. G. Gill, Cornell University Press, Ithaca, NY

Jaggar, Alison (1983) *Feminist politics and human nature*, Rowman and Allanheld, Totowa, NJ

James, Henry (1984) *The Bostonians*, Penguin, Harmondsworth

Keller, Evelyn Fox (1983) *A feeling for the organism: the life and work of Barbara McClintock*, Freeman, New York

——— (1985) *Reflections on science and gender*, Yale University Press, New Haven, CT

Key, Mary Richie (1975) *Male/female language* Scarecrow Press, Meluchen, NJ

Kollantai, Alexandra (1972) *Autobiography of a sexually emancipated woman*, London

——— (1974) *L'opposition ouvrière*, trans. Pierre Pascal, du Seuil, Paris

——— (1975) *Marxisme et révolution sexuelle*, François Maspero, Paris

——— (1977) *Selected works*, ed. Alix Holt, W.W. Norton, New York

Kramarae, Cheris (1981) *Women and men speaking*, Newbury House, Rowley, MA

Krieger, Susan (1983) *The mirror dance: identity in a woman's community*, Temple University Press, Philadelphia, PA

Kristeva, Julia (1974) *La révolution du langage poétique*, du Seuil, Paris

——— (1977a) 'Hérétique de l'amour', *Tel. Quel.*, no. 74

——— (1977b) *On Chinese women*, trans. A. Barrows, Urizen Books, New York

——— (1980a) *Desire in language*, Basil Blackwell, Oxford

——— (1980b) *Les pouvoirs de l'horreur*, du Seuil, Paris

——— (1981) 'Women's Time', trans. A. Jardin and H. Blake, *Signs*, vol. 7, no. 1

——— (1984) *Revolution in poetic language*, trans. M. Waller, Columbia University Press, New York

——— (1985) *Powers of the horror*, trans. L. Roudiez, Columbia University Press, New York

Kuhn, A. and Wolpe, A. (eds) (1978) *Feminism and materialism*, Routledge and Kegan Paul, London

Lacan, Jacques (1966) *Écrits*, du Seuil, Paris

——— (1975) *Encore, le séminaire de Jacques Lacan*, Livre XV, du Seuil, Paris

——— (1977) *Écrits: a selection*, trans. A. Sheridan, Tavistock, London

——— (1982) *Feminine sexuality*, ed. J. Mitchell, and J. Rose, trans. J. Rose, Pitman Press, Beaconsfield, England

——— (1984) *Les complexes femiliaux*, Navarin, Paris

Lakoff, Robin (1975) *Language and woman's place*, Harper and Row, New York

Lenin, V.I. (1966) *The emancipation of women*, International Publishers, New York

——— (1976) *State and revolution*, Foreign Language Press, Peking

Levi-Strauss, Claude (1969) *The elementary structures of kinship*, Beacon Press, Boston, MA

——— (1955) *Tristes tropiques*, Plon, Paris

——— (1973) *Tristes tropiques*, trans. J. Weightman and D. Weightman, Cape, London

Locke, John (1970) *Two treatises on government*, ed. P. Laslett, Cambridge University Press, Cambridge

Lomas, P. (ed.) (1968) *The predicament of the family*, Hogarth Press, London

Luxemburg, Rosa (1951) *The accumulation of capital*, Routledge and Kegan Paul, London

Maruani, M. (1979) *Les syndicats a l'épreuve du féminisme*, Syros, Paris

Marx, Karl (1955) *The communist manifesto*, ed. S. Beer, Appleton-Century Crofts, New York

——— (1967) *Capital*, International Publishers, New York

Masson, Jeffrey (1984) *The assault on truth: Freud's suppression of the seduction theory*, Farrar Strauss and Giroux, New York

Mill, J.S. (1859) *On liberty*, London

——— (1895) *Utilitarianism*, Routledge and Kegan Paul, London

——— (1961) *Principles of political economy*, Kelley, New York

——— (1970) 'The subjection of women' in Alice Rossi (ed.) *Essays on sexual equality*, University of Chicago Press, Chicago

Millett, Kate (1970) *Sexual politics*, Doubleday, New York

Mitchell, Juliet (1971) *Women's estate*, Penguin, Baltimore, MD

——— (1975a) *Psychoanalysis and feminism*, Vintage Books, New York

——— (1975b) *Women and equality*, University of Cape Town Press, Cape Town

Nye, Andrea (1983) 'Alleged freedom of the moral agent', *Journal of Value Inquiry*, no. 17, pp. 17–32

——— (1987) 'The woman clothed in the sun: Julia Kristeva and the escape from/to language', *Signs*, vol. 13, no. 4

Olivier, Christine (1980) *Les enfants de Jocaste: l'empreinte de la mère*, Donoel/Gouthier, Paris

O'Neill, William (1969) *The woman's movement: feminism in the United States and England*, George Allen and Unwin, London

Plaza, Monique (1978a) '"Phallomorphic power" and the psychology of "Woman"', *Ideology and Consciousness*, no. 4, pp. 4–36

——— (1978b) 'Pouvoir phallomorphic et psychologic de "la femme"', *Questions Féministes*, no. 1

——— (1980) 'La même mère', *Questions Féministes*, no. 7

Proudhon, P.J. (1858) *La justice dans la révolution et dans l'église*, Garnier Frères, Paris

Reiche, Reimut (1974) *Sexuality and class relations*, New Left Books, New York

Rich, Adrienne (1976) *Of woman born*, W.W. Norton, New York

——— (1980) 'Compulsory heterosexuality and lesbian existence', *Signs*, vol. 5, no. 4

Romieu, Madame (1859) *La femme au XIX siècle*, Amayat, Paris

Rossi, Alice, (ed.) (1970) *Essays on sex equality*, University of Chicago Press, Chicago

Rousseau, Jean-Jacques (1911) *Emile*, Dent, London

Rowbotham, Sheila (1972) *Women, resistance and revolution*, Penguin, Harmondsworth

Sargent, L. (ed.) (1981) *Women and revolution: a discussion of the unhappy marriage of Marxism and feminism*, South End Press, Boston, MA

Sartre, Jean-Paul (1966) *Being and nothingness*, trans. H. Barnes, Washington Square Press, New York

Saussure, Ferdinand de (1966) *Course in general linguistics*, trans. Wade Baskin, McGraw-Hill, New York

Seccombe, W. (1974) 'The housewife and her labour under capitalism', *New Left Review*, no. 83, pp. 3–24

Smith, Adam (1974) *The wealth of nations*, Penguin, Harmondsworth

Stael, Madame de (1830) *De l'influence des passions sur le bonheur des individus et des nations*, Louis Harimen, Bruxelles

Stanley, Julia (1977a) 'Gender-marking in American English: usage and reference' in A.P. Nilsen *et al.* (eds) *Sexism and language*, Nat. Council of Leaders of Eng., Urbana, IL

—— (1977b) 'Paradigmatic women: the prostitute' in D.L. Shores and C.P. Hines (eds) *Papers in language variation*, University of Alabama Press

—— (1978) 'Sexist grammar', *College English*, vol. 39, no. 1

—— with Robbins, Susan (1978) 'Going through the changes: the pronoun "she" in Middle English', *Papers in Linguistics*, vol. II, nos. 1–2

Stein, Edith (1956) *La femme et sa destinée*, Amiot-Dummont, Paris

Stites, Richard (1978) *The women's liberation in Russia*, Princeton University Press, Princeton, NJ

Taylor, Barbara (1983) *Eve and the new Jerusalem: socialism and feminism in the nineteenth century*, Pantheon Books, New York

Taylor, Harriet (1970) 'The enfranchisement of women' (Orig. 1851) reprinted in Alice Rossi (ed.) *Essays on sex equality*, University of Chicago Press, Chicago

Thiebaux, Charles (1906) *Le féminisme et les socialistes*, Arthur Rousseau, Paris

Turkle, Sherry (1978) *Freud's French revolution*, Basic Books, New York

Vance, Carol (ed.) (1984) *Pleasure and danger: exploring female sexuality*, Routledge and Kegan Paul, Boston MA

Wagner, Georgina (1986) 'Women and neo-liberalism' in J. Evans *et al.* (ed.), *Feminism and political theory*, Sage Publications, London

Weinbaum, Batya (1980) *The curious courtship of women's liberation and socialism*, South End Press, Boston, MA

—— (1983) *Pictures of patriarchy*, South End Press, Boston, MA

Winnicott, D.W. (1965) *The maturational processes and the facilitating environment*, Inter-Universities Press, New York

Wittig, Monique (1971) *Les guérillères*, Viking Press, New York

—— (1975) *Lesbian body*, trans. David Le Vay, Owen, London

Wollstonecraft, Mary (1792) *Vindication of the rights of women*, Walter Scott, London

Zetkin, Clara (1980) *Batailles pour les femmes*, trans. Gilbert Badia, Éditions Sociale, Paris

Zylberberg-Hocquard, Marie-Hélène (1978) *Féminisme et syndicalism en France*, Éditions Anthropos, Paris

Index

Index